THE ELECTION OF 1984

THE ELECTION OF 1984

Reports and Interpretations

Gerald M. Pomper

Ross K. Baker

Charles E. Jacob

Scott Keeter

Wilson Carey McWilliams

Henry A. Plotkin

Marlene Michels Pomper
editor

Chatham House Publishers, Inc.
Chatham, New Jersey

THE ELECTION OF 1984
Reports and Interpretations

CHATHAM HOUSE PUBLISHERS, INC.
Box One, Chatham, New Jersey 07928

PUBLISHER: Edward Artinian
JACKET AND COVER DESIGN: Lawrence Ratzkin
COMPOSITION: Chatham Composer
PRINTING AND BINDING: Hamilton Printing Company

LIBRARY OF CONGRESS CATALOGING IN PUBLICATION DATA

The Election of 1984

Includes bibliographies and index.
1. Presidents—United States—Election—1984—Addresses, essays, lectures. 2. United States. Congress—Elections, 1984—Addresses, essays, lectures. 3. Elections—United States—Addresses, essays, lectures. I. Pomper, Gerald M.
JK526 1984d   324.973'0927   85-4223
ISBN 0-934540-42-X
ISBN 0-934540-41-1 (pbk.)

Manufactured in the United States of America
10 9 8 7 6 5 4 3 2 1

Contents

Tables

Figures

Preface

"To every thing there is a season," the ancient poet teaches us. As the rhythms of our personal lives bring occasions to seek and to lose, for mourning and for joy, our shared societal life provides "a time to love and a time to hate; a time for war, and a time for peace."

The election of 1984 too brought a new season in the changing cycles of American politics. Novel directions in public policy were legitimized by the reelection of America's oldest President. The first woman was nominated for national office, and the first major black candidate sought the White House.

Politics itself changed. The world's oldest political party simultaneously won legislative victories and faced the prospect of long-term decay. The 1984 election was not simply an ambitious pursuit of office; the candidates probed the nation's religious traditions and its ultimate values.

In this volume, six political scientists analyze the meaning of this election. The authors — Ross K. Baker, Charles E. Jacob, Scott Keeter, Wilson Carey McWilliams, Henry A. Plotkin, and Gerald M. Pomper — have been colleagues at Rutgers University. Our frequent discussions have led to previous works on the elections of 1976 and 1980. This year we have again shared our ideas, provoking some differences, many agreements, and great mutual learning.

There is one common theme to these essays: The election of 1984 was a searching of America's soul, not only a race for power. Though their thoughts were disguised in television's sound bites, Reagan and Mondale debated philosophy. Beneath their statistical details, opinion polls revealed new cleavages of race, sex, age, and class. In the coming years, we will witness new party loyalties, new public policies, and renewed political conflicts. We hope these essays contribute to the understanding of those future developments.

The authors of this collaborative work include:

Ross K. Baker, professor, and author of *Friend and Foe in the United States Senate*
Charles E. Jacob, professor, and author of *Policy and Bureaucracy*
Scott Keeter, assistant professor, and co-author of *Uninformed Choice: The Failure of the New Presidential Nominating System*

ix

Wilson Carey McWilliams, professor, and author of *The Idea of Fraternity in America*

Henry A. Plotkin, an independent scholar, currently researching a book, *The Image of the Corporation in America*

Gerald M. Pomper, professor, and author of *Voters' Choice*

We acknowledge the help of many people who have facilitated this early interpretation of the election. Marlene Michels Pomper, as editor, improved both our logic and our syntax. Edith Saks, of the Eagleton Institute, typed much of the manuscript and administered our comings and goings. We are grateful for various services, ranging from help in obtaining opinion surveys to word processing. Our providers include Kathleen Frankovic of CBS News, Brad Bryen, Ron and Erica Cowan, Laurily Epstein, Barbara Farah, Chris von Gruchalla, and Chris Wakeley. We have gained from discussions with wives, friends, and colleagues—particularly Dennis Bathory, Susan Carroll, Anthony Corrado, Daniel Fraire, Irving Louis Horowitz, Marc Landy, Maureen Moakley, Susanne Peticolis, Alan Rosenthal, Stephen Salmore, and Cliff Zukin. Edward Artinian, our publisher, who is also a friend, conceived the project and ably saw it through to completion. The index was compiled by Miles Pomper, assisted by Gregory Brail.

We have just concluded a year marked not only by the election. In an ironic combination, it also celebrated the "year of the teacher" and symbolized George Orwell's warnings of the threat of totalitarianism. Writing about 1984, we remember Orwell's lessons of the importance of language and of political education. In our own lives, we were taught these lessons by rare and gifted teachers, from kindergarten to our doctoral research. Acknowledging their devotion, we dedicate this book to those individuals: Stanley Kelley, Jr., William R. Kintner, Frank Munger, Clinton Rossiter, Adelaide Santor, John H. Schaar, and Howard E. Shaw. We hope we are worthy of their care and skill.

January 1985   GERALD M. POMPER

1

The Nominations

GERALD M. POMPER

The more things stay the same, the more they change.

On the surface, the national nominations seemed a return to normalcy. The midsummer conventions followed traditional forms — delegates zealously applauded partisan rhetoric, pridefully spoke in roll calls of the states, mistily viewed thousands of star-spangled banners, earnestly sang their commitment to America the beautiful. The incumbent President, Republican Ronald Reagan, was renominated without a whisper of dissent — in contrast to the troubles of his predecessors — Jimmy Carter, Gerald Ford, and Lyndon Johnson. The opposition Democrats chose an established figure, Walter Mondale, as their leader. After a decade and a half of "reform" efforts to "open" participation, the party apparently had returned power to its entrenched barons — state governors, congressional chieftains, and labor union leaders.

The appearance was deceptive. Familiar outward settings disguised fundamental changes, much as an old suit of clothes might be worn by an unfamiliar person. President Reagan's renomination marked the transformation of the Republican party into a cohesive organization with a coherent ideology. Mondale's selection paralleled the reach toward political power by newly assertive groups. Dramatically epitomizing the novelties of American politics in 1984, Democrats nominated Geraldine Ferraro for Vice-President, the first woman selected for national office by a major party.

The parties gave the voters not only persons to see and names to hear. Republicans and Democrats invited the electorate to think about significant differences of issues and philosophy. They even challenged Americans to examine their most basic assumptions — their religious beliefs, their roles as men and women, their commitments to self and society. The election of 1984 was not simply an appeal to the senses, or solely a stimulus to the mind. It prompted Americans to probe their very souls.

The Political Setting

As the election year began, discussion among the politically informed dealt more with literature than with nominations and voting. The calendar read 1984, concentrating thoughts on George Orwell's novel of that title. Writing after the Second World War, Orwell had warned of a nightmare future of poverty, thought control, and continual war. Comparing contemporary reality to the fiction of *1984,* most observers gratefully concluded that drastic changes had not occurred.[1]

Totalitarianism had been averted in the United States, but major changes had been made in the brief three years of Ronald Reagan's administration. At his inauguration in 1981, the new Republican President had stated his basic philosophical beliefs: America has a special mission in the world; individualist activity is superior to collective action; government typically threatens, rather than promotes, liberty. Symbolically facing westward, away from the sites of power, Reagan declared:

> Government is not the solution to our problem; government is the problem. . . . Our government has no power except that granted it by the people. It is time to check and reverse the growth of government which shows signs of having grown beyond the consent of the governed. It is my intention to curb the size and influence of the Federal establishment. . . .[2]

Acting quickly to realize this philosophy, Reagan achieved a major change in the direction of the federal government. Income taxes were substantially reduced, a total cut of 25 percent over three years. In keeping with the conservative emphasis on "supply-side economics" and the preference for private investment, tax changes were directed toward increasing investment by businesses and wealthy individuals. Important changes were also made in federal spending programs. For the first time in a quarter century, the national government reduced its grants to states and cities, from $95 billion to $88 billion. Cuts were particularly large in the social services that had grown steadily under previous administrations, both Democratic and Republican. At the same time, the new administration promised to preserve the "social safety net" for the poorest groups in the population.

As if to prove that politics does matter, the new administration made major changes in additional policy areas. Federal regulation of industry was reduced, and wilderness areas opened to fuller economic development. The direction of civil rights activity was sharply altered, with the federal government now arguing against affirmative action plans and — until forced to retreat by Congress and the courts — in favor of tax exemption for private segregated schools. In the area of ultimate significance, foreign policy, American interests were asserted strongly. Over Soviet objections and despite mass protests, intermediate-range missiles were installed in Western Europe, and U.S. troops intervened briefly in Lebanon and Grenada. To close a presumed military "window of vulnerability," defense spending increased rapidly, to nearly $300 billion annually in late 1984.

Inevitably, the election of 1984 would center on the record of the Reagan administration. As a candidate, the President had posed the most important question, "Are you better off now than you were four years ago?" Dissatisfaction with an economy marked by inflation, sluggish growth, and high interest rates had brought him victory, rather than a popular swing to his conservative philosophy. Economic satisfaction was the key to his reelection.[3]

In his programs, the President himself recognized the priority of economics. Issues involving moral philosophy were shunted aside. While Reagan continued to speak in favor of school prayer and to oppose abortion, he took no significant actions to effect these goals. When a vacancy opened on the Supreme Court, he did not simply use the opportunity to appoint a philosophical conservative, but instead improved his public standing by naming the first woman to the nation's highest court. Although the rhetoric of foreign policy became more nationalistic, and the arms budget grew rapidly, the United States continued to maintain both its alliances with the West and its ambivalent relationships with the communist powers.

The Reagan economic program was based on the premise that economic growth came from private, not government, action. A sharp reduction in government spending and taxes would give consumers more money to spend, and businesses more money to invest, while removing governmental hindrances. As the economy grew, moreover, sufficient new tax revenues would be generated to balance the government's own budget. Inflation would be halted by limits on bank credits and by controls over interest rates. By mid-1981, the program was under way.

The first results were discouraging. Philosophically, the program had already been compromised, with more benefits going to the wealthy than originally promised. As David Stockman, Reagan's Director of the Budget and major economic planner, admitted in an unguarded interview, "The hogs were really feeding. The greed level, the level of opportunism, just got out of control."[4] Economically, it wasn't working. Unemployment rose for the first two years of the administration, eventually reaching 10.7 percent, the highest level since the depression of the 1930s. The federal budget deficit rose above $100 billion for the first time, and fears began to be heard about the safety of the Social Security System. Some Republican encouragement could be found, however, in the declining inflation rate and in upturns in long-range economic indicators.

The results of the 1982 elections were a setback for the administration, but not a disaster. Republicans lost 26 seats in the House of Representatives, a high number historically, but less than would be expected on the basis of the poor economic news. In the Senate, the Republicans were able to hold their majority, probably because their well-financed and well-organized national campaign brought them victory in every marginal contest.

The political meaning of the elections was that there was no longer a bipartisan conservative coalition in control of Congress. The President would have to compromise with the legislature. He did, and to his own advantage. Democrats passed new programs to stabilize Social Security funds, reduce the federal deficit, ease unemployment. In so doing, they reduced some of the most obvious economic problems, while easing the political problems of the President.[5]

The midterm elections had other results, less noticed immediately but possibly of greater long-term significance. Reversing a trend of two decades, electoral turnout increased, with 10 million more voters on the rolls. The increase demonstrated critical changes in the political demographics of the United States. For one, the "baby boom" was now maturing, as children born in the population explosion after the Second World War began to approach middle age. The voting increase, however, was not simply a result of callow youths becoming respectable citizens. Participation increased especially among groups previously underrepresented at the polls. New racial consciousness, and the long-term effects of voting rights laws, brought 2 million new blacks and Hispanics to the polls. Unions and welfare organizations mobilized blue-collar workers and the unemployed. Women, already a majority of the electorate, further increased their activity. Overall, these trends promised a historic expansion of the American political universe. They were especially cheering to the Democrats, who read the new enrollments as strengthening their electoral foundation.[6]

Democrats were also encouraged by evidence of a continuing "gender gap" between the two major parties. Through most American elections, women had voted quite similarly to men or even somewhat more Republican. In the 1980 election, however, a difference had become evident. Although a majority of both sexes had backed Reagan, women were far less supportive. Later polls, and the 1982 election, showed the difference continued, with women about 6 percent more favorable to the Democrats. Analysts differed about the nature of the gap—were women more Democratic or men more Republican?— and about its possible causes. Among the explanations were women's greater wariness about the use of force, their greater concern for the disadvantaged, men's greater attraction to Reagan's assertive foreign policy, and the impact of changing life-styles. Sexual politics was almost as mysterious as sex itself.[7]

After the midterm elections, however, the economic news — and the President's political fortunes — improved. Unemployment began to drop, and eventually fell below the level at the time of Reagan's inauguration. Economic growth rates rose to boom proportions, as high as 10 percent annually. Inflation, the sensitive factor known to every consumer, fell dramatically, to annual rates as low as 4 percent. Americans were working more, spending more, and paying lower taxes. Only two economic factors were politically disquieting. Interest rates remained high, and the federal deficit continued to grow and was projected to reach close to $200 billion in the election year. These problems were of little concern to the administration. The critical date was 6 November 1984 — not an unspeakable day in 1985 when an economic reckoning might be necessary. With delight, the Republicans were prepared to again ask voters the challenging personal question, "Are you better off now than you were four years ago?"

As the economy turned up, so did Reagan's personal standing. In January 1983, he had been at his lowest point in national popularity. (See figure 4.2 on page 94.) As the election year opened, Americans overwhelmingly approved of his performance as President, with 57 percent supportive and only 32 percent critical. In contrast to most of his predecessors, Reagan had avoided not only a slump in his ratings during the third year in office but had actually improved. Indeed, his personal standing seemed unaffected by the inevitable policy problems encountered by a chief executive. Even as voters supported him generally, polls found that pluralities disapproved of specific policies, such as his handling of unemployment and budget deficits or his foreign policy in regard to Lebanon, Central America, and the Soviet Union. Democrats began to wonder at the "Teflon factor," the ability of the President to prevent blame for policy problems from sticking to him.[8]

Nominating Politics: The Republican Celebration

Throughout his term in office, President Reagan was aided by a legislative party and an executive staff that showed remarkable ideological coherence. In the most critical votes, on federal taxing and spending in 1981, the Democrats were somewhat less solid, as southern "boll weevils" provided enough defectors to pass the Reagan program. Nevertheless, the legislative order of battle found 99 percent of the Republicans lined up against 89 percent of the Democrats. This party discipline was virtually unprecedented in American history and sharply belied the conventional comment that the political parties had lost their meaning.[9]

Republican unity reflected the development of a truly national political party. Over the past two decades, beginning with Barry Goldwater's campaign in 1964, the party had refined a conservative political philosophy from such ingredients as economic individualism, social order, assertive anticommunism, and traditional morality. Once divided between an eastern "left" and a midwestern "right," Republican activists now spoke in a distinctly conservative accent. Coherence was also evident in the party organization. The Republican National Committee had become an efficient, centralized organ of the party, able to raise $80 million annually, recruiting candidates for state and national office, providing polls, campaign advice, and advertising techniques for these candidates, and defining issue positions through a national journal and regional conferences.[10]

Cohesively and coherently, the party had fought the 1980 election on a common slogan, "Vote Republican — For a Change." It had supported its persuasive ideological spokesman, Ronald Reagan, as he changed the direction of the national government. Despite economic and political problems in the midterm congressional elections of 1982, the party had asked voters to "Stay the Course." As the presidential election neared, Republicans never doubted that they would support Reagan for a second term. Their only doubt was whether the 73-year-old President would run again.

Potential aspirants positioned themselves to replace him, if he should step down. For example, Majority Leader Howard Baker decided to leave the Senate, so as to be free for national campaigning — if not in 1984, then four years later — and Vice-President George Bush made overtures to the right-wing groups that had opposed him earlier. These tentative toes in the water were snatched back when Reagan himself entered the electoral swim in February. Favorably assessing his own record, the President found he needed more time to complete his program and announced his candidacy in February. That ended the tale of the 1984 Republican nomination, aside from some suppressed grumblings over Bush's renomination as running mate. It was a very short story, with no mysteries in its plot and only a single, and familiar, character.

Nominating Politics: The Democratic Constitution

The Democrats provide a more interesting, and more complex, adventure. Like their opponents, albeit less slowly, they were developing a more coherent national party organization. National fund-raising had begun, though the amounts raised were only fractions of the well-established Republican effort, and professional campaign specialists were incorporated within the party. The party's congressional delegations began to develop a national program, first in reaction to the Reagan initiatives, then more originally. The House Democratic caucus developed a common platform for the party's 1982 and 1984 campaigns, and many of these proposals were later included in the presidential manifesto. A small step toward party discipline in the House was taken when Phil Gramm, the most prominent of the Reaganite "boll weevils," was deprived of his Democratic committee assignments, and then resigned to run for reelection as a Republican.

The most important actions toward the development of the national Democratic party concerned its rules on the presidential nomination. Ever since its tumultuous conclave in 1968, in the midst of the Vietnam War, the party had changed its structure and rules every four years. Advocates of change had generally sought to broaden participation in the party, to ground the presidential nomination in the "grass-roots" support for particular candidates, and to limit the power of established party officials, who were often denigrated as "bosses" operating in "smoke-filled" rooms. Critics found that the rules changes had turned control of the party over to unrepresentative elites, damaged its electoral appeal, and hampered its effectiveness in government. The nominations of George McGovern in 1972 and Jimmy Carter in 1976 and 1980 were praised by some as triumphs of popular democracy, while they were condemned by others as examples of political ineptitude.[11]

Regardless of their theoretical merits, the accumulated Democratic rules changes had certainly contributed to some basic changes in presidential nominating politics. One vital change was that the selection of the party's candidates was no longer, in fact, a choice of its organizational leaders or the public officials elected on the party ticket. Instead, the choice was made through presidential primaries or mass caucuses, held in the various states. That choice was heavily influenced by the mass media. They, rather than the parties, informed the voters of the candidates, rated their prospects and abilities, and determined the significance of particular events.

Although the primaries had become decisive, selecting three-fourths of the delegates in 1980, this change did not mean that all voters rationally shared in nominating presidential candidates. Only a minority of the electorate participated. Even that group was dependent for information on mass media, which provided limited useful information, concentrating instead on the "horse race" among candidates. Nor were all voters equal. Particularly important were those voting in the earliest of these contests, held in Iowa in January and New Hampshire in February. A candidate winning these states was likely to gain disproportionate attention from the media, accumulate funds, rise in public opinion polls, and gather enough momentum to control the party's convention, even if his popularity waned in later months.[12]

Rules changes in the Democratic party also changed its basic structure. In the past, the basic power groups at a convention had been the state delegations, which operated as relatively cohesive units. After the period of reform, this was no longer possible. The new rules prohibited bloc voting by states and also required that delegates be divided among presidential candidates in proportion to their popularity in local areas. The downgrading of state blocs was further evidenced by the overriding of state laws in conflict with new national party rules. For example, the party restricted participation in Wisconsin's delegate selection to declared Democrats, thus nullifying the impact of the state's open primary. The Supreme Court supported such actions.[13]

The new basic blocs in the Democratic party were not states but collections of individuals, such as demographic categories and interest groups. National rules now required that half the delegates from each state be women and that the numbers of other groups, particularly racial minorities, approximate their proportions among Democratic voters. Interest groups throughout the nation organized to elect delegates who were union members, or teachers, or environmentalists. At the convention itself, caucuses were no longer held only by state delegations, but by members of these groups and advocates of particular policies. It became more important for a presidential candidate to win endorsement from the women's caucus or to mollify Hispanics than to cut a deal within the California delegation or gain the endorsement of Ohio's favorite son.

Finally, rules changes had the effect of reducing the impact of party and elected officials on presidential nominations. The theoretical premise of the new party legislation was egalitarian and democratic. The party ought to be controlled by its individual and local voters, and the presidential nominee should be the more direct choice of these individual persons. Primaries, proportional representation, demographic allocations were the legal forms through which the egalitarian democracy would operate. The new theory gave less importance to representation or to intermediate institutions, such as the party organization. Officeholders, party leaders, and other elected representatives were not entitled to any assured place in the nominating process. Accorded no specific role, these officials took little part in the national nominations. In 1980, for example, only 38 Democratic congressmen attended the party convention.

After its defeat in the presidential election of 1980, the Democrats again changed their rules. Without reversing the general directions of the previous revisions, or changing the representation of women and minorities, they attempted to deal with some of the problems that had become evident. A reliance on primaries had not brought ideal democracy but had fostered division within the party, burdensome expenditures, and electoral failure. The media environment led to an undue stress on early victories, which quickly foreclosed the nominating choice, leaving the party unable to change its collective mind as the political situation clarified. Uniform national rules left too little flexibility for diverse states. The absence of public officials deprived the convention of their advice and deprived the nation of their expert "peer review" of prospective nominees. A new commission, headed by North Carolina Governor Jim Hunt, addressed these deficiencies.[14]

The Hunt commission had many internal struggles, but eventually agreed on four major changes in the 1984 nominating procedures. First, it attempted to shorten the nominating campaign by requiring all selection of delegates to take place within three months, from early March to early June. By bunching state actions into a shorter period, it hoped to reduce the distorted impact of any single result. The effect of this change, however, was reduced when New Hampshire and Iowa (and later Maine) were allowed to make their selections late in February. Another unintended result was that many state parties moved their selection process to early in the calendar, to gain the attention and influence expected for the first contests. This "front-loading" eventually meant that almost half the states reached decisions by the end of March, affecting the selection of over a third of the delegates.

Second, states were given more flexibility in the method of selecting delegates. They could hold primaries, but they could also use caucuses, local meetings open to all party members. If states held primaries, a variety of systems would be permitted. They could use proportional representation, so that delegates chosen from a local district were divided among presidential candidates in proportion to the preferences of the local voters. Alternatively, they could use a "winner-take-all" system where the leading candidate in a district won all of the delegates at stake. A third possibility was a "winner-take-more" system, by which the leading candidate in a district received a bonus delegate and then the rest were divided proportionately.

With this encouragement, states tried different methods. The number of binding primaries fell, and were held in only 23 states (and the District of Columbia and Puerto Rico). The number of delegates chosen in these contests came to 54 percent of the total, compared to 71 percent in the previous convention. Where primaries were employed, proportional representation was no longer the dominant mode of selection, leading to the selection of only a fifth of delegates elected in primaries. Four additional states held nonbinding primaries, while they and the remaining states chose their delegates in party caucuses, under rules of proportional representation.

A third revision turned out to be of critical importance in the nominating race. This was a statistical criterion, a "threshold." It meant that a candidate must receive a minimum percentage of the vote in a district caucus or state primary, usually 20 percent, before he could receive any delegates. This meant that a candidate with limited or scattered support—perhaps 15 percent in a district or 10 percent throughout a state—would get very few delegates.

Finally, a major effort was made to bring elected and party officials into the process. These persons were allocated 14 percent of the delegates, or 568 out of a total of 3933. Specific seats were allocated for most Democratic senators and members of Congress, as well as Democratic governors, mayors, members of the party's national committee, and each state's chair and vice-chair. Most important, these "superdelegates" were formally uncommitted to any presidential candidate, leaving them with the potential balance of power in a divided convention.

The "experts" soon agreed on the effect of these changes: the early nomination of an established party figure. "Front-loading," the early bunching of state selection, worked to the advantage of a known and well-financed candidate. He would be favored by the party's "superdelegates" and would sweep up delegates under the new nonproportional systems. Any potential rivals would fail to reach the high threshold, and would be unable to capitalize on surprise victories in the early primaries. As Senator Gary Hart concluded, echoing the conventional wisdom, "Democrats will give up their dreams of heroes and realize that they are going to have to pick the party's 1984 presidential candidate from among the familiar faces of 1982."[15]

The most familiar face was that of Walter Mondale, the Vice-President in the previous Democratic administration. As early as election night in 1980, his nomination had been predicted by the staff of the defeated President, Jimmy Carter.[16] In the next three years, Mondale built what was generally conceded to be "the nation's most elaborate presidential campaign organization,"[17] well-financed, in touch with party and group leaders throughout the nation, and poised to take advantage of the new party rules. His most troublesome opponent had been Senator Edward Kennedy of Massachusetts, who had contested the last nomination down to the opening day of the Democratic convention, and had then made a dramatic speech, pledging that "the dream will never die." But Kennedy had surprised the party in late 1982 by firmly withdrawing from the 1984 presidential race. Mondale was ready to line up the support he needed, from interest groups first, and then from the voters and the party.

Only one critical group had not come into Mondale's camp: the media. A year before the first delegates were to be selected, Russell Baker sardonically warned him of the perils ahead:

"Rotten luck," Mondale," I said. "We've made you the front-runner. . . . Without a front-runner, we'd have nobody to suffer surprising setbacks in the early stage of the campaign, and without surprising setbacks we would be stuck with a very dull story. We can't get people interested in a bunch of solemn klunks talking about complicated problems of government, Mondale. We've got to have a horse race or nobody's going to watch. It's tough, but somebody's got to make the sacrifice and be front-runner." . . . We'd probably finish him off in the early political fiddling in Iowa or New Hampshire. "Say you get only 47 percent of that boondocks vote. What we'll do is say, well 47 percent may not be disgraceful, but Mondale had been expected to do better. It looks like he's all washed up. . . . We of the press and TV do the expecting. You do the disappointing. That way we work together to give the country an entertaining story."[18]

The Democratic Carnival

Presidential nominations look like circuses. In the Democratic contest of 1984, there were three rings in the circus, but the rings were not isolated from each other. Acts in one place affected performances in the others. The candidates appeared in each ring, but they played with different casts of performers, and under different ringmasters. In the first ring, theme music was played by public opinion pollsters, measuring the popularity of the aspirants against each other and in hypothetical contests with Ronald Reagan. The most important ring, often unnoticed by the audience, was where the candidates chased delegates, seeking the 1967 votes that would constitute a majority at the party's convention. The spotlighted center ring of the circus was the primaries and caucuses at which the delegates were chosen. In this ring, the whip was cracked by the mass media.

Since political parties exist to win elections, forecasts of the presidential race were critical data for the Democrats. Initially favorable, the polls became discouraging for the party as the economy and Reagan's standing improved. From late in 1983, Reagan held a clear lead—whether paired against Walter Mondale, or John Glenn, or Gary Hart. Still, an optimistic Democrat could find some hope in the polls. They showed great instability within the electorate. In June 1983, Mondale was signficantly ahead of Reagan, by margins of 4 to 9 percent. True, he was down by 16 points within six months, but there might be a chance after all.[19]

Yet the polls also carried other information, messages that were particularly adverse to Mondale's campaign. When a viable alternative was available, voters seemed more attracted to a different face. In the initial period, that alternative was John Glenn, who usually did better in the polls against Reagan than the former Vice-President. When Glenn disappeared from the contest, Gary Hart seemed to be a more viable Democratic candidate. Even after all the primaries had been completed, when Mondale was assured nomination, Mondale trailed Reagan by 15 points, but Hart by only six.

Mondale's more immediate problem was winning the support of Democrats, who would be choosing the delegates in primaries and caucuses. The polls were not consistently encouraging even in this respect. Asked to name their favored nominee, only 14 percent of Democrats spontaneously chose Mondale, while 10 percent selected the withdrawn Kennedy. Even when presented with a limited list, Democrats showed no greater support for Mondale than for Glenn. Mondale's popularity within the party rose later. By January, and again by the end of the primaries, he was the preferred candidate of an absolute majority of Democrats. In the intermediate period, however, he was closely challenged by Gary Hart. These rapid shifts of opinion did not mean that Mondale was unpopular, but they did indicate that loyalty to him was thin and could be easily lost.

In the second ring of the circus, the candidates pursued delegates. Early attention focused on Mondale and Glenn. The first was the most experienced leader of the party, heir to both its liberal heritage and the Carter record, well-regarded by party and interest group leaders. The second was seen as a relatively nonpartisan figure, an American hero since he had flown the first manned spacecraft in earth orbit, able to challenge Reagan's patriotic appeals. Enlivening the race were six other candidates. Alan Cranston gained media attention when he won a straw poll at Democratic conventions in California and Wisconsin. George McGovern, reviving memories of his 1972 campaign against the Vietnam War, captured third place in a Gallup poll. Jesse Jackson began an evangelical campaign, the first significant presidential effort by a black leader. Reubin Askew of Florida, Fritz Hollings of South Carolina, and Senator Gary Hart of Colorado completed the field.

Despite the multiple competition he faced, Mondale consistently led in the chase of delegates. Accumulating almost $10 million in early contributions, and with early organization throughout the nation, he laid the groundwork for his effort in the caucus states. Recognizing the new importance of interest groups within the party, he won the endorsement of the American Federation of Teachers, the National Organization for Women, and the AFL-CIO, the national labor federation. The latter was particularly critical, for it provided field workers and money for the later primaries, and its endorsement carried some, if not decisive, weight with union members, a critical component of the Democratic electorate.

The first delegates were chosen not in the states but in the House of Representatives where 164 "superdelegates" were selected. Supported by these political professionals, who knew him well and admired his abilities, Mondale led in the count of delegates from the very first moment. In the coming months, the Minnesotan would come close to being eliminated from the contest, and-would not gain an assured majority until the last primaries. Still, as shown in table 1.1 on pages 14-15, he consistently led the field, even when the media were discounting his prospects.[20]

Mondale's success in the critical race for delegates was due to both the Democratic rules and his organization's ability. The new group of "superdelegates" provided a resource that was partially insulated from the momentary fads of polls and limited primaries. Even in those states holding primaries, Mondale was able to benefit from the altered means of selecting delegates. The high threshold sometimes meant that Jackson did not always reach the necessary minimum throughout a state, and thus received less than a proportionate share of delegates. In other places, particularly larger industrial states, the winner-take-all or winner-take-more systems meant that Mondale, by carrying a district, won an especially large share. In some states, such as Florida and Pennsylvania, Hart suffered from poor preparation. He received fewer delegates than his vote warranted because he had neglected to file complete lists of supporters. His popular showings therefore were diluted. Jackson and Hart would later complain that these rules were unfair. But the rules had been known in advance. If Mondale made the best use of them, that did not show impropriety. It was evidence of better political skills — and the presidency is, after all, a job for a politician.[21]

In the center ring of the nomination circus were the primaries and caucuses. After the long period of party reform, the script seemed predictable — an early focus on Iowa and New Hampshire, the rapid development of "momentum" for one candidate, a ritualistic convention. But there were new performers in the ring. Labor's formal endorsement broke a tradition of nonintervention before the parties made their formal nominations. By entering directly into the Democrats' selection process, the AFL-CIO was going considerably beyond its historic practice of "rewarding friends and punishing enemies." Like the union movements of Europe, it was redefining itself not only as an economic claimant but as a partisan political force.

Women, even more dramatically, also were ready to claim power. The feminist movement had grown increasingly assertive over the past two decades, altering legislation, life-styles, and even the American language. Within the Democratic party, it had achieved formal equality of representation and the ability, in effect, to veto candidates who opposed such feminist policies as the right-to-choice on abortion or the Equal Rights Amendment. The presidential aspirants needed women's energy and votes, just as the party needed to exploit the "gender gap" to have a chance of victory.

Blacks were a third claimant. Monolithically loyal to the Democrats, blacks were now moving to occupy the seats of power. Two decades earlier, their right

TABLE 1.1

Week	Primary states	New delegates	Total selected	Percent of total
Before 23 February			214	5.4
23 February	NH (18)	18	232	5.9
13 March "Super Tuesday"		510	742	18.9
	AL (52)			
	FL (123)			
	GA (70)			
	MA (100)			
	RI (22)			
20 March	IL (171)	559	1,248	31.7
27 March	CT (52)	174	1,422	36.1
3 April	NY (252)	376	1,798	45.7
10 April	PA (172)	293	2,091	53.2
1 May		382	2,473	62.9
	DC (15)			
	TN (65)			
8 May "Super Tuesday II"		483	2,956	75.2
	IN (77)			
	MD (62)			
	NC (75)			
	OH (154)			
15 May		275	3,231	82.2
	NE (24)			
	OR (43)			
5 June "Super Bowl"		596	3,827	97.3
	CA (306)			
	NJ (107)			
	NM (23)			
	SD (15)			
	WV (35)			
13 June		32	3,859	98.1

SOURCE: Associated Press count of delegates, as reported in *National Journal,* volume 16.

to vote had been violently denied in Birmingham, their choice of housing had been officially restricted in Chicago, and their neighborhoods had been devastated by rioting in Los Angeles. By 1984, all of these cities — and a hundred others — had black mayors. The group's impact at the polls was still not fully tapped. Although their numbers were growing faster than the general population, many had not yet responded to the freedom provided through voting rights laws, and they still voted less frequently than whites. Jesse Jackson would now direct this electoral potential toward national politics.

THE DEMOCRATIC DELEGATE CHASE

Mondale total	Mondale percent of majority	Hart total	Jackson total
118	5.9	7	7
126	6.4	17	7
301	15.3	164	34
627	31.8	351	61
692	35.2	422	88
816	41.4	512	141
1,036	52.6	578	152
1,236	62.8	671	208
1,450	73.7	874	279
1,599	81.2	980	293
1,971	100.2	1,222	372
1,996	101.4	1,229	371

The list could be extended, to include Hispanics, homosexuals, environmentalists, nuclear freeze advocates, Jews. But one group was initially unnoticed. "Yuppies," or "Yumpies," were not a distinct or formally organized group, but these young, urban (and/or upwardly mobile) professionals would have a large impact on the presidential race. The inexorable facts of demography foretold that the children of the baby boom would soon decisively affect American politics. Among this younger generation, those more affluent and more politically conscious had already made their mark in opposition to the Vietnam War, in the McGovern and Carter candidacies, and in the creation of a new "culture of narcissism." In 1984, Gary Hart would give them an identity and a political focus.[22]

Coping with the demands of these different groups was a major problem for the presidential candidates. Jackson explicitly sought their support, as he attempted to build a "rainbow coalition." Ultimately, he failed in this effort, winning overwhelming support from blacks, but from almost no other voters. John Glenn tried to rise above the group claims, asking, "Will we offer a party that can't say no to anyone with a letterhead and a mailing list?" He, and later Gary Hart, would attack Mondale for his ready endorsement of these demands. The Minnesotan lacked a clear response. He defended his support of group claims, saying at one point, "America is about promises," but was also embarrassed by polls showing that public opinion regarded him as too closely tied to labor and other interests. Mondale personified the problem of the Democratic party generally, the need to define a more general vision from the clash of competing factions.[23]

As the season of the primaries began, Mondale was dominant. His expected major challenger, Senator Glenn, was already fading in polls and in the press. A feature motion picture, *The Right Stuff,* had been expected to help his campaign, by reminding voters of his heroism as an astronaut. Instead, by identifying him with the past, it made him irrelevant in the search for a "new face" to challenge Mondale. A foreign observer drew a searching portrait of "a solid, able, tolerably modest fellow, . . . a hero and celebrity, rather, who is doing what he is doing for reasons obscure to the observing eye, and possibly even to him. The legend of heroism carries charisma but Glenn himself—apart from an odd resemblance to the Pope—has no charisma."[24]

No other major challenger was evident. While Jesse Jackson was clearly dramatic, his campaign was disrupted by a series of apparently anti-Semitic incidents. These included his reference to Jews as "Hymies," his delays in admitting or repudiating offensive comments, and his relationship with a demagogic black Muslim, Louis Farrakhan. As the candidates engaged in the first of nine nationally televised debates, Mondale was confident. Acting as if he were already the party's leader, he praised many of his colleagues' comments and avoided opportunites for conflict. The strategy seemed sound when he overwhelmingly won the first test, the Iowa caucuses, gaining 45 percent of the vote. In a national poll taken in the following week, Mondale was the preferred presidential candidate of 57 percent of Democrats, "the most commanding lead ever recorded this early in a presidential nomination campaign by a nonincumbent."[25]

Yet there were problems evident for Mondale, even as he exulted in this first victory. Some problems were hidden in the Iowa figures: He was very weak among younger voters, winning only 19 percent among those under the age of 30, and was seen as lacking "new ideas" and as overly influenced by "special interests." Nationally, it was evident that the former Vice-President had not generated enthusiasm. He was well-known, but not very well-liked. Favorable comments outnumbered critical ones, but the ratio remain fixed at a tepid 3 to 2 level. Even as they prepared to accept Mondale as their party's choice, a majority of Democrats also indicated that they were unhappy with the choices before them. The Minnesotan was vulnerable.[26]

That vulnerability was exploited, even created, by the media. Their emphasis was not on Mondale's decisive victory, but on the "surprising" showing of Gary Hart, who came in second in the Iowa voting, with 15 percent, and the contrasting poor performance of Glenn, with only 5 percent. Hart and the media parroted each other in intepreting the results as evidence that Democrats were looking for an alternative to Mondale. A week later, that interpretation became a self-fulfilling prophecy, as Hart won the New Hampshire primary—another "surprise." The Colorado senator's success was impressive statistically, 37 percent to 28 percent, but it amounted to a margin of only 12,000 votes. "Wait a minute!" warned a political scientist. "Did he say 12,000 votes? That's about half the population of Waterville, Maine, and many of you have never even heard of Waterville. . . . Why should we all be swayed by 12,000 votes?"[27]

Nevertheless, the victory was sufficiently dramatic to carry Hart to successive victories in the Maine and Wyoming caucuses, and in the nonbinding primary in Vermont. Television certainly contributed to this momentum. Even though Mondale had won 3 to 1 in Iowa, his share of video news coverage actually declined. Hart received as much attention as the previous "front-runner," and it was "virtually free of any harsh criticism, unflattering issues, or cynical commentary." All of the other candidates were neglected, and three (Askew, Cranston, and Hollings) formally withdrew after the New Hampshire primary. On the eve of "Super Tuesday," 13 March, when nine states would begin choosing delegates, Hart had become the new "front-runner." As such, however, he was now the target for media attention and attack. Inconsistences in his record, ranging from issue positions to his correct age, were pointed out, critical comments were aired, and one reporter used the public forum of a national interview to ask Hart to do an imitation of Edward Kennedy.[28]

Astonished at his reversed fortunes, Mondale briefly considered withdrawing from the race, and then changed tactics. He aggressively attacked Hart, exaggerating their differences on such issues as nuclear disarmament and industrial reconstruction. He questioned Hart's social commitment, asking, "Where's the guts, where's the soul?" And, borrowing the slogan of a hamburger chain, he asked of Hart's ideas, "Where's the beef?" On "Super Tuesday," Mondale

TABLE 1.2

Date	State	Total vote	Mondale	Percent	Hart	Percent
			State			
28 February	NH	101,131	28,173	27.9	37,702	37.2
13 March	AL	428,283	148,186	34.6	88,655	20.7
	FL	1,160,713	372,588	32.1	464,285	40.0
	GA	684,541	209,785	30.5	186,880	27.3
	MA	630,962	160,895	25.5	246,075	39.0
	RI	44,511	15,312	34.4	20,030	45.0
18 March	PR	143,039	141,751	99.1	858	0.6
29 March	IL	1,659,425	672,067	40.5	584,118	35.2
27 March	CT	220,842	64,265	29.1	116,163	52.6
3 April	NY	1,387,950	621,802	44.8	380,298	27.4
10 April	PA	1,656,294	746,989	45.1	551,546	33.3
1 May	DC	102,731	26,299	25.6	7,294	7.1
	TN	322,063	132,046	41.0	93,720	29.1
5 May	LA	318,810	71,095	22.3	79,703	25.0
8 May	IN	716,955	293,235	40.9	299,687	41.8
	MD	506,886	215,427	42.5	123,173	24.3
	NC	960,857	342,065	35.6	290,179	30.2
	OH	1,444,797	582,253	40.3	608,260	42.1
15 May	NE	148,855	39,595	26.6	86,273	58.2
	OR	377,939	103,177	27.3	222,606	58.9
5 June	CA	2,724,248	1,019,761	37.4	1,121,175	41.2
	NJ	678,893	306,132	45.1	200,525	29.5
	NM	186,635	67,477	36.2	86,819	46.5
	SD	53,155	20,485	38.5	27,238	51.2
	WV	359,744	193,277	53.7	133,329	37.1

SOURCE: *Congressional Quarterly,* volume 22.

achieved his minimum objective—he survived. Although Hart won primaries in Massachusetts, Rhode Island, and Florida, Mondale did well in Alabama and led narrowly in Georgia. Contrary to expectations, "Super Tuesday" ended not with a knockout but as the preliminary to an extended slugfest. As Glenn and McGovern withdrew, the race had become, in fact, a two-man contest. Jesse Jackson remained a candidate and an influence, but he had no realistic chance of nomination.

The drama continued for three months. A series of nine television debates provided new opportunities for citizens to learn, and for candidates to per-

THE DEMOCRATIC PRIMARIES

			Cumulative		
Jackson	Percent	Total vote	Mondale %	Hart %	Jackson %
5,359	5.3	101,131	27.9	37.3	5.3
83,943	19.6				
143,928	32.1				
143,754	21.0				
31,548	5.0				
3,872	8.7				
		3,050,141	30.6	34.2	13.5
0	0.0	3,193,180	33.7	32.7	12.9
348,479	21.0	4,852,605	36.0	33.6	15.7
26,501	12.0	5,073,447	35.7	34.4	15.5
355,315	25.6	6,461,397	37.7	32.9	17.7
265,007	16.0	8,117,691	39.2	33.0	17.3
69,128	67.3				
81,482	25.3				
		8,542,485	39.0	32.5	18.2
79,703	42.9	8,861,295	38.5	32.2	19.1
98,223	13.7				
129,256	25.5				
244,058	25.4				
236,947	16.4				
		12,490,790	38.8	33.5	19.2
13,458	9.1				
35,904	9.5				
		13,017,584	38.3	34.5	19.7
532,952	19.6				
160,281	23.6				
22,257	11.9				
2,745	5.2				
24,005	6.7				
		17,020,259	38.7	35.6	19.5

suade. The voters certainly took the opportunity to think anew, as half of the Democrats changed their preferences in the month of March. The amount of learning and commitment was less impressive. Decisions were made late, and sometimes on the basis of chance comments by the candidates. In midcampaign, only half of the primary voters had strong preferences. Much attention was directed to Hart's "new ideas," but only 9 percent of all voters, and only one of six Hart supporters, could identify any specific proposal.[29]

Mondale had recovered. As delegate selection moved to the large industrial states, he scored a series of victories, in Michigan, Illinois, New York, and Penn-

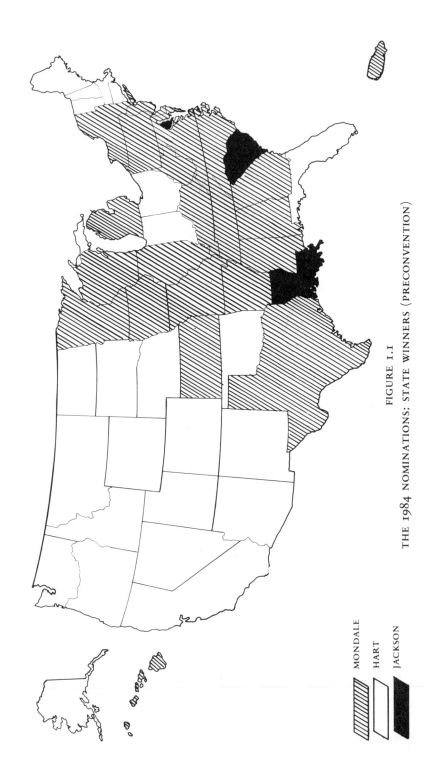

FIGURE 1.1

THE 1984 NOMINATIONS: STATE WINNERS (PRECONVENTION)

MONDALE

HART

JACKSON

sylvania (see table 1.2 on pages 18-19). From this point, he also consistently led the polls again as the preference of Democratic voters, and he was accumulating large numbers of delegates. As the revived front-runner, however, he again assumed the burden of that position. Four primaries were held on 8 May, "Super Tuesday II." Hart won narrow victories in two of the contests—Indiana and Ohio—then swept western primaries and caucuses, while maintaining his criticism of Mondale's campaign financing and programs. On the last day of primaries, the "Super Bowl" of 5 June, Hart made his last stand, winning decisively in California and two other states. By this point, however, Mondale needed only his overwhelming success in New Jersey to clinch the nomination.

Mondale had won, but the primaries had shown his personal weaknesses and the party divisions that darkened the chances for electoral victory. Geographically, Mondale's base was constricted. As can be seen in figure 1.1, he won virtually no states west of the Mississippi basin, and lost all of New England, as well as important parts of the Midwest and South. With this narrow support, he would lose the November election against Reagan, even if he could hold all of the states that formed his nominating coalition. Mondale also faced continuing divisions within the party. These differences are evident in table 1.3 on page 22, which presents the voting patterns evident in the combined vote of all the Democratic primaries.[30]

Jesse Jackson presented both a problem and an opportunity. His impact went beyond his total capture of the black vote. Its immediate effect was to complicate Mondale's efforts, since the Minnesotan lost black votes he probably would have received otherwise. For the longer run, Jackson had stimulated extraordinary increases in the group's vote, particularly among the young, so that blacks constituted nearly one out of five voters in the primaries. These numbers meant that the policy spectrum of the party would need to be extended to the left, to include programs he advocated for the disadvantaged. Jackson himself would need to be wooed, because his enthusiastic followers were critical to a Democratic victory. Too much wooing of Jackson, however, risked alienating the affections of other members of the party coalition, particularly white southerners and Jews.

Hart symbolized a very different element. He was weak in the traditional constituency of the Democratic party—blacks, union members and their families, the elderly, Catholics. At the same time, his candidacy raised the possibility that he would bring new groups into the party, since he attracted independent, young, better-educated, and more affluent voters. As one reporter found, they saw in Hart "many qualities they see in themselves: independence from old ideas and political structures; a pragmatic, nonideological approach to problems and a rejection of the cynicism that developed in the Vietnam and Watergate eras."[31]

TABLE 1.3

VOTING IN THE DEMOCRATIC PRIMARIES

(in percent)

	Primary electorate	Mondale	Hart	Jackson
Totals	100	38.2	35.6	18.6
Sex				
Men	46	38	36	17
Women	54	39	35	20
Race				
White	78	42	43	5
Black	18	19	32	77
Age				
18-29	17	26	39	26
30-44	30	30	38	23
45-59	24	41	34	18
60 and over	28	52	31	10
Family income				
Under $25,000	54	40	32	22
$25,000 and over	46	36	40	15
Education				
Less than high school	14	51	26	18
High school graduate	33	43	34	16
Some college	27	33	38	21
College graduate	26	31	41	20
Party				
Democrat	74	42	33	20
Independent	20	28	44	16
Ideology				
Liberal	27	34	36	25
Moderate	47	41	37	15
Conservative	21	37	34	16
Union household	33	45	31	19
Catholics	NA	50	40	7

SOURCE: Adam Clymer, "The 1984 National Primary," *Public Opinion* 7 (August/September 1984): 53.

Yet these very qualities of his constituents also limited Hart's appeal to the broader Democratic party. Independent voters might temporarily support Hart, but would they actually vote Democratic? Self-reliant, they showed less loyalty to the party. Hart supporters gave Reagan relatively higher approval ratings, indicating their possible defection in November. Furthermore, Hart voters were more likely to be "sore losers." More of them would vote against

Mondale in a race with Reagan than Mondale supporters would vote against Hart. In rejecting "the establishment," they sometimes evidenced a hostility to the union movement that had long served both workers and the party. Advanced in their own work, they stressed development of high-technology industry. They showed limited empathy with those too poor or too immobile to abandon the smokestack industries. The California primary vote underlined the nature and limits of Hart's constituency. The Coloradan won more than half the votes from persons who used computers at home or at work, but he was beaten 3 to 1 among persons who had been unemployed in the previous year.[32]

Mondale's support was more firmly rooted in the basic constituency of the Democratic party. He won the nomination in the end because he was the most consensual candidate available. Not only did he lead opinion polls among Democrats for most of the primary period, Mondale also won the most votes in all of the primaries, as well as the support of experienced party leaders. Moreover, he came in either first or second in virtually every state contest, while both Hart and Jackson sometimes ran far behind.

The Minnesotan presented the most balanced appeal of the three major aspirants. Hart's advocates stressed foreign policy issues, and Jackson's social concerns, while Mondale won votes on both grounds. Ideologically, he was not always favored by self-identified liberals, but he did win support across the spectrum. While he did not come across as well as Jackson to blacks or as a "caring" person, he far outdistanced Hart in these respects. If seen as deficient in new ideas, he was rated as superior in experience and leadership.[33] Mondale was the most appropriate person available to carry the Democratic banner. His broad support in the party proved to be a decisive strength in seeking the nomination, but it could also be a major limitation in later attempting to expand that constituency toward a presidential majority.

The Democratic Consensus

The primaries over, the Democratic party began to move toward unity. Whatever their abstract philosophy, Hart and Jackson knew that realistic arithmetic gave Mondale a convention majority. The erstwhile competitors edged toward consensus, surely spurred by opinion polls predicting a Reagan triumph. While Hart continued to argue that he would be a stronger candidate, he dropped his legal complaint over Mondale's campaign financing, and eliminated personal attacks on the former Vice-President. Jackson, mollifying some of his critics, repudiated a virulent anti-Semitic comment by Louis Farrakhan, and asserted his loyalty to the party. McGovern and Edward Kennedy endorsed Mondale, adding to his consensual support.

For his part, Mondale acted to conciliate his defeated opponents. He supported the creation of a party "Fairness Commission" to rewrite the nominating rules for 1988 to meet Jackson's and Hart's objections. As the party platform was being drafted, the dominant Mondale faction accepted major points of the other factions, especially large parts of Hart's economic program. The result was that the platform totaled a record 45,000 words, but only five items of disagreement were left for the convention to decide.[34]

Consensus was relatively simple to achieve because the Democrats were not divided ideologically. Although the party did contain competing factions, the competition was for power rather than for programs. All of the final three candidates—and the platform—favored limiting defense expenditures, a nuclear freeze, expansion of civil rights, affirmative action, abortion and other feminist goals, higher social spending, greater taxes on the wealthy, environmental protection, and government involvement in economic planning. Convention delegates shared this consensus, being "strikingly unified on the major issues," with over 90 percent favoring limitations of defense spending, expanded public jobs, and affirmative action programs. There were also electoral dangers in this agreement, for the delegates did not mirror the party's rank and file. While two-thirds of the delegates labeled themselves liberals, only a third of Democratic voters did. On the other hand, only 7 percent of the delegates were self-identified conservatives, compared to a quarter of all Democrats.[35]

The remaining question for the Democrats was the vice-presidential nominee. In accord with recent practice, it was understood Mondale would designate his preference, for formal ratification by the convention. Seeking to maintain public and media interest, Mondale began a process of interviewing potential candidates at his Minnesota home. As each group within the party pressed its claims, Mondale enlarged the list to include women and minority groups, but only one white male. The open process particularly encouraged feminists, who threatened a convention floor fight if a woman was not selected. This threat made Mondale seem indecisive. As George Will saw it, "Mondale bought his own paint and then painted himself into a corner. . . . He has no choice but to pick a woman, and he must not do it. If he does not, he will have got half the population up on its tiptoes and then not kissed it. If he does, he will be the wimp who was bullied by the National Organization for Women."[36]

Mondale turned away the scorn when he made his choice, New York Congresswoman Geraldine Ferraro, the chair of the platform committee. The selection of a woman guaranteed a harmonious convention. The unique action gave the Democrats the attention and novelty they needed to improve their trailing position in public opinion. Beyond her gender, Mrs. Ferraro soon showed herself to be a lively personality who would attract attention and provide a desirable contrast to the stolid personality of the presidential candidate. Mondale used this new appeal to advantage. When the running mates arrived at the opening Democratic rally in San Francisco, she gave the climactic final speech.

The Democratic convention itself was a surprising success. Although no major decisions were left to be made, it was vibrant. Although the primaries had been hard-fought, the party was unified. Although delegates were uncertain of their electoral chances, they left San Francisco inspired by remarkable oratory that stated new themes for the party.

Vibrancy came from the emergence of new groups within the party. Jackson's oratorical theme, "Our time has come," expressed the elation of women delegates that Ferraro's nomination marked their achievement of full political equality, the pride of blacks that they now had a national spokesman and national role, the hope of Hispanics that they had begun to climb the ladder of immigrant mobility, the confidence of "Yuppies" that they inevitably controlled the future.

Unity was promoted by the shared dislike of Reagan, by the efforts of defeated candidates to build support for the future by graciously accepting their loss, and by further compromises on the platform. The Mondale forces accepted a Hart proposal to restrict the President's authority to use military forces abroad, and a Jackson proposal to omit opposition to racial quotas in programs of affirmative action. On three remaining issues, the convention defeated pledges to renounce the first use of nuclear weapons, to cut defense spending below current levels, and to eliminate southern runoff primaries. By defeating these three proposals, all sponsored by Jackson, Mondale and his supporters hoped to increase their appeal to moderate voters. Table 1.4 on pages 26-27 presents the roll call on the first of these issues, which caused the most division. The table also shows the similarity between this vote and the later roll call on the presidential nomination.[37]

In a series of notable speeches, the Democrats stressed the themes of coalition politics and positive government. Jackson expressed these themes evocatively, using the stirring cadences of the black church. Evoking the imagery of Christian saintliness, he asked Jews and others to forgive any errors: "Charge it to my head and not to my heart . . . which is boundless in its love for the human family. I am not a perfect servant. . . . As I develop and serve, be patient. God is not finished with me yet." Jackson pleaded for "the desperate, the damned, the disinherited, the disrepected, and the despised." Prophesizing political success, he urged the extension of his "rainbow coalition": "When blacks vote in great numbers, progressive whites win. It's the only way progressive whites win. If blacks vote in great numbers, Hispanics win. If blacks, Hispanics and progressive whites win, women win. When women win, children win. When wom-

TABLE 1.4
DEMOCRATIC CONVENTION ROLL CALLS

State	Totals	Nuclear "First Use" Ban		Presidential Nomination		
		Yes	No	Mondale	Hart	Jackson
Alabama	62	15	46	39	13	9
Alaska	14	7	7	9	4	1
Arizona	40	20	19	20	16	2
Arkansas	42	13	29	26	9	7
California	345	149	84	95	190	33
Colorado	51	31	16	1	42	1
Connecticut	60	28	24	23	36	1
Delaware	18	1	17	13	5	0
District of Columbia	19	15	4	5	0	14
Florida	143	47	76	82	55	3
Georgia	84	40	33	40	24	20
Hawaii	27	1	26	27	0	0
Idaho	22	9	0	10	12	0
Illinois	194	42	145	114	41	39
Indiana	88	31	46	42	38	8
Iowa	58	22	36	37	18	2
Kansas	44	14	29	25	16	3
Kentucky	63	14	48	51	5	7
Louisiana	69	24	32	26	19	24
Maine	27	7	16	13	13	0
Maryland	74	20	51	54	3	17
Massachusetts	116	89	24	59	49	5
Michigan	155	43	105	96	49	10
Minnesota	86	37	41	63	3	4
Mississippi	43	15	26	26	4	13
Missouri	86	20	62	55	14	16
Montana	25	8	15	11	13	1

Nebraska	30	2	25	12	17	1
Nevada	20	6	14	9	10	1
New Hampshire	22	10	12	12	10	0
New Jersey	122	9	113	115	0	7
New Mexico	28	7	19	13	13	2
New York	285	134	140	156	75	52
North Carolina	88	28	56	53	19	16
North Dakota	18	13	5	10	5	1
Ohio	175	71	103	84	80	11
Oklahoma	53	16	35	24	26	3
Oregon	50	32	13	16	31	2
Pennsylvania	195	42	153	177	0	18
Puerto Rico	53	0	53	53	0	0
Rhode Island	27	11	15	14	12	0
South Carolina	48	21	23	16	13	19
South Dakota	19	7	12	9	10	0
Tennessee	76	31	41	39	20	17
Texas	200	53	137	119	40	36
Utah	27	17	10	8	19	0
Vermont	17	11	4	5	8	3
Virginia	78	29	48	34	18	25
Washington	70	49	18	31	36	3
West Virginia	44	12	27	30	14	3
Wisconsin	89	28	45	58	25	6
Wyoming	15	2	12	7	7	0
Latin America	5	0	5	5	0	0
Democrats Abroad	5	1.5	3.5	3	1.5	.5
Virgin Islands	6	1.2	4.8	4	0	2
American Samoa	6	0	6	6	0	0
Guam	7	0	7	7	0	0
TOTALS		1,405.7	2,216.3	2,191	1,200.5	465.5

SOURCES: *New York Times*, 20 July 1984, A12; and *Congressional Quarterly* 42 (21 July 1984): 1800.

en and children win, workers win. We must all come up together. We must come up together."

The candidates added to the message. Receiving the most emotional reception, Ferraro used the opportunity to appeal to ethnic and blue-collar voters who were critical in the coming election. "Tonight," she said firmly to misty-eyed women and men, "the daughter of working Americans tells all Americans that the future is within our reach—if we're willing to reach for it. Tonight the daughter of an immigrant from Italy has been chosen to run for Vice-President in the new land my father came to love."

Accepting his nomination, Mondale attempted to broaden his appeal beyond the party forum. As the Democrats waved thousands of American flags to show their patriotism, Mondale professed a "new realism." Rather than new programs, he made an unusual promise: "By the end of my first term, I will reduce the Reagan budget deficit by two-thirds. Let's tell the truth. . . . Mr. Reagan will raise taxes, and so will I. He won't tell you. I just did." Returning to the convention's theme of the promotion of social mobility, he concluded, "America is a future that each generation must enlarge; a door that each generation must open; a promise that each generation must keep."[38]

The Democrats left San Francisco enthusiastic, and were soon encouraged by a flash Gallup poll that showed their candidates had actually moved slightly ahead of Reagan and Bush. Four Fs defined their coming campaign. Family values required government to accept social responsibilities. Fairness necessitated change in social programs. Fear of nuclear holocaust demanded a new President committed to a nuclear freeze. Ferraro would provide a unique personal appeal on the ticket. But it was still uncertain whether the voters would endorse a fifth element, Fritz Mondale.

The Republican Competition

Republicans met a month later, in Dallas. Where their rivals had struggled to achieve unity, Republicans were mired in agreement. Where the opposition had provided the excitement of change, Republicans stretched to fill the free media time. Where the challengers sought to recover their past glories, Republicans began to contest their party's future.

Outwardly, there was no division in the Dallas meeting. President Reagan and Vice-President Bush were praised by every speaker, festooned on placards in every corner, unanimously favored by every state delegation. The party's platform was adopted without vocal dissent. Ideologically, the delegates were cohesively conservative—only one of a hundred called themselves liberals, and only one of four even claimed to be moderates.

Behind the smiling agreement, competition for the future of the party had begun. Proposals to give northeastern states more equitable representation in future conventions were buried. Conservatives in control of the platform held only one day of public hearings, and denied any concessions to the other factions. Illustratively, they rejected not only the Equal Rights Amendment but even language supporting "equal rights and equal responsibilities" for women. On taxes, the platform writers went beyond the President's own policy, opposed all increases in levies, and encouraged the abolition of progressive income tax rates.

The conservatives were looking to 1988, when the party's leadership would again be open. Finding even Ronald Reagan suspect, they complained that "he has substantively abandoned his Main Street constituency and embraced his party's Wall Street wing." They hoped for the creation of an "antiliberal" majority party, which would further reduce taxation and government intervention, as a means to enhance individual economic opportunities, while promoting traditional social morality and assertive foreign policies. The outnumbered moderates could only warn, with Iowa Congressman Jim Leach, "The country is a progressive, moderate nation. Yet our party is becoming ideologically narrow."[39]

Conservative domination of the convention was personally demonstrated in the speech of the faction's ideological progenitor, Senator Barry Goldwater. Returning to the rhetoric of his own presidential campaign two decades earlier, he castigated Democrats as "ashamed of our freedom" and blamed the party for the nation's four wars in the twentieth century. He deliberately repeated his aggressive motif of 1964: "Extremism in the defense of liberty is no vice." Once controversial, the statement now brought only nodding agreement from the delegates.[40]

For 1984, at least, the party remained united, and optimistic. The Democratic gains of July had disappeared, and the Reagan-Bush ticket again enjoyed comfortable poll leads. The President himself set the tone for the party in a film biography and in his acceptance speech. Ideology was subordinated to an emphasis on the administration's achievements, the Reagan personality, and the revival of American patriotism. On the critical economic issue, Reagan took up Mondale's challenge:[41]

> In 1980, the people decided with us that the economic crisis was not caused by the fact that they lived too well. Government lived too well. It was time for tax increases to be an act of last resort, not of first resort. . . . America is on the move again, and expanding toward new eras of opportunity for everyone. . . . Our opponents are openly committed to increasing your tax burden. We are committed to stopping them, and we will.

The Republican campaign was defined by four *P*s. Prosperity was wide-spread for most Americans, especially voting Americans. Peace had been maintained, and was attributed to the administration's defense buildup. Patriotism had become fashionable again, evident in national pride in Olympic victories and in new respect for the military. President Reagan was personally popular, even among those disagreeing with him on some issues. With these advantages, Republicans left Dallas maneuvering for 1988 but confident about 1984.

The Parties and the Choices of 1984

The election would be a competition between two pairs of candidates, but it would also be a contest of ideas and attachments.

The Ferraro nomination encapsulated these contests. Most obviously, it highlighted the uncertainties Americans had felt for at least two decades about the proper roles of the sexes. Was politics a "man's job," or could women also fill the highest offices? Did women who devoted themselves to home and children shirk social duties, or actually meet the most precious responsibilities? Were men willing to accept equality not only by words, and not only by the division of housework, but by accepting female rulers? Polls suggested that the congress-woman would bring new votes to the Democrats, but no poll could probe the voters' hearts.

Religious values were also contested. The American doctrine of the separation of church and state had prevented the joining of these two authorities, but the ethical teachings of religion had always affected our politics. In 1984, the relationship was more open. As a minister, Jackson spoke explicitly in religious accents, while the Republicans gave Jerry Falwell, leader of the right-wing "Moral Majority," a conspicuous place at their convention. Among the candidates, Ferraro questioned the President's commitment to Christian values of charity and caring, while Reagan found politics "inseparable" from religious morality.

Reagan's Christianity, sincerely held, was that of Protestant individualism. It emphasized the responsibility of each person for his or her own salvation, and defined charity and good works principally in terms of interpersonal relationships. Ferraro, representing more the Italian Catholic and Jewish traditions, put greater emphasis on good works than on faith alone, and on meeting social responsibilities through collective action. These differences had once defined the principal lines between the parties, when nineteenth-century Republicans were more likely to be temperance advocates, and Democrats were more likely to endorse the crude social welfare programs of the urban machines. In 1984, the voters again were asked to relate their partisanship to their basic values.[42]

Value differences led to philosophical and political conflicts. The two parties in 1984 were defining themselves as parts of two divergent American traditions. The Republicans fully embraced the usually dominant tradition, that of liberal individualism. It sees society as composed of distinct persons, each entitled to "life, liberty, and the pursuit of happiness." Government is to be restrained from interfering with individual liberties and rights or, at most, is to eliminate obstacles to individual opportunity. Together, these persons comprise one united society, in which group interests are suspect as invasions of individual needs and social cohesion.

The Republican keynoter, Katherine Ortega, stated these themes concisely: "America stands for freedom. For opportunity. For the right of every individual to fulfill his or her potential as members of the family of God, not creatures of an almighty government."[43]

The individualist tradition stresses liberties against government and rights to be respected by government. Another tradition emphasizes community, leading to the mutual obligations of citizens to one another and to claims upon society and government. From the Mayflower Compact and the Declaration of Independence's pledge of "our lives, our fortunes, and our sacred honor," it also has inspired Americans. The communitarian tradition derives from the ancient Roman extended household, whose head was "responsible for the well-being of everyone, related or not related, who can legitimately be considered a 'familiar.' "[44]

The Democratic keynoter, New York Governor Mario Cuomo, eloquently invoked this responsibility: "We believe we must be the family of America, recognizing that at the heart of the matter, we are bound one to another [and] that the failure anywhere to provide what reasonably we might, to avoid pain, is our failure."[45]

Both these traditions are accepted by Americans, who believe simultaneously in individual liberty and in community responsibility, who distrust government even as they rely upon it. Each tradition has conflicting effects. While individualism can undergird the entrepeneurial spirit of Silicon Valley, it can also neglect the uneducated. While communitarianism can stimulate a concern for the poor, it can also legitimize unrestrained demands on government.

The significance of the 1984 election was that these two traditions became the competing programs of the major political parties. No longer could cynics complain that they wanted "a choice, not an echo." The United States no longer had a consensual politics in which the parties imitated each other's appeals to moderate opinion. It was closer to the academicians' dream of a "responsible party system," in which the parties "provide the electorate with a proper range of choice between alternatives of action."[46]

Americans now had a real option before them, but also a real dilemma. Accepting the Republican program could mean not only less government interference but also less government help. Endorsing the Democratic agenda could mean not only solving social problems but also creating social demands. Time would tell if these new political alternatives were any better than the choice between the pit and the pendulum.

NOTES

1. See Irving Howe, ed., *1984 Revisited* (New York: Harper & Row, 1983).
2. Gerald Pomper et al., *The Election of 1980* (Chatham, N.J.: Chatham House, 1981), 190f.
3. Various analyses of the 1980 election support this view, including Paul Abramson et al., *Change and Continuity in the 1980 Elections* (Washington, D.C.: Congressional Quarterly, 1982); Ellis Sandoz and Cecil V. Crabb, *A Tide of Discontent* (Washington, D.C.: Congressional Quarterly, 1981); Pomper, *The Election of 1980*, chaps. 3, 4.
4. William Greider, "The Education of David Stockman," *Atlantic* 248 (December 1981): 51.
5. See Thomas Mann and Norman Ornstein, *The American Elections of 1982* (Washington, D.C.: American Enterprise Institute, 1983), chap. 5.
6. *Congressional Quarterly Weekly Report* 41 (23 July 1983): 1503-7. The leading analysis of voting turnout is Raymond Wolfinger and Steven Rosenstone, *Who Votes?* (New Haven: Yale University Press, 1980).
7. Two different interpretations are found in Kathleen Frankovic, "Sex and Politics: New Alignments, Old Issues," *P.S.* 15 (Summer 1982): 439-48; and William Schneider, "The Democrats Are Counting on the Gender Gap, But It May Not Be Much Help," *National Journal,* 23 June 1984, 1242-43.
8. The popularity of Reagan can be traced in the CBS News/New York Times polls. Results reported here are from surveys of January 1983 and January 1984. Gallup poll results are reported in *National Journal* 16 (28 January 1984): 190. The disparity between Reagan's personal popularity and evaluations on specific issues is evident in the Gallup poll of 10-13 February 1984, reported in the *New York Times,* 14 March 1984, 27. (See also figure 3.2.)
9. See the critical votes in *Congressional Quarterly Almanac* 37 (1981): 40H-43H. On the cohesion of the White House staff, see John Kessel, "The Structures of the Reagan White House," *American Journal of Political Science* 28 (May 1984): 231-58.
10. On the ideology of party activists, see John S. Jackson III et al., "Herbert McClosky and Friends Revisited: 1980 Democratic and Republican Party Elites Compared to the Mass Public," *American Politics Quarterly* 10 (April 1982): 158-80; Martin Plissner and Warren Mitofsky, "Political Elites," *Public Opinion* 4 (October/November 1981): 47-50. On Republican party organization, see John Bibby, "Party Renewal in the National Republican Party," in *Party Renewal in America,* ed. Gerald M. Pomper (New York: Praeger, 1980), chap. 7.

11. The history of these changes is presented by William Crotty, *Party Reform* (New York: Longman, 1983). They are criticized by Nelson Polsby, *Consequences of Party Reform* (New York: Oxford University Press, 1983).
12. The limitations of the primaries are analyzed in Scott Keeter and Cliff Zukin, *Uninformed Choice* (New York: Praeger, 1984). The effects of the mass media are critiqued by Michael Robinson, *Over the Wire and on TV* (New York: Russell Sage, 1983).
13. *Democratic Party of U.S. v. Wisconsin ex. rel. LaFollette,* 450 U.S. 107 (1981).
14. The work of the commission is described and defended by its executive director, David Price, in *Bringing Back the Parties* (Washington, D.C.: Congressional Quarterly, 1984).
15. *New York Times,* 30 December 1982, A10.
16. Hamilton Jordan, *Crisis* (New York: Putnam, 1982), 417.
17. Howell Raines, *New York Times,* 26 September 1983, B8.
18. "Handicappers," *New York Times Magazine,* 6 February 1983, 12.
19. *Los Angeles Times,* 8 July 1983; CBS News/New York Times poll, completed 28 January 1984.
20. Table 1.1 is derived from the delegate estimates made weekly by the Associated Press and published regularly in *National Journal* during the campaign. AP's estimates were relatively low, compared to that of the other media. The figures include projected estimates of the delegates to be selected in later meetings in caucus states.
21. For analyses of the impact of the rules, see *National Journal* 16 (23 June 1984): 1236; and *Congressional Quarterly Weekly Report* 42 (23 June 1984): 1504-5.
22. The name was created by the Hart organization and soon spread by the media. Its origin may have been "Yippie," the acronym for the Youth International Party, a radical protest group of 1968. "Yuppie" was probably appealing because it combined a rhyme for adorable "puppies" with nostalgia for "hippies."
23. At the state dinner of the Iowa Democratic party, reported in *New York Times,* 9 October 1983, 31, and in the New Hampshire debate.
24. Peter Preston, "Glenn of This World," *Manchester Guardian Weekly,* 4 December 1983, 8.
25. New York Times/CBS News poll, *New York Times,* 28 February 1984, A1.
26. CBS News/New York Times poll, concluded in Iowa 20 February 1984, and concluded nationally 21 January and 25 February 1984.
27. L. Sandy Maisel, "Should Mice That Roar Decide the Nomination?" *New York Times,* 7 March 1984, A23.
28. William C. Adams, "Media Coverage of Campaign '84: A Preliminary Report," *Public Opinion* 7 (April/May 1984): 9-13. The Hart lead was found by the CBS News/New York Times Poll, in interviews held 5-8 March 1984.
29. New York Times/CBS News Poll, reported in *New York Times,* 27 March 1984, A1.
30. The table was developed by Adam Clymer from a model of the electorate based on exit polls from all of the primaries except Louisiana. The figures for Catholics are the median percentages reported in CBS News/New York Times exit polls from the states of Illinois, New York, Pennsylvania, and Ohio, the only states in which religion was asked.
31. Steven Roberts, *New York Times,* 18 March 1984, 26.
32. California exit poll, CBS News/New York Times poll, 5 June 1984.

33. These conclusions are based on the CBS News/New York Times exit polls in six states holding later primaries: Illinois, New York, Pennsylvania, Ohio, North Carolina, and California. The differences among the candidates are illustrated by the percentage of their supporters who cited, respectively, foreign and domestic social issues as reasons for their votes. The median figures (with each respondent allowed two choices) are: Mondale, 47 percent and 78 percent; Hart, 62 percent and 62 percent; Jackson, 28 percent and 119 percent.

34. See *National Journal* 16 (30 June 1984): 1278; and *Congressional Quarterly Weekly Report* 42 (30 June 1984), 1572-75.

35. *Los Angles Times,* 15 July 1984.

36. "Machiavelli from Minnesota?" *Newsweek,* 16 July 1984, 88.

37. *Congressional Quarterly Weekly Report* 42 (21 July 1984): 1800; and *New York Times,* 20 July 1984, A12. The votes on the other platform issues were similar, with the exception of relatively higher support for the ban on first use of nuclear weapons by delegates from California, Colorado, Iowa, Massachusetts, Ohio, Oklahoma, and Washington. The minority position on defense spending received 1128 votes, and that on runoff primaries received 1253.

38. Texts of the speeches can be found in *Congressional Quarterly Weekly Report* 42 (21 July 1984): 1781-95.

39. The contest over the platform is covered in the *New York Times,* 14-19 August 1984. The conservative program is presented by Howard Phillips and Congressman Newt Gingrich in the *New York Times,* 19 August 1984, sec. 4, p. 19.

40. *New York Times,* 23 August 1984, A28.

41. *New York Times,* 24 August 1984, A12.

42. See Paul Kleppner, *The Cross of Culture* (New York: Free Press, 1970); and Richard Jensen, *The Winning of the Midwest* (Chicago: University of Chicago Press, 1971).

43. *New York Times,* 21 August 984, A20. The tradition is traced by Louis Hartz, *The Liberal Tradition in America* (New York: Harcourt, Brace, 1955).

44. Dean Maria J. Falco, Loyola University of New Orleans, letter of 13 September 1984.

45. *New York Times,* 17 July 984, A16. This intellectual heritage is analyzed by Wilson Carey McWilliams, *The Idea of Fraternity in America* (Berkeley: University of California Press, 1973).

46. Committee on Political Parties, American Political Science Association, *Toward a More Responsible Two-Party System* (New York: Rinehart, 1950), 1.

2

Issues in the Campaign

HENRY A. PLOTKIN

The conventional wisdom about American politics instructs candidates to occupy the center of the ideological spectrum. Yet the election of 1984 matched two candidates who were classically liberal and conservative. Not since Lyndon Johnson trounced Barry Goldwater in 1964 had the two major parties presented candidates whose positions on the issues differed as markedly as those of incumbent President Ronald Reagan and former Vice-President Walter Mondale. Both candidates argued strenuously for two very different conceptions of the purposes of governmental domestic policy and of America's role in the world. To be sure, the campaign of 1984, like its predecessors in recent decades, suffered from the massive intrusion of television with its tendency to trivialize substantive differences and emphasize personality differences. Nevertheless, despite the electronic medium's shadowy presentations of reality, much like those in Plato's cave, the candidates still conveyed starkly different sets of political ideas and different visions of the nation's future.

The Philosophies of 1984

The presidency of Ronald Reagan represented a sharp departure from assumptions about public policy that had shaped American politics since the New Deal. The Reagan administration sought to reverse a half century of activist national government by returning power to the states. At the heart of the "Reagan revolution" was a desire to "get government off the backs of the people" and to allow the private sector to function as freely as possible. And while Reagan was not able to make all the budget cuts he wanted, he was still able to substantially slow the growth of many domestic programs.

The real battle that raged during Reagan's first term was a battle over ideas. The Reagan administration was soon to learn that the rhetoric of policy change was much easier than its implementation. Government programs develop over years. They obtain congressional, bureaucratic, and constituency support, making them resistant even to the pressures of a popular President. The deep cuts gained by Reagan in social welfare still did not permanently alter the logic and priorities of the national budget. Yet, although the budget battle was inconclusive, the war of ideas was quite another story. In this arena the administration may well have had the greatest impact on American public thought since Franklin Roosevelt's New Deal.

Indeed, there are certain parallels between the New Deal and Reaganism. Both, as Samuel Beer has pointed out, are revolutions in political ideas.[1] For the generation of Roosevelt, the call for a strong central government to raise the nation out of the depression was at the heart of a new political consensus. Innovative policies in rural electrification, trade union policies, Social Security, banking and farming were all promulgated in the hopes of getting the economy moving again. None of these and other initiatives wholly succeeded in their task until the Second World War generated a booming economy. The measure of success of the Roosevelt years was to make welfare state liberalism the new public philosophy of America.[2]

The victory of liberalism in politics had enormous consequences for the development of American society over the next 50 years. What began in the 1930s as a series of ad hoc responses to the horrors of the depression ended with the "nationalization" of American politics. The old public philosophy of liberal capitalism declined. Its beliefs—individual market success, the "invisible hand" leading to prosperity and progress, the absence of governmental interference—came to exist only rhetorically. A growing welfare state, which sought substantial redistribution of income, regulation of the economy, and a reduction of the role of the several states, was enshrined in both doctrine and reality.

The intellectual and political legacy of the New Deal was maintained without regard to party. The election of Dwight Eisenhower, the first Republican to become President in 20 years, did not signal any attempt to "roll back" the New Deal. Nor did the administrations of Richard Nixon and Gerald Ford make any such attempt. Once the welfare state was established and its legitimacy accepted by the public, elected officials of both parties become "operational liberals," delivering the most desirable pieces of the national pie to their constituencies. Electoral success in the welfare state era is achieved, and reelection insured, by providing the electorate with the subsidies and entitlements they have come to expect.

The Reagan revolution has done much to change the language of American politics, giving it a decidedly conservative accent. The free market economy so derided by welfare state liberals is now heralded as the necessary precondition for political democracy. Conservatives had been railing against what they saw as excesses of the federal government for decades. Reagan's victories transformed their ideas from the isolated meanderings of discontented intellectuals into the clarion call of a popular chorus. For, in Reagan, conservatives had not only an articulate spokesman for their cause but the "bully pulpit" of the presidency as well. And while it is arguable that the Reagan victory of 1980 was not a victory of conservative ideas but a judgment that the presidency of Jimmy Carter had failed, the past four years have seen a President set forth in no uncertain terms a powerful conservative agenda that augurs to transform American politics permanently.

Presidents are always political educators to some extent, but Ronald Reagan, perhaps because he has stood so far outside the liberal consensus, seems to have had more impact than most. Even Walter Mondale admitted in the first debate that President Reagan had done much to improve the morale of the nation. This was no mean feat in a nation that had suffered through the traumatic '70s of Watergate, Vietnam, double-digit inflation, soaring interest rates, and the humiliation in Iran. The simple patriotism of Reagan with its bounding optimism about America's future and its glorification of America's past was welcomed by a public that had grown weary of years of criticism and self-doubt. The Reagan message played well in America and succeeded in altering the way the nation saw itself and saw its government.

This change was reflected in many ways, not the least of which was the unbridled enthusiasm Americans expressed toward the Olympics. Much to the surprise of many, the Soviet-inspired Olympic boycott did little to dampen the interest Americans had in the Los Angeles games. As the Olympic torch passed through city after city, unexpectedly large crowds hailed its passing. The nation was swept up in a patriotic fervor inspired by a President who himself was unabashedly patriotic and sentimental about America.

This change in national attitudes can also be seen in such recent films as *Uncommon Valor* and *Missing in Action,* both of which portray successful attempts to rescue American soldiers still held prisoner in Vietnam. Not only do they center on Vietnam, a recently unmentionable topic, but these films also applaud the bravery of the military and decry the brutality of the communist regime. At the level of popular culture, at least, a view of heroic America is presented in stark contrast to the terrors of totalitarian regimes. One other movie, *Red Dawn,* makes this contrast even more graphic, as it describes the heroic resistance of American high school students to a combined Soviet, Cuban, and Nicaraguan invasion of the United States.

Instructively, all these films celebrate American virtue and condemn communist tyranny—themes rarely heard in recent years. It would be a mistake to underestimate the meaning of these social and cultural events by assuming they are merely ephemeral, or worse, jingoistic. For what this campaign demonstrated was the importance of traditional values—religion, patriotism, family, morality—to the American psyche. While many substantive issues were raised by both sides, their tones were overwhelmed by the emotional chord struck by Reagan.

Perhaps Reagan's greatest accomplishment was to soothe an anxious nation—"to slow the tempo of change" that threatened to destroy what was familiar and comforting. Rapid social, cultural, and political change made many fear that the nation was deteriorating. Soaring divorce rates, drugs, crime, pornography, teenage suicides—all pointed to a society in decay. Reagan told the nation that the answer to these problems could be found in a religious and moral revival and by a return to basic American values. As Theodore White observed:

> He saw the future in the lost summertime of the nation's past, when neighborhoods were safe, when families held together . . . when U.S. power bestrode the world. He wrapped both past and future in the American flag.[3]

Reagan's major issue in the election of 1984 was his vision of America. The President's America consisted of the successful entrepreneurs, the Horatio Algers of Silicon Valley, creating great enterprises; of citizens voluntarily helping the needy; of a morally just nation doing battle with "the evil empire"; of the individual doing battle with the state; and of a nation grounded in deeply felt religious values. The appeal of these sentiments was widespread—his vision became what the vast majority of Americans knew was not their present, but hoped was their future.

Reagan tapped into a powerful need of many Americans to forget the struggles of the past and present. The moral, religious, and patriotic revival of Reagan fit nicely into the nostalgic mood of Americans. Reagan sought, not to repress past history, but to redefine it in a way that pleased a nation grown weary of its own conflicts. Christopher Lasch argues that the great danger of "revivals" is that they "deny any link with past objects." He asserts "they endow those objects with the charm of distance and inconsequence. Our sense of discontinuity is now so great that even very recent periods, like the '50s or the '60, have become objects of nostalgic retrospect. Eager to deny that events in those decades continue to hound our politics and our culture, we consign them to the irrelevance of the good old days."[4]

Reagan's success, in no small measure, was his ability to redirect the memory of many Americans away from painful experiences toward more pleasant ones. As he had done in 1980, Reagan often referred to America as John Winthrop's "City Upon a Hill"—the focal point for the "eyes of all people." Thus

Reagan made an implicit case for "American exceptionalism," of an America "as mankind's last best hope." His success in bringing the economy back to life was used by his supporters as proof of the success of Reagan's philosophy and as a rebuke to welfare state liberalism.

Perhaps the most powerful attempt to refute Reagan's appeal came not from the Democratic standard bearer, Walter Mondale, but from the convention keynoter, Governor Mario Cuomo. While not denying Reagan's vision of America's splendor, Cuomo drew a picture of "another city," which existed alongside the "city upon a hill." That city Cuomo asserted was one,

> where some people can't pay their mortgages and most young people can't afford one, where students can't afford the education they need and middle-class parents watch the dreams they hold for their children evaporate. . . . There are more poor than ever, more families in trouble . . . there are elderly people who tremble in the basements of houses.[5]

Mario Cuomo's "Tale of Two Cities" goes on to describe the plight of the ghettos "where thousands of young people, without jobs or an education, give their lives away to the drug dealers every day."[6]

The "other" America described by Cuomo was populated by the millions who did not benefit from the Reagan recovery and indeed were directly injured by the cuts in federal programs designed to assist the poor. The Democratic party platform and presidential nominee would stress this issue during the campaign. He fought an uphill battle to remind Americans that, because of the huge budget deficit, the economy was not as good as it seemed and that many had been excluded from improvement in the economy. Most important, Mondale tried to remind Americans of the historic contribution the Democratic party had made to the nation's affluence. Yet as the election results clearly indicated, Americans were of a different opinion and saw the welfare state, not as the vehicle for their individual success, but as an avaricious consumer of taxes for purposes they did not necessarily approve (e.g., welfare, food stamps).

The Democratic party found itself in a paradox as it attempted to remind groups that had become economically secure of the historic mission of the party to assist the "left out." The issue of economic fairness did not play well in the America of 1984. It implicitly asserted that many who had entered the middle class recently did so because of government programs and not individual initiative. Moreover, any extension of the welfare state threatened the economic security of this postwar middle class. Americans were no longer convinced that governmental expansion meant greater economic progress. Successive presidential campaigns had helped to persuade much of the nation that government was not worthy of their support. The Reagan victory of ideas both taught citizens to be skeptical of the benevolence of the federal government and persuaded many that government had hampered, not assisted, the upward mobility most Americans desired.

Indeed a basic tenet of the conservative consensus was a mistrust of all the New Deal organizational engines of progress—trade unions, political activities, governmental programs—that replaced a belief in the efficacy of individualism. The picture of individuals competing in the marketplace was the Republican talisman of success, while the idea of collective action as the route to a more just society remained the standard of the Democratic party.

The Economy

In an obvious sense the Reagan landslide can be attributed to one single issue—the economy. Clearly, the behavior of the middle class demonstrated a certain faith in the economy, reflected in their buying and saving patterns. Indeed, much of the economic recovery can be attributed to record levels of consumer shopping and borrowing and low savings. Ironically, this contravened the assumption of "supply-side" theorists, who had posited that the substantial cuts in income taxes would lead to greater savings and more capital expansion. Instead, a classic "demand-side" recovery took place during the Reagan years, fueled by a middle class so eager to purchase desired goods that even high interest rates did not dim its ardor.[7] Nor, apparently, did the long-term effects of record budget deficits seem to weigh heavily on the mind of the public.

Apparently, public confidence in the economy was restored by the lowered inflation rate. The Carter years were remembered as the time of high inflation with the concomitant fear of erosion in the value of money. An inflationary psychology gripped the nation as soaring prices caused people to panic and to become uncertain as to where it would all end. Inflation, unlike other economic factors, has an immediate effect on the entire population: senior citizens on fixed incomes see their savings melt away; taxpayers are pushed into higher brackets with no increase in disposable income; and an individual's understanding of the "monetary" worth of a product is left without an anchor. When Ronald Reagan asked the nation: "Are you better off now than you were four years ago?" the answer was seemingly a resounding "yes," a "yes" attributable to the political potency of the inflation issue.

It is worth noting that, aside from the inflation rate, the Carter administration's economic performance was superior to that of the Reagan administration along several major dimensions. Economic growth over four years was higher (13.6 percent vs. 10.3 percent); home mortgage rates on the average were lower (10.6 percent vs. 13.86 percent); the four-year unemployment rate was lower

(6.4 percent vs. 8.6 percent); and the percentage of those falling below the poverty line was smaller (13 percent vs. 15.2 percent). However, a major difference was that Carter sought reelection as the indicators of economic health were declining, while Reagan ran for a second term when they were improving. Probably the most significant difference was the federal deficit, which approached the $200 billion mark under the Reagan administration as opposed to $59 billion under Jimmy Carter.[8]

The political lesson we can draw from these figures is that the nation feared the ravages of inflation more than higher unemployment rates and bloated deficits. A curious reversal regarding economic policy took place in this campaign, with Reagan defending deficits, traditionally anathema to Republicans, while Mondale attacked them in a fashion uncharacteristic of Keynesian Democrats. Still, the economic context of the election of 1984 was one in which the Republicans could declare a momentous victory over inflation while the Democrats had to battle the public's memories of inflation during the Carter-Mondale years.

The major debate about the economy concerned whether its apparent health was real or illusory. For Reagan, economic growth was sustainable in a context of low inflation and a reduction in unemployment. The result of that economic growth would be increased government revenues, which in turn would allow the deficit to be decreased and a balanced budget achieved. Mondale sharply disagreed with this scenario, arguing instead that the economic recovery was an illusion that would be shattered at the Waterloo of the deficit.

In Mondale's terms, the economic recovery was accomplished by a deep recession, which, while it lowered inflation, did so by increasing the rate of unemployment. Hence, the recovery was artificial, born from the pain of the unemployed and ultimately stimulated by mammoth increases in the national debt. At its core, then, in Mondale's view the Reagan recovery was ephemeral and its real cost would be paid in the future.

THE REPUBLICANS

Republicans presented the electorate with an optimistic view of the economy's future and urged the public to "stay the course" by continuing to support the President's economic program. Reagan emphasized his opposition to increased taxes. For the Republicans, the tax cuts of 1981 were the main cause of the nation's return to economic health. On the issue of taxes and economic growth, the Republicans staked out their firmest position:

> Our most important economic goal is to expand and continue economic recovery and move the nation to full employment without inflation. We, therefore, oppose

any attempt to increase taxes which harm the recovery and reverse the trend to restoring control of the economy to the American people.[9]

The President's belief in the efficacy of tax cuts had a metaphysic all its own. For, at root, the "supply-side" vision of the world had as much to do with a theory of the just society as it had to do with economic efficacy.[10] Tax policy differences during this election reflected various theories about the proper role for the federal government: how to motivate rational economic behavior; the ethics of redistribution; and, finally, the degree of autonomy of the private sector. The Reagan position on these issues was clear: The size of the government ought to be reduced; individuals should judge how to spend; redistribution of income will only lead to higher unemployment; the maximization of private sector autonomy will insure both economic growth and political freedom.

Beyond the issue of tax cuts, the Republicans also hinted at a much more serious assault on the logic of the graduated income tax itself. David Gergen argued:

> There are voices on the right who believe the progressive tax system does not promote savings, does not promote investment, and they even question the fairness of it.[11]

The graduated income tax has historically reflected an egalitarian ethic which states that those who earn more ought to pay proportionally more in taxes. Republican objection to this redistributive principle was emblematic of their skepticism about the efficacy of using revenue policies to achieve economic equality. Many Democrats have argued for a "flat tax," which would lower the tax rate and radically reduce a slew of special tax breaks, ranging from investment tax credits to consumer interest deductions. However, their proposals would not fundamentally alter the progressive slope of the tax system. The Republican support of a "simplified" tax system also included a call to "eliminate the incentive destroying effects of the graduated tax."[12]

Implicit in the Reagan tax policy were two reinforcing principles: that redistribution of wealth is not government's purpose, and that graduated tax policies destroy incentives to economic productivity. This view was consistent with the Reagan revolution in its contention that economic progress is spurred by incentives that allow individuals to retain most of their income. It is a view of society where the common good is the sum of individual goods. Put another way, the Republican tax program represented a major departure from the consensus between the two parties that had existed since the New Deal. That consensus saw government as having the major responsibility for managing the "macro" economy through good and bad times. It assumed that government fiscal policy would be utilized to insure stability and growth in the economy. This consensus further assumed that income generated by the government would be applied to redressing the imbalance between the rich and the poor.

What essentially defined the Reagan alternative was an economic perspective that predated the New Deal. It harked back to a classical laissez-faire view that counted on the private sector to distribute economic rewards. The "invisible hand" of Adam Smith found a renewed life in the economic theories of Ronald Reagan.

For the President the welfare state was not a benign force but represented through its continued growth, a real threat to political liberty. In his acceptance speech, the President made this point in no uncertain terms:

> Isn't our choice really not one of left or right, but of up or down: down through the welfare state to statism, to more and more government largesse, accompanied always by more government authority, less individual liberty and ultimately totalitarianism, always advanced for our own good.[13]

The Reagan economic program was a clarion call for a dramatically reduced governmental role in the economy and a greater reliance on the free market. This was true in agriculture where he called for an eventual end to government subsidies; in trade policy where he rejected domestic content legislation and supported free trade; in energy where he advocated allowing private corporations to explore for oil and natural gas on federal lands; and in his call for a series of regulatory reforms that would stem the "flood of regulations" that erect "artificial barriers" to entry into the marketplace.[14]

Underlying these Reagan positions was an assumption that "virtue" is found in a citizenry unfettered by restrictive policies and that "vice" is found in a government that seeks its own aggrandizement at the expense of individual freedom.[15] For the Republicans of 1984, America needed to return to her past — a past where the American dream was nourished, not by what government did, but what it did not do. As the platform's basic premise states: "From freedom comes opportunity, from opportunity comes growth, from growth comes progress."[16]

THE DEMOCRATS

Walter Mondale and his party were in a quandary. Republican success in reducing inflation created, in their view, inappropriately high deficits. Clearly, Reagan had won the battle of inflation. Since no candidate was going to to argue seriously for higher rates of inflation, some other issue was needed. That issue was the deficit, and how to reduce it. While Reagan could assert that "supply-side" policies along with budget cuts would ultimately balance the federal deficit, allowing him to essentially discount its importance, Mondale had no such luxury. Instead he argued that the deficit mortgaged the nation's future, and proposed immediate steps to reduce it. His policy recommendation, unusually courageous during an election, was to raise taxes in order to cut the Reagan deficit by two-thirds after Mondale's first term.[17]

In his tax program, Mondale promised to generate $85 billion by imposing a 15 percent minimum corporate tax, setting limits of eligibility for the Reagan tax cut. He also proposed a 10 percent surcharge on those making over $100,000 a year, deferral of indexing of tax brackets, and elimination of those tax loopholes that allow the rich to shield their true income.[18]

Mondale's tax proposal had two major goals: to reduce the deficit and to maintain the principle of fairness in the tax code. By fairness, an issue Mondale stressed during the campaign, he meant retaining and expanding the principle of redistribution of income as a principal maxim of the federal government. While American politics has rarely made "class" a major issue, Walter Mondale sought to reassert, in the face of the philosophy of Reaganism, the traditional Democratic beliefs that taxes should be progressive and that revenue should go to those who are most in need. In significant ways the Mondale tax plan was symbolic of the values of the New Deal for the past half century. Its rejection by the public constituted, perhaps, a true barometer of Reagan's victory in the "war of ideas."

CONSTITUENCIES: LABOR AND BLACKS

The redistributionist thrust of Mondale's tax plan represented more than simply a restatement of previous Democratic party positions. It was also an acknowledgment of the nature of the political coalition Mondale was trying to shore up. The "Roosevelt coalition," consisting as it did of labor, blacks, Jews, ethnics, and the poor, compelled Mondale to support a host of policies that would rebuild that coalition. Rather than being a "tool" of the special interests, as Gary Hart and others had charged during the primaries, Walter Mondale was attempting to breathe new life into those programs that were critical to the survival of those groups and hence of his own party.

The Democratic party had come to be the party of labor, and its decline correlates strongly with labor's decline. The transformation of the American economy from a manufacturing to a service economy had severely weakened the power of industrial unions. Labor's support of Mondale before the onset of the primaries represented a dramatic and desperate act on its part to place a "labor" man in the presidency. Having borne much of the burden of America's "technological revolution," unions felt they had to find a political formula that would protect their constituency, caught between the economy's past and future.[19] Mondale would forsake the free trade position of his party in order to protect labor from the hazards of cheaper imported goods. Mondale's message to capital and labor was clear:

> To big companies that send our jobs overseas, my message is: We need those jobs here at home. And our country won't help your business — unless your business helps our country.[20]

Mondale argued against the export of American jobs, in favor of a domestic content bill, and, most critically, for policies that would punish those nations that closed their markets to American goods. He promised he would be a "President who stands up for American workers" and that the United States would "not be pushed around anymore" by those nations who put unreasonable barriers in the way of American exports.[21] Although Mondale did not articulate a long-range industrial policy for the nation, his advocacy of a jobs program for the chronically unemployed and job retraining showed his commitment to the cause of labor.

That labor could help deliver the Democratic nomination to Mondale, but not the general election, showed its decline as a political force. Labor's inability to deliver its members' votes demonstrated an elite-mass split in the labor movement. Indeed, it can be said that labor unions themselves are an issue in American politics. Outside the industrialized northern states, unions are not seen as acting in the interests of workers, but rather as impediments to economic progress, hostile to the interests of young workers without seniority. Whatever labor's power might be within the Democratic party, its power outside has declined as rapidly as the economic sector it traditionally dominated.[22]

A second important element in the Mondale "coalition" was blacks, vital support for any Democratic presidential victory. Unlike labor, blacks did not see voting Republican as a viable alternative; hence, their support for Mondale was assured. What was not assured, however, was the enthusiasm of that support. Many blacks felt the Democratic party had taken them for granted and had not supported those policies necessary to pull them out of numbing poverty. Galvanizing and capitalizing on these feelings, the Reverend Jesse Jackson emerged as a significant issue in this election.

Jesse Jackson and the Issue of Race

Nothing enervated the Democratic party during and immediately after its primary season more than the candidacy of the Reverend Jesse Jackson. The

Jackson candidacy was noteworthy in several ways: He was the first black candidate to run a serious primary campaign for his party's nomination; his campaign style was evangelical with its roots firmly embedded in the black church; and he strongly implied that, unless taken seriously, he might lead a withdrawal of black support from the Democratic party. This last threat caused the Democratic party establishment, particularly Mondale, to treat Jackson gingerly. Mondale walked a narrow line between assuaging Jackson's ego and not appearing to capitulate to demands that would offend other elements of the party's electoral coalition.

The rise to prominence of Jackson signaled both the success and failure of Democratic party liberalism. The alliance between the Democratic party and blacks was solidified during the civil rights struggle. That coalition had a remarkable string of political and social successes. The civil rights acts of the Johnson administration, along with other initiatives involving education and affirmative action, had all served to redress many of black Americans' legitimate grievances. By 1984, while blacks still endured discrimination, their overall position in society was much improved from what it had been 25 years ago. Yet, the fact of black poverty remained.

Jackson's basic appeal was to the frustration many blacks felt about the inability of the welfare state to deliver its promise of economic equality. The economic gap between blacks and whites remained substantial and was exacerbated by the Reagan administration's economic programs. Jackson's economic message was clear in its demand for a radical redistribution of income from the rich to the poor. He called for an increase in the corporate share of taxes and for federal programs to distribute these funds to the nation's poor.

Jackson's domestic program was similar to that of the "liberal left" faction of the Democratic party. Clearly Jackson was more "liberal" on the economy than were Mondale and the party's platform. Yet his ideas were not so radical as to be beyond the scope of ordinary policy debate in the nation. He explicitly called for a more steeply graduated income tax, which used surcharges as a way of generating more revenues. This tax increase, along with his proposed 20 percent reduction in the defense budget, would, he argued, free the necessary resources to address the problems of the nation's poor.[23]

Jackson saw himself as the conscience of the Democratic party and constantly reminded his audiences that he spoke for those who were forgotten by American society—the "rainbow coalition"—an amalgam of groups of different hues but all united by the bond of oppression. Jackson's "rainbow" was wide:

The white, the Hispanic, the black, the Arab, the Jew, the woman, the Native American, the small farmer, the business person, the environmentalist, the peace activist, the young, the old, the lesbian, the gay and the disabled make up America's quilt.[24]

This was the cause of Jesse Jackson—to give a voice to those who had none and to remind his party and the nation that the work of the welfare state was not completed until its writ was extended to all Americans. There was much that was powerful in the Jackson appeal. It reminded many of the words from a distant era—"one third of the nation, ill-housed, ill-clothed, and ill-fed." Yet, behind his call for a revitalization of the ideals of the party's left was a darker side—black separatism, anti-Semitism, prototalitarianism—which haunted his campaign.

Jackson's well-publicized visits to Syria and Cuba, along with his sympathy for the Palestinian cause and the Sandinista revolution in Nicaragua, raised questions about his foreign policy. His assertion that the Sandinistas were "on the right side of history,"[25] combined with other comments that flattered Third World regimes often hostile to American interests, staked out a foreign policy perspective well to the left of Mondale. More serious was the implicit threat in Jackson's campaign of a separatist black politics, which not only endangered any possible Democratic electoral victory but menaced the pluralistic basis of American politics. For many, the prospect of the Democrats becoming "the party of Jackson" was frightening because it promised to push the party so far to the left that it could no longer appeal to those constituencies it needed for survival—conservative Catholics, Jews, and moderates.

Jackson's controversial relationship with the Nation of Islam leader, Louis Farrakhan, along with his references to Jews as "Hymies," brought the issue of anti-Semitism squarely into the campaign. For Jews, historically sensitive to issues of religious prejudice, Jackson's behavior was anathema. They responded with great hostility, raising the possibility of withdrawing their support from any Democratic leader who did not repudiate Jackson. This issue left the Democratic party in some turmoil up until the time of the convention. It subsided as the "bad Jesse" of "Hymietown" and "Farrakhan" was replaced by the "good Jesse" who argued for reconciliation and cooperation during the fall campaign.

Still, the Jackson controversy was a serious one because it dramatically raised the issue of race in America. It is arguable that Jackson is a "loose cannon," that the Farrakhan flap, along with his off-the-cuff comments about Jews and Israel, are simply his own idiosyncrasies, not reflective of the opinion of the black masses. Nonetheless, the question of race he raised is not ephemeral and goes to the heart of the crisis facing the Democratic party and the nation.

The issue of race perpetually exists below the surface of American politics. In a fundamental way, the attack by the Republicans on the welfare state can be seen as an attack on black aspirations as well. For many Americans, the welfare state and blacks are seen as coterminous, so that talk of dramatically cutting social programs is merely a subtle form of racism. This is not to say that the President is a racist; rather it is to argue that criticism of the welfare state and the reluctance to expand it have a disproportionate effect on black America. Blacks are wedded to the welfare state and do not trust the mechanisms of the marketplace to undo their economic inequality. Conservative Democrats like Richard Scammon dismiss Jackson by calling him "a black George Wallace — a Rodney Dangerfield. He wants respect." Scammon asserts that Jackson "has no real program and he doesn't know what he is doing."[26] But whatever the quality of Jackson's policies, the enthusiastic support he received from blacks ought to be sufficient warning that the United States may be fragmenting into two separate societies, one white, the other black.[27]

The Social Issues

If the issue of race bubbled below the surface of American politics, religion erupted like a geyser in the election of 1984. America, as Walt Whitman had noted, was not a nation but rather a "nation of nations," and of races, ethnicities, and religions as well. Americans historically learned tolerance, if not out of liberal instinct, then out of prudence. Such prudence acknowledged that the price for one's own freedom of religion was the granting of that same right to others. And while this principle was often abused, it was still a major element in the "liberal consensus" of the past half century. In general, the consensus held, religion ought to remain as part of the private order and be kept out of the public order. Americans would probably not accept Mark Twain's wry observation that the United States has "freedom of speech, freedom of conscience, and the prudence never to practice either of them." In practice they would agree that both, and religion in particular, ought not be practiced too zealously.[28]

Yet, just as the old consensus concerning economic policy seemed to have shattered, so did ideas about the proper role of religion. The high wall that separated church and state in America was attacked by members of the "new right," who felt the trend toward secularization of society had gone so far as to threaten religion. Accounts of the destructive effects of "secular humanism" were pronounced daily by a new breed of "electronic ministers" who used the advanced technology of television to warn their "congregations" about the coming apocalypse. Powerful forces had awakened in secularized America, intent on bringing religious issues into the public order.

Participation by religious leaders in America is nothing new, as demonstrated by the wave of clergy who participated in the civil rights struggles of the 1950s and 1960s. The conservative religionists differ, however, in their overt alliance with the "new right" of the Republican party. While issues like abortion and prayer in the schools are not logically tied to questions of capitalism and the free market, they have become politically joined in the 1980s. The fundamentalist ministers teach a theology that combines a literal interpretation of the Bible with an interpretation of American history through the eyes of Horatio Alger.

The religious revivalism that overlay the election of 1984 helped shape the Republican platform and became a major issue in the campaign itself. The Reverend Jerry Falwell strenuously opposed political participation by ministers in the 1960s. By 1980, he had become the leader of the Moral Majority which sought to bring America "back to basics" by opposing homosexuality, abortion, the Equal Rights Amendment, the Supreme Court decision on school prayer, and busing.

They saw America becoming a new Sodom and Gomorrah—a land where the pornographers, atheists, and socialists held sway, threatening to destroy all that was virtuous. Therefore, their participation in electoral politics was not that of just another pressure group but was a holy cause.[29]

Abortion was stressed by the Moral Majority. Finding support among prominent Catholics and Orthodox Jews, the Moral Majority advocated a constitutional amendment that would override the prochoice decision made by the Supreme Court in 1973. The opposition to abortion also found a powerful voice in the newly appointed Catholic archbishop of New York, John J. O'Connor. Archbishop O'Connor raised the concern of many Catholic politicians when he called abortion the critical issue in the campaign and then stated the teaching of the Catholic church:

> It is the task of the church to reaffirm that abortion is death. It is the killing of innocent creatures. Consequently, the church considers all legislation in favor of abortion as a serious offense against primary human rights and the divine commandment: "You shall not kill."[30]

The archbishop went well beyond simply reflecting Catholic teaching, implicitly taking a partisan stance when he wondered "how a Catholic in good conscience can vote for a candidate who explicitly endorses abortion."[31] This statement had a partisan tinge because the only two prochoice candidates running for national office were Walter Mondale and his Catholic running mate, Geraldine Ferraro. The implicit alliance among conservative theologians had vast significance: Not only did it dominate headlines during the campaign, but it raised complicated philosophical questions about the role of private religious belief and conscience in a highly pluralistic society.

For Walter Mondale and Geraldine Ferraro, the necessity of separating private religious belief from the strictures of the law made them choose a prochoice position on abortion. The Democratic platform asserted that "reproductive freedom is a fundamental human right" and, while recognizing "the religious and ethical concerns many Americans have about abortion," supported the principle that "a woman has the right to choose whether or when to have a child."[32]

On other social issues Mondale also sharply disagreed with Reagan, and his campaign echoed the historic Democratic belief in the rights of the individual against unwarranted intrusion by governmental institutions. Mondale was direct on this point:

> I believe in an America that honors what Thomas Jefferson called the "wall of separation between church and state." That freedom has made our faith unadulterated and unintimidated. . . . Today the clauses of the First Amendment do not need to be fixed; they need to be followed.[33]

The First Amendment was Mondale's primary justification for opposing prolife, antihomosexual, proprayer, and similar thrusts by the Reagan campaign. While affirming his own deep religious convictions, Mondale, in the tradition of liberalism, did not think it proper to impose those beliefs on others. Nor did Mondale accept the apocalyptic visions of those who attributed America's decline to the state's undercutting of religious behavior. For Mondale the solution to the nation's ills was to insure that each citizen was fairly treated by the government. Hence he stressed affirmative action, ERA, fair housing, enforcement of the civil right laws, and educational opportunity. The Reagan record on these issues was the basis of Mondale's attacks on the President. Holding up the banner of fairness, Mondale attacked the incumbent for supporting those policies that favored the powerful and for ignoring those laws meant to protect the weak.

The battle over social issues reflected both current divisions in American politics and portended future ones. Clearly, the politics of religion in 1984 did not hurt the Reagan candidacy, and his ability to link patriotism with religion may have benefited his campaign. Equally clear, however, was the uneasiness that many Americans felt about the issue of religion in politics.[34] It may well be that Jews overwhelmingly voted for Mondale because they feared Falwell more than they feared Jackson. Too, the agreement between the Catholic hierarchy and fundamentalist Protestants on abortion masks a much deeper division on other issues, most notably economic justice. Hence, it is arguable that despite appearances to the contrary, continued attempts to use the authority of religion to endorse specific candidates and specific policies may erode religious authority. Ronald Reagan may be correct when he states that "politics and morality are inseparable," and since religion is "morality's foundation," citizens "need religion as a guide."[35] The question that the election of 1984 raised is, What will become of the spiritual purpose of religion if it becomes the captive of partisan politics?

The focus on religious issues was a consequence of deeper concerns about the radical changes that had occurred in America. In one sense, the "religious issue" was a symbol for the need many felt for some moral high ground from which they could judge the tumultuous changes around them. The transformation of America over the past decades made individuals feel they had little control over their lives. The changes in the worlds of technology, sexuality, and criminal justice made many yearn for a simpler time in America when there was a greater consensus over basic values. In no area did these changes have a greater impact than in the "feminist revolution." Not only were women now a major force in the economy, but attitudes about women's role in society and the family had undergone a profound alteration. The "woman's issue" was a point of major disagreement between the two parties.

Walter Mondale's selection of Geraldine Ferraro as his running mate was of obvious historical importance. It acknowledged both the political power of women within the Democratic party and the potential of the "gender gap" to provide the margin of electoral victory.[36] The Democratic party had defined itself as the "party of feminist aspirations," and promised programs that would meet the needs of modern women. These programs included support for the ERA, equal pay for equal work, equal pay for comparable work, day care centers, abortion, and political equality. The Democrats of 1984 tried to link their support of women's issues with traditional family values—arguing, for example, for "flex time" so "women—and men—could shape even full-time jobs around their family schedules."[37] Nonetheless, it was clear the Democrats heartily endorsed the "liberation" of women, while the Republicans were far less enthusiastic.

As in 1980, the Republican platform of 1984 did not endorse the ERA, which had become the primary symbol of the women's movement. Although the Republicans supported "equal pay for equal work," the major thrust of their appeal to women was that the economic recovery freed women from the legacy of Carter-Mondale: "a shrinking economy, limited job opportunities and a declining standard of living." The Reagan record, by contrast, had led to an economic expansion that "produced a record number of jobs so that women who want to work outside the home have an unmatched opportunity."[38] The Republicans thus acknowledged the importance of women in the labor market but still, implicitly, tended to idealize woman in her traditional role as homemaker.

The Republicans were not the party of Gloria Steinem but of Phyllis Schlafly. Despite appointing the first woman—Sandra Day O'Connor—to the Supreme Court, the President presented himself to the public as the advocate of "the family as the natural and indispensable institution for human development."[39] No American politician would ever disagree about the centrality of family life in promoting decent values. In the lexicon of modern American politics, however, "family values" has come to mean, more pointedly, an opposition to the goals of liberal feminists, who measured themselves by standards other than their roles in families.

The positions of the two candidates on the social issues were the reverse of their economic stances. On the economy, Reagan stressed individual freedom and curtailed governmental regulations. In contrast, when it came to abortion and prayer in the public schools, he urged a more activist government role legitimized by constitutional amendments. Mondale wanted a more interventionist government for the economy and less government interference with presumed "private" matters such as prayer and abortion. This juxtaposition is not unprecedented in American politics, since ideological consistency has never been the hallmark of our political parties. It does underline two very different philosophical perspectives. Reagan feared a tyrannical government emerging from a welfare state that stifled individual initiative in the economy, while Mondale worried about a tyrannical government emerging from the stifling of individual choices in society. Ironically, in principle, neither was reluctant to use state power; they just differed over the arena in which to apply that power.

Foreign Policy and Defense

The debate over foreign policy and defense allowed each candidate to stake out different views about American interests in international relations. Foreign policy issues were a central theme in Reagan's victory over Jimmy Carter in 1980. Reagan argued that the United States was becoming a second-rate power and that the policies of the Democratic party were akin to a global surrender. The Republicans in 1980 were unabashedly apocalyptic as they warned that if Democratic policies continued, the "American experiment . . . would come strangely, needlessly, tragically to a dismal end in our third century."[40] The Republicans of 1984 continued their blistering attack on "weak" Democratic foreign policy. At their convention, UN Ambassador Jeane Kirkpatrick asserted:

> When Marxist dictators shoot their way to power in Central America, the San Francisco Democrats don't blame the guerrillas and their Soviet allies, they blame U.S. policies of 100 years ago. But then, they always blame America first.[41]

The "San Francisco Democrats" Kirkpatrick derided were her symbol for alleged liberal naiveté about the threat of Soviet expansionism. The Democrats were criticized for advocating "unilateral restraint" in the face of "massive Soviet weapons buildup," of not recognizing the danger of Soviet influence in a host of countries from Afghanistan to Grenada, and, most important, for neglecting the grave threat that totalitarianism posed for Western democratic values. For Kirkpatrick and her conservative brethren, Ronald Reagan represented an antidote to the West's penchant for "self-criticism and self-denigration." He enunciated a patriotism that "declared to the world that we have the necessary energy and conviction to defend ourselves."[42]

Much of the foreign policy debate in 1984 dealt with such illusive issues as America's prestige or image in the world. Foreign policy conservatives saw a steady decline in America's power vis-à-vis the rest of the world. It is arguable that this perception of America's decline was only a perception, and that what had actually occurred was an equalizing of the power disparity that existed after World War II. Whatever the empirical basis of these perceptions, the Republicans flailed away at the Democrats as a party unable to confront the Soviet menace effectively.

Foreign policy debates always suffer from an obvious limitation: As a presidential candidate it is difficult to reveal to the public how one would act in specific circumstances. Secrecy shrouds foreign policy discussions and makes them far less revealing than debates over domestic issues. Yet it is also true that the public needs to understand how each candidate defines American national interests. The foreign policy issues discussed by the candidates in this election were not especially helpful in this regard. As Flora Lewis pointed out:

> The trouble with the foreign policy debate nearly 40 years after World War II is that it does not address the questions for decision. Building consensus that "they can't push us around any more" and that "the United States is standing tall" isn't difficult. Of course the nation will not abandon its vital interests.[43]

President Reagan's consistent attacks on the Carter administration's lack of strength made the foreign policy and defense debate less informative than it might have been. Indeed, the categories of "tough" and "weak" so often employed by the Republicans missed the mark. Was Jimmy Carter weak in the wheat boycott? Was Ronald Reagan strong for refinancing the Polish debt? The presidential debate on foreign policy suffered from a lack of conceptual clarity about what the national interest of the United States ought to be.

Nevertheless the two candidates expressed sharply divergent opinions. For Mondale, the Reagan record on foreign policy was flawed. Reagan's handling of Central America, the deaths of the marines in Lebanon, and arms control were attacked by Mondale. He also criticized waste in the defense budget and urged more resources be allocated for conventional forces rather than the B-1 bomber and the MX missile. Mondale's essential objection to the President's policies had as much to do with Reagan's abilities as it had to do with specific policies. In the second debate, Mondale centered on presidential leadership:

> The bottom line of national strength is that the President must be in command. He must lead. And when a President doesn't know that submarine missiles are [not] recallable, says that 70 percent of our strategic forces are conventional, discovers three years into his administration that our arms control policies have failed because he didn't know that most Soviet missiles were on land—these are things a President must know to command.[44]

For Mondale, being "tough" was not sufficient in making foreign policy; a President must also "be wise and smart."[45] Mondale was raising the essential question of Reagan's competence. Mondale focused on this issue because of the President's poor performance in the first debate, when he often seemed distracted and not in full command of the facts. Clearly the fear of nuclear war fueled speculation as to whether this President was capable of making rational decisions on such monumental questions. Yet almost as quickly as it arose, the age issue seemed to melt away, helped, no doubt, by the President's improved performance in the second debate.

Aside from personal abilities, differences over the nation's external relations did raise important questions. The Reagan presidency had made the containment of Soviet ambitions its highest priority. To make this policy credible, it substantially raised the defense budget. The first Reagan budget was $36 billion higher than Carter had planned, and the military budget as a percentage of the national budget increased from 22.6 percent in 1981 to 26.8 percent in 1984. This spending represented a substantial reallocation of resources from domestic programs to defense.[46]

The Reagan camp also believed that arms negotiations could occur only after the United States had persuaded the Soviet Union that we were willing to spend as much as necessary to insure security. Given this thesis, the lack of an arms control agreement with the Soviet Union was not an important strategic consideration for the United States.

The Reagan plan was to build up America's strategic forces to the point where the Soviet Union felt that it was compelled to negotiate. Coupled with this plan was the improvement of NATO's defenses by introducing Pershing and Cruise missiles into Western Europe. Again, the thesis was that arms negotiation could only take place once strategic parity with the Soviet Union was achieved.

Mondale had a much different approach to this issue. He advocated a verifiable nuclear freeze. He announced:

> On my very first day as President, I will call on the Soviet leadership to meet me within six months in Geneva for fully prepared, substantive negotiations to freeze the arms race and to begin cutting back the stockpiles of nuclear weapons.[47]

The hard-line rhetoric of the Reagan administration made many people worry that there had been a fundamental change in U.S. nuclear policy that made the "unthinkable" now "thinkable." Fearing a nuclear confrontation, a well-organized movement emerged, seeking a nuclear freeze. This movement dovetailed with similar groups abroad, particularly in Germany and England, which protested the deployment of Cruise and Pershing missiles in Western Europe. These movements were bolstered by such popular television programs as "The Day After," which graphically portrayed the horrors of nuclear war. Also, scientists speculated that a nuclear war would lead to a "nuclear winter," making the earth unfit for human life. Another significant contribution to the nuclear debate was the publication of Jonathan Schell's *The Fate of the Earth,* which gave freeze advocates a philosophical and historical framework.

The combination of tough anti-Soviet rhetoric and increased defense budget and publicity about the consequences of nuclear war had made the public jittery. It began to question the adequacy of sophisticated theories of deterrence when the stakes were so high. In one sense, deterrence theory was always anomalous, resting heavily as it did on the subjectivity of decision makers, as opposed to the objective criterion of security. The nuclear age does not allow for even the illusion of security because of the nature of the weapons involved. Hence, strategic improvements are always matched by the other side, resulting in greater insecurity on both sides.

An exchange over "Star Wars" in the second debate illustrated this dilemma. Reagan, searching for a way out of the unbending logic of nuclear deterrence, argued that weapons in space would allow the United States to "defend against a nuclear war by destroying missiles instead of destroying millions of people."[48] The "Star Wars" concept sought to find a technological, instead of a political, solution for the arms race. Mondale worried about the propriety of sharing this advanced technology with the Russians, as the President suggested. Instead, he argued that the placement of weapons in space would "bring about an arms race that is very dangerous indeed" and favored ending this "madness now [to] keep the heavens free from war."[49]

While the debate about "Star Wars" had a certain science fiction quality to it, the controversy over arms control did not. The election of 1984 did not decide which course was better, Mondale's call for an immediate freeze or Reagan's call for strength prior to negotiation. Their divergent views may turn out, in time, to have been irrelevant to resolution of the arms race. The future of this issue may well be more affected by the leadership crisis now confronting the Kremlin. Certainly the rapid shift in leadership—Brezhnev to Andropov to Chernenko—has not provided the Soviets with the internal stability to engage in substantive talks over arms control and reduction.

Clearly, what the United States needs is a foreign policy strategy, of which defense is a critical part, and one responsive to a rapidly changing international environment. The precondition of a bipartisan foreign policy consensus had been shattered by the war in Vietnam. The hard realities of international affairs —starvation in Africa, terrorism, Third World indebtedness, trade policy—require policy foundations that reflect the natural interests and the values of a democratic nation. This is difficult enough to develop. It is made more difficult by the atmosphere of partisan acrimony currently dominating foreign policy and defense discussions.

The Reagan Mandate

Ronald Reagan nearly swept the nation, but his policy mandate is ambiguous. The results show Democratic strength in Congress and an astounding personal popularity of the President, but no obvious public support of his positions on the issues. We doubt the nation will really favor official prayers in the public schools, a constitutional amendment banning abortion, further increases in the current defense budget, or continued cutting of domestic programs.

The President has succeeded in shifting the political agenda of the nation significantly to the right. He has also managed to leave the Democrats in disarray—unsure if they should maintain, diminish, or change their historic support for the welfare state policies that address the needs of the disadvantaged. The Democrats must decide whether their massive defeat was due to their issue positions or to the popularity of the incumbent. They also must learn why they were so unceremoniously abandoned by those constituencies whose support they had come to expect.

The President had such emotional appeal that even many who disagreed with him on particular issues voted for him. His popularity may mask deeper issue concerns, about the environment, Social Security, and the arms race, as well as the demographic issues of age and gender. There are many "issue publics" in America: the aged and Yuppies, poor blacks and upwardly mobile ethnics, environmentalists and trade unionists. All have issue agendas of their own. The future ability of either party to satisfy these sometimes conflicting groups remains open to question.

There is a mystical ring to much of the debate about the future of American politics. Each of the parties had its own particular image of America's past that it invoked to justify its future policies. There is much to be said for the appeal of the Reagan vision of America's past—it presents a picture of the courageous individual struggling against great odds to build a political democracy and economic abundance. Americans are socialized to think of themselves as exceptional, and as part of a nation that is destined for greatness. In this sense, Reagan was able to identify his values with those of the nation. Whether the Republicans in a post-Reagan era can maintain this association is still moot.

The Democrats, because they lost, face an even greater series of challenges. As the historic keepers of liberalism's flame, they must redefine what that liberalism now means. Surely there will be those in the Democratic party who will argue that the old welfare state has outlived its historic mission and that "new ideas" are needed to insure electoral victory. The serious conflict within the party is itself proof of the success of the Reagan revolution of ideas. Perhaps a Democratic agenda will emerge that is simply a vague reflection of the Reagan agenda, which might make the Democratic party "a movement without a purpose and without a constituency."[50]

Democrats would do well to remember the cyclical nature of American politics. Present defeat will become future victory. Until then Democrats need to revivify their basic faith. What defines the soul of the party has been its commitment to reform. Eric Goldman reminded another generation of liberals of this same truth:

> For almost a century the modern American reformer has been the gadfly and the conscience, to a large extent the heart and mind, of the only nation in man's history which has dared to live by the credo that any individual's rendezvous with his destiny is a rendezvous with a better tommorow.[51]

The party of Reagan has been true to its past in arguing for the autonomy of the private economic sector and in resisting secular encroachment on traditional values. To maintain a decent pluralism, Democrats too must remain true to their past in contending that economic bounty be fairly distributed. If the Democrats do this, they will have contributed to the democratic dialogue essential to the health of the republic.

NOTES

1. Samuel Beer, "Memoir of a Political Junkie," *Harvard Magazine,* September-October 1984, 65-70.

2. See Theodore J. Lowi, *The End of Liberalism: The Second Republic of the United States* (New York: Norton, 1979), for an informed discussion of "interest group liberalism" and its consequences for American politics.

3. Theodore H. White, "The Shaping of the Presidency 1984," *Time,* 19 November 1984, 70.

4. Christopher Lasch, "The Politics of Nostalgia," *Harpers,* November 1984, 70.

5. Mario Cuomo's Keynote Address, *Congressional Quarterly Weekly Report* 29 (21 July 1984): 1781.

6. Ibid.

7. Peter T. Kilborn, "Four Years Later: Who in U.S. Is Better Off," *New York Times,* 9 October 1984, A10.

8. Ibid.

9. 1984 Republican Platform, *Congressional Quarterly Weekly Report* 34 (25 August 1984): 2097.

10. The entire administration was not enamored by supply-side theory. Budget Director David Stockman was skeptical about the impact of the tax cuts on the deficit. See William Greider, "The Education of David Stockman," *Atlantic Monthly* 248 (December 1981): 27-54. See also George Gilder, *Wealth and Poverty* (New York: Basic Books, 1981), for a systematic justification for supply-side economic theory.

11. Quoted in the *New York Times,* 24 September 1984, D12.

12. 1984 Republican Platform, 2097.

13. Reagan's Acceptance Speech, *Congressional Quarterly Weekly Report* 34 (25 August 1984): 2125.

14. 1984 Republican Platform, 2098.

15. See Milton Friedman and Rose Friedman, *Free to Choose* (New York: Harcourt Brace Jovanovich, 1980), for a contemporary exposition of this classic conservative position.

16. 1984 Republican Platform, 2096.

17. Mondale's Acceptance Speech, *Congressional Quarterly Weekly Report* 29 (21 July 1984): 1792-94.

18. Ibid.

19. Much has been written about what the Democratic party's agenda ought to be during this period of economic change. A notable example of the "new" thinking among Democrats can be found in Gar Alperovitz and Jeff Faux, *Rebuilding America: A Blueprint for the New Economy* (New York: Pantheon, 1984).

20. Mondale's Acceptance Speech, 1793.

21. Ibid.

22. Even within the Democratic party there was less than enthusiastic support for labor's early endorsement of Mondale. During the primary debates, Gary Hart tried to brand Mondale as simply a tool of labor who never disagreed with labor's policies.

23. Evan Thomas, "Pride and Prejudice," *Time,* 7 May 1984, 30-40.

24. Jackson Convention Speech, *Congressional Quarterly Weekly Report* 29 (21 July 1984): 1786.

25. "Pride and Prejudice," 40.
26. Ibid. In important ways, Jackson had always been an anathema to both conservative Democrats and Jews. His "embrace" of Yasir Arafat in the mid-1970s along with his criticisms of Jews for their opposition to affirmative action were points of conflict that predated Jackson's behavior during the campaign.
27. A point made over a decade ago by the U.S. Commission on Civil Disorders Report, (the Kerner Commission), 1.
28. This point is verified by the New York Times/CBS News poll, which found "most Americans . . . uncomfortable about the way politics and religion became intertwined in this . . . election." *New York Times,* 19 September 1984, B9.
29. For an interesting discussion of the "New Christian Right" and American democracy, see Richard John Neuhaus, *The Naked Public Square* (Grand Rapids, Mich.: Eerdmans, 1984).
30. Quoted in the *New York Times,* 10 September 1984, B9.
31. Ibid.
32. 1984 Democratic Platform, *Congressional Quarterly Weekly Report* 29 (21 July 1984): 1767.
33. Quoted in *New York Times,* 7 October 1984, 30.
34. New York Times/CBS News poll.
35. Quoted in *New York Times,* 7 October 1984, 30.
36. See, for example, June Perlez, "Woman, Power and Politics," *New York Times Magazine,* 24 June 1984. The selection of Geraldine Ferraro also brought to the surface the issue of her personal finances, which dominated the headlines for several weeks and took some of the luster off her nomination. See Marie Brenner, "Gerry Rides It Out," *New York Magazine,* 3 September 1984, 23-33.
37. Democratic Platform, 1767.
38. Republican Platform, 2108.
39. Ibid., 2109.
40. 1980 Republican Platform, *Congressional Quarterly Weekly Report* 38 (18 July 1980): 2030.
41. Kirkpatrick Convention Speech, *Congressional Quarterly Weekly Report* 34 (25 August 1984): 2121.
42. Ibid.
43. Flora Lewis, "Let's Debate Foreign Policy," *New York Times,* 16 October 1984.
44. Second Presidential Debate, *New York Times,* 22 October 1984, B4. See also Strobe Talbott, *Deadly Gambits* (New York: Knopf, 1984), a book that Mondale quoted extensively during the debate.
45. Ibid.
46. *New York Times,* 23 October 1984, A26.
47. Quoted in the *New York Times,* 6 September 1984, A1.
48. Quoted in the *New York Times,* 22 October 1984 B5.
49. Ibid.
50. Marc Landy and Henry Plotkin "The Limits of the Market Metaphor," *Society,* Spring 1982, 17.
51. Eric F. Goldman, *Rendezvous with Destiny* (New York: Vintage, 1955), 347.

3

The Presidential Election

GERALD M. POMPER

I can call spirits from the vasty deep.
Why so can I, or so can any man,
But will they come when you do call for them?

Henry IV, Part I

Ronald Reagan did evoke some spirit, whether friendly sprite or fearsome demon.

Winning the presidential election against Walter Mondale, Reagan gained 59 percent of the popular vote. He achieved a record high of 525 electoral votes, losing only those of Minnesota and the District of Columbia. Supported by nearly 55 million Americans, the incumbent President accumulated majorities in virtually every group in the population. In so doing, he obtained more votes for his Republican candidacy than had ever been cast for a U.S. politician.[1]

While the results of the election are clear, their meaning is more clouded. What genie has been released from that bottle? Will it bring war and social disharmony, or national strength and prosperity? Is it only a pleasant phantom bearing the likeness of the reelected President? Or does it also carry political flesh and blood?

Ronald Reagan may have achieved no more than a great personal triumph over an ineffective opponent. Or he may have won, more substantively, an endorsement of his policy proposals. Perhaps the voters, looking backward, simply judged the Reagan record and found it good. Or, looking forward, they may have moved the nation toward a new conservative and Republican alignment. All of these explanations have some validity, but we see the election of 1984 as neither a triumph of personality nor a policy referendum. Rather, in approving the conduct of the Reagan administration, the voters prepared the way to a new American politics.

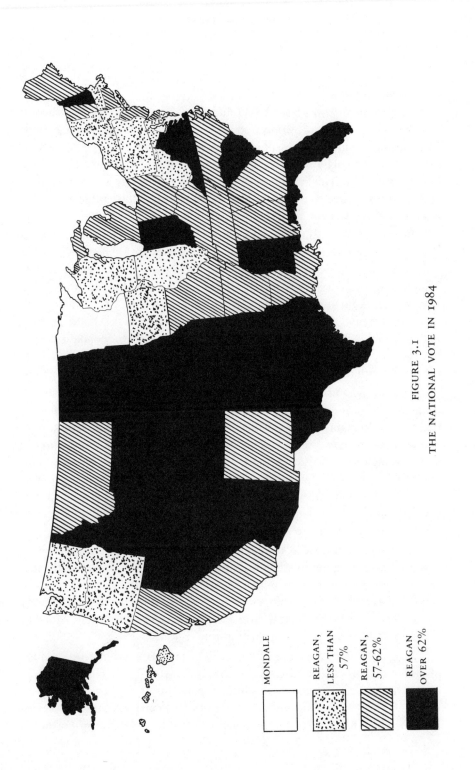

FIGURE 3.1

THE NATIONAL VOTE IN 1984

MONDALE

REAGAN,
LESS THAN
57%

REAGAN,
57–62%

REAGAN
OVER 62%

The Results

GEOGRAPHY

The Reagan victory was both broad and deep. Even in Minnesota, the one state he lost, he fell short by only 4000 votes, a fraction of a percentage point. (The detailed results are presented in table 3.1 on pages 64-65.) The national results were certainly a landslide, but in some states they were more like a political earthquake. The President won by margins of nearly 2 to 1 in such diverse areas as Yankee New Hampshire, Sunbelt Florida, the hard plains of Nebraska, and the soaring mountains of Utah.

Beneath the nearly unanimous victory, however, there are significant variations. Although the rain of presidential defeat fell on the Democrats throughout the nation, they could find some silver linings in the unfriendly clouds. They did relatively well in two areas of the country. The first was the Northeast, where they had a traditional base of support among city residents, factory workers, and members of minority and ethnic groups. Of the 13 areas in this region, including the District of Columbia, seven gave Mondale relatively large proportions of their vote, and only New Hampshire provided a large margin for Reagan. (These variations can be seen in figure 3.1 on page 61.)

The second source of Democratic consolation could be found in an unusual location. Mondale, contrary to tradition, did well in areas originally settled by New England Yankees, which had long supported liberal Republicans. These included states such as Wisconsin and Iowa in the Midwest, Oregon and Washington on the Pacific Coast, as well as southern New England. These tended to be the places where John Anderson had done best in the 1980 election, adding to poll evidence that much of his support, once Republican, had been converted to the Democratic cause over four years. It is one indication, although limited, that the 1984 balloting registered partisan change.

On the Republican side, there were also significant geographical variations, and two notable regions of strength. Most prominent on the map was the party's strength west of the Mississippi. In all but two of the 14 states from the Great Plains to the western slopes of the Rockies, from the Texas empire to the wilderness of Idaho, Reagan won at least five votes out of eight. Mondale had no notable support in any state in this region.

Reagan's other geographical base was in the more advanced economies of the South, particularly Virginia, Florida, and, again, Texas. His large pluralities in these states were, in part, simply expansions of the Republicans' past bases in Dixie. They also showed the party's particular appeal to areas that combined high technology, recent industrial growth, and a low proportion of black voters. (The same favorable combination for Republicans could be found in New Hampshire, their redoubt in the Northeast.)

The remaining 19 states were quite similar in their vote, coming within three percentage points of the national average. Despite the significant regional differences we have noted, the election was more striking for this relative uniformity. The states close to the national average were quite diverse, including old Yankee Republican strongholds such as Maine, as well as the Democrats' former industrial heartland in the Midwest. Perhaps most significantly, most of the former Confederacy, the once-solid South, reflected the general mood of the nation, although the overall Dixie results masked severe internal racial divisions in the region.

Between Reagan's two elections, the nation had become more unified—at least electorally, if not ideologically. Individual states shifted in opposite directions, but toward a common Republican majority. Compared to 1980, Reagan actually lost proportionate support in 12 states, almost all in places where he had done extremely well in the earlier contest. In contrast, he gained particularly in 10 states. Seven of these were in the South, where 1980's close contests had been converted to 1984's large victories.

The geographical results of the election, in summary, show that there is a distinct regional cast to each major party's support. Not only is the Republican coalition obviously the larger one in 1984, but it also shows signs of being a stable and widespread coalition.[2] The regional pattern of the Reagan vote persisted over the four-year period, indicating that the Republican support has some depth.* At the same time, voter reactions were more similar from state to state in 1984 than in 1980, indicating that the Republican party had achieved some breadth as well.†

DEMOGRAPHY

The social bases of the Reagan victory are both self-evident and hidden. The President won majorities among virtually every population group—the landslide contained rocks of almost every description. Of the demographic groups listed in table 3.2 on page 67, Mondale won only among blacks, Hispanics,‡

---

*The linear correlation of the results in the two elections is .87, a historically high figure, indicating stability in party coalitions.

†The standard deviation of the vote measures the similarity of votes among the states. In 1984, it was 8.8 percentage points, compared to 9.9 in 1980, again suggesting greater political similarity across the nation.

‡Because of their small numbers, it is difficult accurately to estimate the vote of Hispanics. Other polls reported that Reagan had won as much as 47 percent of this group.

TABLE 3.1
THE 1984 PRESIDENTIAL VOTE

State	Electoral vote		Popular vote		Percentage 1984 (two-party vote)		Percentage 1980 (two-party vote)	
	Reagan	Mondale	Reagan	Mondale	Reagan	Mondale	Reagan	Carter
Alabama	9	—	872,849	551,899	61.3	38.7	50.7	49.3
Alaska	3	—	138,392	62,018	69.1	30.9	67.3	32.7
Arizona	7	—	681,416	333,584	67.1	32.9	68.2	31.8
Arkansas	6	—	534,774	338,646	61.2	38.8	50.3	49.7
California	47	—	5,467,009	3,922,519	58.2	41.8	59.5	40.5
Colorado	8	—	821,817	454,975	64.4	35.6	63.9	36.1
Connecticut	8	—	890,877	569,597	61.0	39.0	55.6	44.4
Delaware	3	—	152,190	101,656	60.0	40.0	51.3	48.7
District of Columbia	—	3	29,009	180,408	13.8	86.2	15.2	84.8
Florida	21	—	2,730,350	1,448,816	65.3	34.7	59.0	41.0
Georgia	12	—	1,068,722	706,628	60.2	39.8	42.4	57.6
Hawaii	4	—	185,050	147,154	55.7	44.3	48.9	51.1
Idaho	4	—	297,523	108,510	73.3	26.7	72.5	27.5
Illinois	24	—	2,707,103	2,086,499	56.5	43.5	54.4	45.6
Indiana	12	—	1,377,230	841,481	62.1	37.9	59.8	40.2
Iowa	8	—	703,088	605,620	53.7	46.3	57.1	42.9
Kansas	7	—	677,296	333,149	67.0	33.0	63.4	36.6
Kentucky	9	—	821,702	539,539	60.4	39.6	50.7	49.3
Louisiana	10	—	1,037,299	651,586	61.4	38.6	52.8	47.2
Maine	4	—	336,500	214,515	61.1	38.9	51.9	48.1
Maryland	10	—	879,918	787,935	52.8	47.2	48.4	51.6
Massachusetts	13	—	1,310,936	1,239,606	51.4	48.6	50.1	49.9
Michigan	20	—	2,251,571	1,529,638	59.5	40.5	53.6	46.4
Minnesota	—	10	1,032,603	1,036,364	49.9	50.1	47.8	52.2

Mississippi	7	—	582,377	352,192	62.3	37.7	50.7	49.3
Missouri	11	—	1,274,188	848,583	60.0	40.0	53.6	46.4
Montana	4	—	232,450	146,742	61.3	38.7	63.7	36.3
Nebraska	5	—	459,135	187,475	71.0	29.0	71.6	28.4
Nevada	4	—	188,770	91,655	67.3	32.7	69.9	30.1
New Hampshire	4	—	267,050	120,347	68.9	31.1	67.0	33.0
New Jersey	16	—	1,933,630	1,261,323	60.5	39.5	57.4	42.6
New Mexico	5	—	307,101	201,769	60.3	39.7	59.9	40.1
New York	36	—	3,664,763	3,119,605	54.0	46.0	51.5	48.5
North Carolina	13	—	1,346,481	824,287	62.0	38.0	51.1	48.9
North Dakota	3	—	200,336	104,429	65.7	34.3	70.9	29.1
Ohio	23	—	2,678,560	1,825,440	59.5	40.5	55.7	44.3
Oklahoma	8	—	861,530	385,080	69.1	30.9	63.4	36.6
Oregon	7	—	685,700	536,479	56.1	43.9	55.5	44.5
Pennsylvania	25	—	2,584,323	2,228,131	53.7	46.3	53.9	46.1
Rhode Island	4	—	208,513	194,294	51.8	48.2	43.8	56.2
South Carolina	8	—	615,539	344,459	64.1	35.9	50.6	49.4
South Dakota	3	—	200,267	116,113	63.3	36.7	65.6	34.4
Tennessee	11	—	990,212	711,714	58.2	41.8	50.2	49.8
Texas	29	—	3,433,428	1,949,276	64.1	35.9	57.2	42.8
Utah	5	—	469,105	155,369	75.1	24.9	78.0	22.0
Vermont	3	—	135,865	95,730	58.7	41.3	53.6	46.4
Virginia	12	—	1,337,078	796,250	62.7	37.3	56.8	43.2
Washington	10	—	1,051,670	807,352	56.6	43.4	57.1	42.9
West Virginia	6	—	405,483	328,125	55.3	44.7	47.6	52.4
Wisconsin	11	—	1,198,584	995,740	54.6	45.3	52.6	47.4
Wyoming	3	—	133,241	53,370	71.4	28.6	69.1	30.9
TOTAL	525	13	54,450,603	37,573,671	59.17	40.83	55.3	44.7

SOURCE: *New York Times*, 22 December 1984, 10.

Jews, members of union households, residents of large cities, and persons either unemployed or with the lowest family incomes. These were not only minorities in an ethnic or political sense; even when added together, they constituted only a minority of the total population. However strongly Mondale won their support, he could not—and did not—win the presidency through their loyalty alone.

While Reagan won majorities in most groups, he did not show the same depth of support in all elements of the population. These relative differences are more significant for the long run, for they reveal the character of the 1984 Republican majority and provide hints about its durability and policy directions. Three points are important: the continuity of a shrunken New Deal coalition; the particular strengths of the newer Reagan coalition; and the significant shifts of some groups over the four-year period between his two national victories.

The New Deal coalition developed 50 years ago in the era of Franklin D. Roosevelt. Democrats won enduring support from a number of overlapping groups: ethnic minorities, particularly Catholics, blacks, and Jews; blue-collar workers, especially those in unions; urban residents; and white southerners. First forged in the political heat of the Great Depression, the alliance was solidified as new voters entered the electorate with strong Democratic loyalties, and strengthened through the policy actions the party's leaders. Even in 1965, two decades after the death of Roosevelt, Democrats held a lead over Republicans of almost 2 to 1 in basic party loyalties, and had lost the presidency only twice in nine contests.[3]

The outlines of that coalition are still evident in the 1984 results, if we focus on the relative position of groups. Racial minorities and Jews voted Democratic. Catholics did support Reagan, but in much lower proportions than Protestants, maintaining the established religious division. Union members and their families stayed with the Democrats, and blue-collar workers provided only a thin Republican plurality.

The most dramatic change from the past is among white southerners. Previously, Democratic loyalty was as traditional in Dixie as fried chicken. By 1984, tastes had changed, and the white vote in the South was more solidly for Reagan (at 72 percent) than in any region. Among the other New Deal groups, the Democratic problem was not dramatic losses but drift—the slow erosion of numbers and loyalty. There are now fewer blue-collar workers, urban residents, union members, and therefore a smaller obvious base of support. Other groups, such as Catholics, maintained their numbers but lessened their loyalty. Economic growth and the Democratic programs of the welfare state enabled many of the party's faithful to achieve security and prosperity, and to turn their attention to new political appeals.[4]

TABLE 3.2

THE PRESIDENTIAL VOTE IN SOCIAL GROUPS, 1984 AND 1980

Percent of 1984 total		1984		1980		
		Reagan	Mondale	Reagan	Carter	Anderson
	Party					
38	Democrats	26	73	26	67	6
26	Independents	63	35	55	30	12
35	Republicans	92	7	86	9	4
	Sex and marital status					
47	Men	61	37	55	36	7
53	Women	57	42	47	45	7
68	Married	63	37	Not available		
32	Not married	51	47	Not available		
	Age					
24	18-29	58	41	43	44	11
34	30-44	58	42	54	36	8
23	45-59	60	39	55	39	5
19	60 and older	63	36	54	41	4
8	First-time voter	60	39	Not available		
	Occupation					
30	Professional/manager	62	37	57	32	9
13	White-collar	59	40	50	41	8
14	Blue-collar	53	46	47	46	5
3	Unemployed	31	68	39	51	8
21	Use computer home/job	62	37	Not available		
26	Union household	45	53	43	48	6
	Income*					
15	Under $12,500	46	53	42	51	6
27	$12,500-$24,999	57	42	44	46	8
21	$25,000-$34,999	59	40	52	39	7
18	$35,000-$50,000	67	32	59	32	8
13	Over $50,000	68	31	63	26	9
	Education					
8	Less than high school	50	49	46	51	2
30	High school graduate	60	39	51	43	4
30	Some college	60	38	55	35	7
29	College graduate	59	40	52	35	11
	Race and ethnic group					
86	White	66	34	55	36	7
10	Black	9	90	11	85	3
3	Hispanic	33	65	33	59	6

TABLE 3.2 *(Continued)*

Percent of	1984		1980		
1984 total	Reagan	Mondale	Reagan	Carter	Anderson
	Religion				
51	White Protestant	73	26	63	31	6
26	Catholic	55	44	49	42	7
3	Jewish	32	66	39	45	15
15	White Born-again				
	Christian	80	20	63	33	3
	Region				
24	East	52	47	47	42	9
28	Midwest	61	38	51	40	7
29	South	63	36	52	44	3
18	West	59	40	53	34	10
	Community size				
12	Large cities	36	62	35	54	8
55	Suburbs-small cities	57	42	53	37	8
33	Rural and towns	69	29	54	39	5

*Family income categories in 1980: under $10,000, $10,000-$14,999, $15,000-$24,999, $25,000-$50,000, and over $50,000.

SOURCES: The New York Times/CBS News poll; *New York Times*, 8 November 1984.

This weakening of the Democrats is evident in two other long-term trends. The first is the gradual decline of party loyalty itself, as Independents become a larger part of the population. Until recently, this trend did not affect the Democrats alone, as they were able to maintain a rough 3 to 2 advantage among those who stayed loyal to either major party. Nevertheless, they were more likely to suffer from this tendency. As the majority party, they were more subject to defection. Furthermore, the Democrats have been less adept at using advertising and the campaign technology that is critical in appealing to an independent electorate. They have relied more on party loyalty and mass organization to win their votes, and were therefore more vulnerable to declines in these influences.

Young voters have been a second problem for the party. As the children of the "baby boom" and the succeeding "baby bust" entered adulthood, they did not simply take on their parents' partisanship, but frequently declared themselves Independents.[5] By 1984, they held enormous potential for change in national politics. Comprising two of every five voters, but without firmly established loyalties, they were readily susceptible to new strategies and arguments. Until 1984, Democrats had renewed their strength each year by doing relatively well among political neophytes. In this election, youth turned toward the Republicans, as three of every five new voters chose Reagan.

Furthermore, this group was more likely to identify with the Republican party (by a 39-34 margin) and to vote for the Republican party in House elections (by a 50-41 edge). These results are a dark portent for the Democratic future. The party might be able to dig out after Mondale's landslide defeat, but it could not easily sustain a continuing hail of rocks.[6]

The Reagan coalition in 1984, while broad, was not simply a cross-section of the nation. In part, it was the reverse image of the remaining elements of the New Deal coalition, with particular strength among whites, Protestants, persons of higher income, and those in higher-status jobs. It also comprised more novel elements. The best way to see this characteristic is to look, not at the voting in 1984 alone, but to compare this election to others, by focusing on shifts among some groups from their voting in 1980 and 1976.

In table 3.3, we have isolated those demographic groups that increased their Republican vote by over 10 percentage points, either between the two Reagan victories or over the longer period from 1976 to 1984. Clearly, the Republicans have become a more defined conservative party over the past four years, relying strongly on an ideological appeal and on groups responsive to such appeals. However, elections cannot be won in the United States by such narrow

TABLE 3.3

MAJOR CHANGES IN REPUBLICAN VOTE, 1976-1980-1984

	Change 1980 to 1984	Change 1976 to 1980
Men	+4	+9
Conservatives	+9	+2
White Protestants	+10	+6
Born-again Christians	+17	NA
Catholics	+6	+5
High-school graduates	+9	+6
Blue-collar workers	+6	+6
Moderate income*	+10	+1
White southerners	+11	+9
Independents	+8	+2
Age 18-29	+15	-4
Age 60 and older	+9	+2
White (non-Hispanic)	+11	+3
Rural and town residents	+15	+1

*In 1976-80, 44 percent of population, earning $10,000-$25,000. In 1980 and 1984, 48 percent of population, earning $12,500-$35,000.

coalitions. More significant may be the longer, eight-year drift to the party of "middle America"—blue-collar workers, high-school graduates, and persons of moderate income.

There have been few trends over this period in the Democratic direction. Blacks, Jews, and the unemployed have increased their support, but they have no other companions on their lonesome partisan road. While Hispanics remain Democratic, their loyalties have become less intense. In comparison to men, women voted relatively Democratic, but the "gender gap" (which we discuss more fully in chapter 4) fell below the party's expectations. Another unfavorable straw in the wind was the large Republican plurality (62-37) among computer users.[7]

These data do not in themselves demonstrate that there was fundamental political change in the 1984 election, but they do raise the possibility. We have considered only the presidential election, and a full analysis must also take into account the congressional results and other trends (see chapters 5 and 7). We will reconsider the meaning of the election results after describing the course of the presidential campaign.

The Campaign

For all the difference it made, America could have skipped the 1984 campaign. Whether the election had been held in the preprimary winter, after the summer conventions, or in November's fall, Ronald Reagan would have won an overwhelming victory.

Almost half the voters had made their decision at the beginning of the year, and only a fourth even waited for the televised debates.[8] As a result, as seen in figure 3.2, there was little change in sentiment over the course of the year. There were some variations, particularly rallies toward Mondale after the Democratic convention in San Francisco and after the first debate. The dominant trend, however, was simple consolidation, as the electorate crystallized its sentiments into a rock-hard majority for Reagan.

THE REPUBLICAN MOOD

Generally, campaigns can be waged on issues or personalities. The Reagan effort used both. The President was credited with achieving prosperity for the nation, with the economy registering an astonishing growth of over 10 percent early in 1984, along with low inflation. In foreign policy, Reagan boasted that "America is back, standing tall," citing the successful American intervention in Grenada and increased military capability. Even setbacks such as the lost lives of marines in Lebanon were presented as honorable deaths.

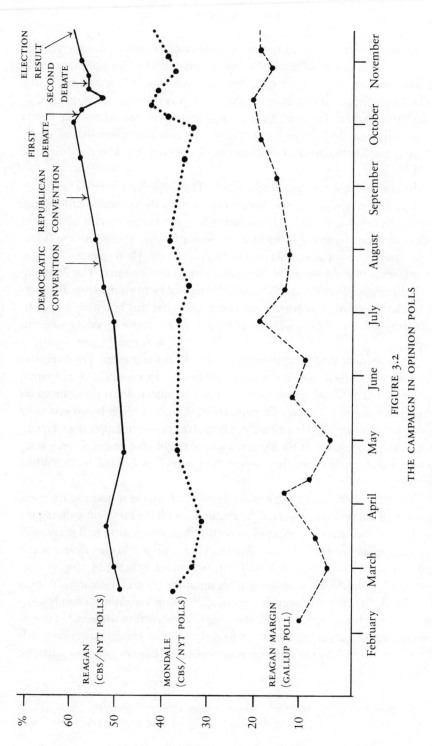

FIGURE 3.2

THE CAMPAIGN IN OPINION POLLS

SOURCE: CBS News/New York Times poll and the Gallup poll.

Beyond his record, Reagan was personally attractive. In the government of the United States, the President is not only the head of the government but the head of state. In the latter role, Reagan was a superb "cheerleader," using his ceremonial position to enhance the nation's congenital optimism and to underline its beliefs. He was "America as it imagined itself to be—the bearer of the traditional Main Street values of family and neighborhood, of thrift, industry, and charity instead of government intervention where self-reliance failed."[9]

Reagan did not rely on charm alone. The considerable resources of an incumbent administration were used to make appeals to various groups and to rebut the opposition. Mondale criticized Reagan's failure to meet with Soviet leaders. Reagan countered by inviting the Soviet foreign minister to the White House. Democrats attacked his environmental record. He responded by signing wilderness legislation at the bird sanctuary in the Potomac. The President was berated as callous toward the needy. He replied by opening a housing project for the elderly in New York. Farm complaints were met by a new loan guarantee program, and industrial unemployment by a promise to reduce steel imports.

The President made conspicuous use of his formal powers. The executive rose garden became a telegenic background for the appointment of Hispanics and the visit of the Israeli prime minister. The administration tried to gain credit for encouraging news, such as a national increase in college board scores or a decrease in crime rates. It avoided potential bad news until after the election, such as its tax program or the expected size of the budget deficit. Even a wary press could do little more than report "the news," as defined by the White House.[10]

The Republican campaign artfully promoted both the record and the man, equating all the positive aspects of American life with the President individually and with administration programs generally. Advertisers who had previously produced upbeat commercials for Pepsi-Cola now filmed "scenes from a sunlit land in which no one was sick, sad, fat, infirm, or afflicted by ring around the collar." As the President spoke of a "springtime of hope," the television spots proclaimed, "It's morning again in America," showing a wedding, a family moving into a new home, fertile fields, and rugged construction workers.[11] Literally wrapping Reagan in the American flag, the longest advertisement concluded with a virile policeman raising the star-spangled banner to a new patriotic anthem:

I'm proud to be an American, where at least I know I'm free,
And I won't forget the men who died who gave that flag to me;

And I'll gladly stand up—next to you—
And defend her still today,
'Cause there ain't no doubt I love this land;
God bless the U.S.A.

THE DEMOCRATIC MESSAGES

In their search for an upset, the Democrats changed strategies a number of times. These revisions made the Mondale campaign appear to be uncertain and mismanaged. There were embarrassingly bad decisions, such as opening the formal campaign at a New York Labor Day rally hours before the parade began. The fundamental problem, however, was not so much the defects of the Democrats but the advantages of the Republicans. Each effort by Mondale and Ferraro was met by the frustrating polls, which continued to show a steady Reagan lead.

The first Democratic problem was a self-inflicted wound. As was usual for national candidates, Ferraro had promised to make her income tax returns public, as well as those of her husband, John Zaccaro, a wealthy real estate broker. A week before the statements were due, however, she announced that her husband had refused to release his personal returns, leading the press and public to assume that the couple had something to hide. Eventually, Ferraro achieved a press victory from the controversy. In a 100-minute televised conference, she disclosed all of her finances, showed that she and Zaccaro had paid large income taxes, and won the open admiration of her questioners. Nevertheless, the campaign was damaged, costing the Democrats time they needed to maintain their postconvention momentum.

More fundamentally, the financial disclosures tarnished the luster of Ferraro, who was being held to particularly high standards as the first woman running nationally. Democrats and feminists could legitimately complain that financial disclosure rules were written on the sexist assumption that men were the chief wage-earners in a family. Still, most voters probably shared that assumption, and they became permanently suspicious of the Democratic running mate. Before the controversy, the congresswoman was relatively unknown but favorably regarded by a 2 to 1 margin. From that point, she became familiar to the public, but 35 percent regarded her critically, almost as many as were favorable. Ultimately, Ferraro may have gained a few votes for the Democratic ticket, but what had once seemed to be an asset became little more than a balance of gains and losses.[12]

The campaign then turned back toward issues, or, at least, jogged in that direction. Mondale's challenge on taxes and the federal deficit had originally upset the Reagan camp. Contradictory statements were made by Republican leaders, continuing the division evident at the party convention. To counter

Mondale, the President said he would increase taxes only as a "last resort" and promised that individual income tax rates would not increase. To correct the deficit, he left open the possibility of increasing revenues through "tax simplification." Reagan then dismissed the problem, optimistically quipping, "To our opponents every day is April 15; to us, every day is the Fourth of July."

Governmental finance was one of the many issues Mondale attempted to address. Because polls showed that Reagan policies were less popular than the President himself, the Mondale organization believed that a continued "issues strategy" would eventually lead to a national day of revelation. Voters would come to understand that only Mondale would do what a majority wanted in regard to deficits, or a nuclear freeze, or environmental controls, or civil rights. The flawed premise of this strategy was that it viewed a presidential election as a gigantic public opinion poll on an accumulation of issues. A presidential election does involve issues, but it is most simply a choice of leadership to deal with recognized societal needs by acceptable means. While voters did recognize the problems cited by Mondale, they continued to see Reagan as the better leader to resolve these problems.[13]

Tax increases were hardly likely to win the election for Mondale. Not only are they unpopular, they are technical and unemotional. Religion, the second major issue of the campaign, was more evocative. Reagan, appearing at a prayer breakfast after the Republican convention, condemned opponents of compulsory school prayer as "intolerant," and argued that "religion and politics are necessarily related," raising fears of a mingling of church and state. Mondale attacked evangelist Jerry Falwell, arguing that the fundamentalist minister would influence the choice of Supreme Court justices. Opponents of abortion shadowed Ferraro on the campaign trail, vehemently presenting their right-to-life position against her advocacy of women's right-to-choice. As a devout Catholic woman, Ferraro was particularly vulnerable to these attacks.

In these controversies, the Democratic candidates again were on the popular side. Strong majorities opposed Falwell's Moral Majority and the absolutist right-to-life position. However, few votes were cast on this basis, so the issue of religion did not aid the ticket. The larger effect was to distract attention, preventing the Democrats from making a coherent attack on the strong Reagan fortress. As one Republican leader put it, "You don't win many votes by raising taxes and arguing with archbishops."[14]

A third Democratic emphasis was on the danger of nuclear war. A television ad inspired by rock videos showed the "red alert" telephone at the White House ringing, foretelling an imminent foreign attack. Reagan's program for a "Star Wars" missile defense, it warned, would mean that computers, not the President, would be in charge, making a nuclear holocaust more likely. While the nuclear freeze movement had shown strong popular support in the past, foreign and defense policy was not stressed consistently by the Democrats. In the conflict with Reagan's patriotic themes, Mondale was unable to gain any advantage.

In the last weeks of the campaign, although still unable to make substantial gains, the Democrats recovered the enthusiasm and the message of their national convention. Mondale found an appealing theme, speaking now of his philosophy instead of his programs, emphasizing fairness instead of finances, displaying emotion instead of expertise, invoking values instead of advertisements. To larger and more enthusiastic crowds, he declared, "I would rather lose a race about decency than win one about self-interest." In his closing effort, wrote David Broder, Mondale rested his case "on the best of the Democratic tradition which he embodies," while showing himself to be "an effective, attractive and decent politician."[15]

THE TELEVISION DEBATES

The Democrats' only true opportunity to gain victory against the overwhelming odds was in the televised debates, which were actually joint press conferences. To win Reagan's consent to the debates, the Democrats had to accept limitations on their number, timing, and format. Still, they had gained an equal forum. Now national television audiences of more than 100 million people would see Reagan and Mondale (twice, on 7 and 21 October) or Bush and Ferraro (only once, on 11 October) answering the same questions, on the same austere platform, before the same nonpartisan audience of the League of Women Voters.

Simultaneously, the debates sent two kinds of messages. The manifest message was the positions of the candidates on the issues, as posed by news reporters (see chapter 2). The contenders informed viewers of their stands on matters as diverse as the likelihood of Armageddon and the control of illegal immigration, while questioning each other's records. Previous research has shown that voters do learn from these discussions, and this effect probably occurred in 1984 as well.[16]

More dramatic was the latent message. Most viewers would find it difficult to sort out the claims, statistics, and refutations of the debaters. They could more easily judge their competence, trustworthiness, and abilities. This meant more than the candidates' images, or personalities; it meant their character, their leadership and vision, their basic fitness for the highest offices the electorate could confer. Voters could sense these qualities with their own eyes and ears — and the news media were more than willing to help the audience by providing instant analyses of "Who Won?"

On these grounds, the debates provided surprises. In the first, Mondale made a strong impression by combining courtesy toward the President with a pointed attack on his policies and, even more, his competence. Mondale's theme was, "There's a difference between being a quarterback and a cheerleader." He gibed at the President, "It's not what he doesn't know that bothers me, it's what he knows for sure [that] just ain't so." In closing, Reagan added to his problems, by admitting that he was "confused," and by giving a rambling statement, cluttered with statistics, as if he were a college student who had crammed too much for a final exam.

In the most dramatic moment of the debate, made more dramatic by later television editing, Mondale responded to Reagan's use of a line from the 1980 debate with Jimmy Carter:

> *Reagan:* You know, I wasn't going to say this at all, but I can't help it: There you go again. . . .
> *Mondale:* Now, Mr. President, you said: "There you go again." Right. Remember the last time you said that?
> *Reagan:* Um hmm.
> *Mondale:* You said it when President Carter said that you were going to cut Medicare. And you said: "Oh, no, there you go again, Mr. President." And what did you do right after the election? You went out and tried to cut $20 billion out of Medicare.[17]

The harmful effects of the President's mediocre performance were exaggerated by adverse press commentaries. As the week went on, the public came to believe not simply that Mondale had won one contest but that there had been no contest. The *Wall Street Journal,* usually a bastion of conservatism, then further worsened the Republican situation by printing a long-prepared article that raised the question of the President's age. Was his mediocre performance in the debate an indication that the nation's oldest chief executive was unable to continue?

The Republicans took a number of steps to limit the damage from the first debate. Reagan campaigned more vigorously to demonstrate his health. Mondale's criticisms on Social Security were rebutted by a firm pledge to maintain present and future benefits. Negative advertising against Mondale began to appear on television. Particular attention was directed toward the next debates.

The Bush-Ferraro confrontation became a preliminary bout before the rematch of the presidential candidates. The incumbent took an aggressive stance, to emphasize his experience in office. To undo the Reagan losses, he tried to stress the President's command of the government. In enthusiastic, even sycophantic tones, he told of Reagan's meeting the Soviet foreign minister: "I wish everybody could have seen that one—the President, giving the facts to Gromyko in all of these nuclear meetings—excellent, right on top of that subject matter."

Ferraro's purpose was to prove her competence, and to dispel doubts raised by her sex and relative inexperience. She presented herself more as a lawyer and a Mondale advocate, rather than the feisty campaigner she was on the road. Only once did she allow herself to display anger. Responding to Bush's position on U.S. policy in Lebanon, she shot back, "Let me just say, first of all, that I almost resent, Vice-President Bush, your patronizing attitude that you have to teach me about foreign policy."

The second presidential debate centered on foreign policy. Mondale again stressed Reagan's competence, repeatedly insisting that he did not meet the basic standards of the presidential office, "to be in charge of facts and run our government and strengthen our nation." On this occasion, however, Reagan was more than equal to the challenge. Presenting himself as an advocate of nuclear disarmament, he stated a simple credo, "A nuclear war cannot be won and must never be fought." On the critical issue of his age, he ended all discussion with the best one-liner of the campaign: "I will not make age an issue in this campaign. I am not going to exploit for political purposes my opponent's youth and inexperience."

The overall effect of the debates was to assure Reagan's victory. At the first confrontation, Mondale had changed the tone of the campaign. He was now taken seriously by the public and press, and party leaders, once reluctant supporters, became open backers. While he performed less strongly in the second trial, he still showed his competence and knowledge. Among those voters who relied on these shows to decide their vote, the Democratic candidate gained three out of four votes. His problem was that less than a tenth of the electorate used the debates to determine their choice.[18]

By the time of the second debate, expectations had changed. Mondale was like a pole-vaulter, facing a higher challenge with each success. He now needed a spectacular second performance to make further gains. Particularly important was the question, raised for a brief moment after the first debate, of the aging President's competence. Reagan no longer had to meet high standards. He needed only to reassure the electorate that he was of sound mind. Ultimately, these forums served only to bring the campaign back to the central focus, the Reagan record. "By revealing more of both men," wrote one journalist, "the debates cut down to size some of the issues that [had] been dominating the campaign: Mondale's image as a wimp, Reagan's as an unparalleled communicator. . . . But by pruning back these personal issues, the debates suggested how secondary they may be."[19]

Polls underlined the debates' limited impact. Mondale gained both a more favorable personal evaluation and higher standing in the expected vote. Nevertheless, Reagan still won personal approval from two-thirds of the voters, and his expected vote barely changed. Rather than changing minds, the debates helped people to settle their minds. The first debate brought Mondale the voters who were likely to mobilize behind him eventually, just as the second debate reinforced the support Reagan already had. Television provided the stage for a drama whose ending was already foreshadowed."[20]

THE CAMPAIGN'S MEANING

Despite its limited impact on the final vote, the campaign was more than sound and fury. The mood and messages of the candidates signified something, the future direction of American public policy.

As they campaigned, Reagan and Mondale sometimes followed the established signposts of American politics as they moved toward the center of the political road. Both camps tried to depict the opposition as extremist, yet both imitated each other's proven appeals. With the fervor of a New Dealer, Reagan made heroes of Roosevelt and Truman. The President defended the Social Security System, praised the former Shah of Iran for his low-income housing projects, and deplored the exploitation of Mexican immigrants. Mondale often adopted the language of traditional conservatism. He treated federal budget deficits as a mortal sin, ridiculed the possibility of sharing antimissile defense systems with the Soviet Union, and enshrined the independence of the Supreme Court.

These movements toward the center still left the candidates far apart on different sides of the political road. William Safire correctly advised the voters the day before the balloting: "Do not be misled: The persuasive leaning-centerward during the campaign is all a lie, while the phony-sounding professions about different 'visions of America' is the truth."[21] In his presidency, Reagan had provided ample evidence of his beliefs in limited government and assertive foreign policy. In a consistent public life, Mondale had faithfully shown his commitment to social welfare and diplomatic accommodation.

The candidates spoke, and the citizenry responded decisively. But what was its reply?

Meanings and Theories

Interpreting a presidential election is different from scientific explanation. We cannot design a controlled experiment, or repeat the campaign while varying the candidates, the issues, or the environment. Politics is not physics. It is more like meteorology, where we try to understand the causes of hurricanes while recognizing that winds are sometimes inexplicable. In reviewing the 1984 election, we will deal with four interpretations.

A TRIUMPH OF PERSONALITY

The most common explanation of Reagan's victory is Reagan himself. The President's success is not due to his record or his philosophy, but to his "image." In this interpretation, tens of millions of Americans voted for a likable individual, who successfully combined stirring if vague rhetoric, a confident personality, an actor's communication skills, and a verbal commitment to religion and family.

The personal emphasis was evident in Reagan's campaign. A film biography of the President, the keynote of his effort, pictured him as an attractive individual, ceremoniously and dramatically representing the nation. Reagan was shown meeting American troops in Korea, walking toward the sunset with his wife, commemorating the Normandy invasion of World War II, cheerfully surviving the 1981 assassination attempt, and celebrating the American Olympic victories. Almost nothing in the film dealt with specific programs and objectives.

Reagan's critics often share this personal interpretation. Indeed, it is comforting to Democrats to believe that they lost only to a "great communicator," who will soon be gone from politics. His success is denigrated by these critics as indicating that Americans have abandoned their judgment to a "kindly grandfather." Walter Mondale himself felt compelled to profess his personal liking for the President, even as he attacked Reagan's policies and his inattention to the duties of the chief executive.

In an extension of this emphasis on personality, Mondale gets the personal blame for the Democrats' defeat. As a campaign joke had it, when Reagan met with the Cabinet, the President fell asleep, but in a Mondale administration, the Cabinet would fall asleep. The former Vice-President was seen as dull "Norwegian wood," a poor performer on television, beset by inefficient campaign organization, and harmed by inchoate advertising. The problem for the Democrats was not the message, but the messenger.

Certainly this interpretation has some validity. The Reagan effort did focus on his personal attributes, as summarized in the repeated slogan, "Leadership That's Working." The President's campaign stops featured ceremony, flags, and good feelings, while avoiding issues and drowning reporters' questions in the noise of helicopter engines. The Mondale organization's deficiencies were also evident, in poor scheduling and in its handling of the Ferraro financial issue. The Democratic slogan, "They're Fighting for Our Future," was neither memorable nor effective, since it conveyed no symbolic meaning and defined no difference between the major parties. (Did voters need to be assured that Mondale and Ferraro were in favor of the future? Would anyone believe that Reagan and Bush were against it?)

All this can be granted without seeing the election as decided on personal grounds. In the glow of election victory, Reagan appears greatly loved, but the evidence is not consistent. During the depths of the 1982 recession, his popularity in the Gallup poll fell below all recent chief executives. Even when he recovered his popular standing, he stood little better at the beginning of the election year than Jimmy Carter at a comparable point in 1980, and below Richard Nixon's level in 1972. Moreover, the President also had high levels of *dis*approval, and some of these antipathies showed in the election vote. A universally admired person would not have 91 percent of a major voting bloc (blacks) in opposition. Reagan did arouse passion, but also division.[22]

Reagan's popularity, while substantial by election day, was also substantive. His vaunted communication skills would have done him little good if unemployment had remained at the painful levels of 1982, or if the United States were involved in a Vietnam-like war in Central America, or if the Social Security System had gone bankrupt. To show the limited impact of simple imagery, Amitai Etzioni suggested, "One need simply imagine that instead of talking about God, family and country, the President was extolling Zen Buddhism, unilateral disarmament and sexual license. His rating would of course crash within a week."[23] Reagan was, to be sure, a good salesman, and his product may have been wrapped attractively, even deceptively, but there still was a product.

Criticism of Mondale also seems exaggerated. Within his party, the Minnesotan was not an extremist candidate, who might be expected to alienate mainstream Democrats. Rather, Mondale was a very appropriate Democratic candidate, personifying the party's philosophy and recent history. His nomination was not a personal coup but the choice both of the leadership and a plurality of the rank and file. His legitimacy was further validated in the election, when he won the votes of 73 percent of identified Democrats, more than Carter, even in the face of Reagan's swollen vote.

Despite complaints after the election, Mondale was not regarded by the public as a poor candidate—except in comparison to his opponent. Even at the nadir of his campaign, in September, pluralities thought the Democrat more caring and less reckless than Reagan. Although the President was considered better on other qualities, Mondale still was rated better than either Jimmy Carter or the 1980 version of Ronald Reagan on five of six other qualities, such as competence, judgment, and understanding of problems.[24]

Postelection complaints about the Mondale organization conflict with earlier descriptions of its awesome efficiency. Blaming it later for the election defeat is a search for scapegoats rather than a discovery of causation. The basic feature of the campaign, after all, was that very little changed after the conventions, and that a Reagan victory was almost preordained. To the extent that there was change, particularly in the last month, the trend benefited the Democrats. Mondale could claim the credit for these limited gains because of his performance in the debates and his vigorous closing efforts. The election was a victory for Reagan, but not a personal defeat for Mondale.

A POLICY CHOICE

A second interpretation of the 1984 balloting pictures it as a "mandate" for the President's program. After the 1980 elections, Reagan used this argument to gain his legislative program, even though most observers saw the result more of a repudiation of Jimmy Carter than an endorsement of the Republican platform.[25] Victorious politicians prefer such explanations, for they provide the legitimacy of popular approval for their programs.

Policy choices in elections are difficult to accomplish. They require, at least, that candidates take definable positions, that the voters correctly perceive these positions, and that the voters then cast their ballots on the basis of these positions. Even when all of these conditions are met, an election may still not be clearly the result of issue voting.[26]

In 1984, Reagan's campaign gave little attention to future policy directions. Proclaiming in victory that "you ain't seen nothing yet," Reagan left the electorate to wonder what would follow, other than "four more years" in the same direction. Even at the general level of philosophy, it is difficult to interpret the election as a mandate. Only a fraction of Reagan's voters defended their vote as the choice of a "real conservative," even fewer than in 1980. Furthermore, compared to the previous contest, both the congressional elections and voting on state referendums evidenced less of an ideological character.

When voters dealt with specific policies for the future, they made little connection between their vote for Reagan and their issue preferences. Table 3.4 on page 82 demonstrates the point by summarizing the results of two polls. On five significant issues, Reagan's position was backed only by minorities, usually small, of the voters. Nevertheless, the President was endorsed by a majority of these respondents. The Republican campaign successfully evaded an election based on future policy decisions. The focus became the President's ability to drive the engine of national government, perhaps in reverse gear, rather than the particular road he would travel.

Tax policy provides an important specific example. Voters agreed that taxes would go up, but also blamed the Democrats for the budget deficit. On election day, government spending and the deficit had become the most important

TABLE 3.4

POLICY POSITIONS AND THE VOTE IN 1984

	Favor Reagan, favor position	Favor Reagan, oppose position	Oppose Reagan, oppose position
Equal Rights Amendment	32%	27%	34%
Pollution controls	10	42	39
Nuclear freeze	23	29	37
Aid to the poor	34	14	46
Abortion	28	31	32

SOURCES: Harris poll of 24 July 1984, as reported in *National Journal* 16 (11 August 1984): 1542; for abortion issue, the *New York Times,* 19 August 1984, A1.

issues, stressed by a fourth of the electorate. By then, however, some of these citizens had apparently become convinced that Reagan would find a way to restrain taxes, others were expressing such hopes rather than convictions, and still others wanted Reagan even if it meant higher taxes. Whatever the motives, even these fiscal worrywarts gave Reagan 59 percent of their votes.[27]

On other issues as well, the Reagan coalition included substantial proportions that disagreed with the President on the issues. Overall, two-thirds of his backers agreed with him on an issue they considered of major importance, but a fifth disagreed with their chosen leader on some vital question. For example, 13 percent of the President's own backers stressed defense policy and also favored a nuclear freeze; another tenth both emphasized poverty as a national problem and wanted to increase aid to the poor.[28]

These patterns make it difficult for the President to claim a prospective mandate from the voters for any policy innovations. He did not present the electorate with a new agenda, and it, therefore, could not endorse an innovative program. Columnist Mark Shields correctly concluded, "In Reagan's last campaign he once again ran against the past, making the 1984 vote a referendum on the 1980 results." In so doing, he achieved "a landslide without a mandate." The landslide itself still needs an explanation.[29]

A RETROSPECTIVE JUDGMENT

Theoretical explanations of voting behavior emphasize that voters are likely to vote retrospectively rather than prospectively. They judge the past records of candidates and parties rather than look toward the future. This makes sense for an electorate that has relatively little time or inclination to devote to political thought, and that inevitably cannot know the future. Of course, voters do worry about what will happen in the next four years, but they use past performance as a means to choose future leadership. If unforeseen problems arise—as they surely will—it is better to have a trusted executive dealing with these problems.[30]

The electoral situation in 1984 was particularly appropriate for this kind of judgment. An incumbent President was running, so his performance and programs could be taken as a good indication of his later course—especially in the case of Reagan, who had a consistent public record and ideology. His opponent, Walter Mondale, had been Vice-President in the previous administration, so a direct comparison could be made between the two parties' achievements. Furthermore, using the immense control of the White House over the news, the Republicans resolutely focused attention on a matching of the records of the Reagan and "Carter-Mondale" administrations.

The retrospective quality of the election is evident throughout the results and can be documented in four ways. The first is the signficance of the economic situation, which we will discuss more fully in chapter 4. Reagan's victory was directly correlated to the voters' belief that their own financial situation, and that of the nation, had improved in his term. If the vote had been confined to those who saw the economy as stable or declining, Mondale would have been elected. The effect was the same, but in the opposite direction from 1980, when the perceived decline in the economy was a strong cause of the Carter-Mondale defeat.

A second demonstration of a retrospective vote is found in the stability of the vote from 1980 to 1984. There was relatively little switching between the two elections. As voters were focusing on the past, they reaffirmed their past ballots. Only a tenth of all voters in 1984 changed their electoral choice. However, Reagan got the better of these changes, by 6 to 4. By holding his previous support, and adding new voters, he was able to increase his vote to landslide proportions.*

The third indication is the way voters dealt with policy issues. There was no clear electoral mandate on policy directions. However, there was considerable coherence in evaluations of the ability of the two candidates and the two parties to deal with these issues. Voters might not know *what* to do about a particular policy problem, but they showed far more agreement on *who* they believed more trustworthy and competent in handling the problem. In mid-October, by a 4 to 3 margin, the electorate was more inclined "to trust the future of this country" to the Republicans. The voters considered Reagan and

---

*Of Reagan's 59 percent of the total ballots, 41 percent came from his 1980 supporters, 6 percent from 1980 Carter backers, 10 percent from previous nonvoters, and 2 percent from Anderson voters. Mondale's 41 percent total included 25 percent who had supported Carter, 4 percent who switched away from Reagan, 9 percent previous nonvoters, and 3 percent recruited from Anderson. See *National Journal* 16 (10 November 1984): 2131.

Bush better able to handle the economy, control inflation and the federal budget deficit, keep the nation out of war, stand up to Russia, maintain strong military defenses, and deal with prayers in schools. Democrats were preferred in regard to providing fairness, aid to the poor, and Social Security, but these were not the dominant concerns as the electorate judged the record of the past four years.[31]

Finally, the voters themselves acknowledged the retrospective basis of their judgment. Three out of five cited "strong leadership" and "experience" as major reasons for their decisions, and heavily supported Reagan, who was the only experienced presidential leader in the race. In assessing Reagan's qualifications, the voters were far more favorable in 1984 than in 1980, as actual performance in office led them to give him higher ratings for intelligence, a command of the issues, ability to maintain peace, and even, despite his advancing years, physical capability. As William Schneider wrote, "Voters acknowledge that Reagan has done the two things he was elected to do: curb inflation and restore the nation's sense of military security," and the electorate then followed "its traditional inclination—'You don't quarrel with success.' "[32]

A PARTY REALIGNMENT

All elections are significant, but some are more significant, for they may be "realigning" votes, in which "new and durable electoral groupings are formed."[33] We have already reviewed the shifts in the geographical and demographic bases of the 1984 vote that suggest a new Republican majority coalition in presidential elections. The durability of this majority remains uncertain until future ballots are counted, but there are some indications of relative permanence.

There have been 10 presidential elections since the death of Franklin Roosevelt and the end of the Second World War. Strikingly, the Democrats have won only one of these contests convincingly, the Johnson landslide of 1964. While the party has managed three other narrow victories, it has lost the remaining six contests, including all but one election since Johnson. This is hardly the record expected of a national majority party. Moreover, the Democrats' losses cannot be laid simply to the faults of individual candidates, even if these men could be separated from the party that nominated them. Overwhelming defeat has been the common fate of Democrats from the party's left (McGovern), right (Carter), and center (Mondale).

Despite this electoral record, Democrats have still ranked as the majority party because of their strength in nonpresidential elections and their lead in the underlying partisan identifications of the voters. Despite its weakened effect in recent years, partisan loyalty remains the single best predictor of vote. The 1984 results, however, point to cracks even in this foundation of the Democratic monolith. After the election, as many citizens considered themselves Republicans as Democrats (32 percent for each party). When those who "lean" to a party are added in, Republicans actually commanded a plurality, 47-44. Although the figures were unreliable, because of the immediate effects of the Reagan landslide, they still made much better news for Republicans than Democrats.[34]

When realignments do occur, they are particularly evident among the young and other new voters. The Republicans therefore had special reason to cheer in their advantage (50-42) among the most impressionable younger group, aged under 30. New registrations in 1984 showed the same trend. Although the Democratic efforts got the most publicity, Republicans actually enrolled more new voters, particularly in the party's southern and western strongholds. Nationally, the new 1984 registrants gave Reagan a 61-39 majority. While the total vote was barely higher than in 1980 (52.9 percent of the voting age population, a slight increase of 0.3 percent), the Democrats found even less favor among the nonvoters.[35]

A final hint—not proof—of realignment can be found in the closer relationship between the voters' partisanship and their ideological positions, as specified in table 3.5. The entries in the table show the vote for Mondale for various combinations of party loyalty and self-declared ideology. The numbers in parentheses show the percentage received by Carter in 1980 among the same group. Thus, among liberal Democrats—the first entry—Mondale won 88 percent, compared to Carter's 70 percent.

TABLE 3.5

PARTY AND IDEOLOGY IN THE PRESIDENTIAL VOTE
(in percent voting for Mondale)

	Partisanship			
	Democrats	Independents	Republicans	Total
Ideology				
Liberals	88 (70)	60 (50)	11 (25)	70 (68)
Moderates	76 (66)	41 (31)	7 (11)	46 (45)
Conservatives	56 (53)	13 (22)	4 (6)	18 (24)
TOTALS	73 (72)	35 (34)	7 (10)	

Reading through the figures, we can see that Mondale's support was affected by both factors. Compared to 1980, ideology has become more important—although still less of an influence than party. Mondale consolidated the liberal vote, especially among Democrats and Independents, yet he did worse than Carter among the growing ranks of conservatives. Increasingly, the parties on the presidential level seem to be not only historical labels but coalitions of like-minded men and women.*

These indications of a turn toward the Republicans should not be exaggerated, since the Reagan sweep was not accompanied by a general Republican victory or a clear policy direction. It is possible that the presidency has now become completely nonpartisan, individualized and distinct from the general political system, so that elections for the chief executive have no larger import. Evidence for this view includes Reagan's lack of coattails to aid other Republicans, widespread ticket-splitting, and the victories of Democrats and incumbents for other offices.

In the long run, however, the presidency cannot be totally isolated from the rest of American politics. In his second term, Reagan's actions are likely to strengthen the Republican position (see chapter 6). In economic policy, the party's constituency will be reinforced by 1988 through tax laws likely to give even more emphasis to business incentives and less to redistributing income to the poor. Reagan is likely to appoint two to four Supreme Court justices, providing a long-term bulwark for conservative values. The reallocation of electoral votes after the 1990 census will probably show a further shift toward the Sunbelt strongholds of the Republicans. With a skilled political leader and efficient organization, the party will have the opportunity to extend its gains beyond the White House, toward control of the state governments, and, after 1990, the redistricting and capture of Congress.

Parties and Philosophy

Controversies over ideas will be at the foundation of future party struggles. In 1984, these philosophical differences were unusually evident, even if they weren't always clear in the personal arguments between Mondale and Reagan. The differences between Democrats and Republicans were captured in two different pictures, or images, used by party leaders.

The Republican philosophy could be painted as the 1984 Olympic Games — an event that President Reagan, in fact, did glorify in his acceptance speech. America's athletes gave splendid individual performances, matching the Republican emphasis on individual economic enterprise. The Los Angeles spectacle was turned over by the local and federal governments to private entrepreneurs.

---

*Another indicator is the ideological composition of the voter coalitions of each candidate. Fully half of Reagan's vote in 1984 came from self-declared conservatives, and only 8 percent from liberals. These figures compared to 42 percent and 10 percent, respectively, in 1980. Mondale received 30 percent of his vote from liberals, and 17 percent from conservatives, compared to 27 percent and 18 percent, respectively, for Carter. The remaining voters are "moderates."

Its financial and artistic success seemed to support Reagan's desire to shift programs away from government. Nor did complaints about discrimination or demands for affirmative action intrude on the Olympic celebration. The path to Olympic success was the same as that suggested by Republicans in the broader society. Women competed fully and well, but totally separated, posing no threat to men. Blacks were offered the role model of Carl Lewis, combining natural talent, intense work, and family support to gain four victories, national recognition, and personal wealth.

The Games allowed us to bask in national glory, stirred by repeated raising of the flag, much as the President tried to do in the campaign. For two weeks, because of the Soviet boycott, communism simply disappeared from the world. The President seemed to wish it could happen in reality. The Olympic image of the athlete's lonely struggle to master the physical world was matched by the campaign image of the President's solitary battle to master the political world. Even the Olympic slogan, "Higher, Faster, Stronger," was adapted by the Republicans.

The contrasting Democratic philosophy was pictured well by Governor Mario Cuomo's image, in his Democratic convention keynote speech, of a covered wagon moving toward a new frontier. He identified the occupants of the wagon, not by individual names, but as members of groups—Catholics, minorities, women, the disabled. The wagon's journey, he suggested, in keeping with Democratic party philosophy, requires more than individual effort. Even reaching the frontier involves a common defense against the "red" menace (of Indians, if not communists), and the need for cooperation continues after reaching the promised land.

The world of the frontier is a harsh world. Resources are scarce, so mutual aid is required, to reap crops, raise barns and build schools, pave roads and care for the poor. For Democrats, these activities require government and sacrifice. Taxes will be collected, and sometimes raised. Social standards of "fairness" will be applied, meaning that some people's income will be reduced, and other people will receive benefits. Women and men both work hard on the frontier. With this picture in mind, Democrats see equal rights legislation not as a theoretical issue but as a recognition of reality.

These two pictures, although somewhat exaggerated, do resemble the different portraits drawn by the parties. Republicans stress individualism, optimism, the virtues of economic accumulation, a national melting pot. Democrats stress communalism, the need for sacrifice, social concern, and ethnic diversity. Both are patriotic; both quote Jefferson, Lincoln, and the two Roosevelts; and both champion "family values"; but they speak from different traditions, and offer different visions of the future.

At present, Republican ideas also seem more congenial to the American people. Polls show more people willing to call themselves conservatives, and fewer concerned with promoting social welfare and minority rights. A return to traditional values stressed by Republicans is evident outside of politics, in earlier marriages, an increase in the birthrate, higher enlistments in the military, and nostalgia for the more quiet music of the 1950s. Individuals stress material gain, not social concern, as the themes of the 1970s "me generation" replace those of 1960s activists. Nationalistic pride is evident, from cheers of "U.S.A." at the Olympics to widespread approval of American intervention in Grenada.

Democratic opportunities remain. A new generation of leaders will take over the party by 1988, building on its successes in state and congressional campaigns. Problems of organization and adaptation to the new technology of politics are remediable. The party can also find encouragement in population trends: More women are working and accepting feminist ideas; more minority youth will enter the electorate; more workers are feeling economic constraints.

The basic need for the Democrats, however, is not leadership, organization, or demographic advantage — it is intellectual. Imitating Republican calls for fiscal restraint or rapid armament would make the party little more than a "me too" party, a pale moon in the political solar system, reflecting the light of the opposition's dominant sun. Democrats need not be extremist, or the apparent captive of "special interests," but they do need to be different to obtain different results at the ballot box.[36]

"Fairness" may be the best Democratic answer to the Republican slogan of "opportunity." The electorate responded well to the theme at the Democratic convention and during the campaign, and even Reagan voters acknowledged Mondale's and his party's superiority on this standard. It symbolizes the party's tradition, and resonates in the American tradition. Like the patriotic optimism of Reagan, the cause of fairness can capture the idealism of youth and the imagination of Americans. It means more, however, than dealing with the valid grievances of racial groups, feminists, and other organized groups. A party of fairness also must consider the needs of blue-collar workers barely meeting mortgage payments, white southerners tentatively meeting the demands of a changing society, and women intentionally meeting their schoolchildren at home.

The data of the 1984 election, and the trends they reveal, do still show a likely Republican dominance in presidential elections. But future events are not fully predictable, and leadership and ideas can change politics. Geraldine Ferraro offered the party a theme to combine its ideals with traditional values: "When we find jobs for . . . the unemployed in this country, you know we'll make our economy stronger and that will be a patriotic act. When we reduce the deficits and we cut interest rates, . . . young people can buy houses, that's pro-family and that will be a patriotic act. . . . When we stop the arms race, we make this a safer, saner world, and that's a patriotic act."[37]

Ferraro is emblematic of the Democrats' possibilities. Her nomination extended opportunities for women and a white ethnic group. Her words may suggest the best way for the party to counter a new Republican majority.

NOTES

1. Walter Mondale's defeat in the Electoral College was not quite as severe as that of Alfred E. Landon, who won only the eight electoral votes of Maine and Vermont in 1936. Since that time, however, seven electoral votes had been added, with the admission of Alaska, Hawaii, and the District of Columbia, enabling Reagan to surpass Franklin Roosevelt's total of 523.
2. See Gerald Pomper, "Classification of Presidential Elections," *Journal of Politics* 29 (August 1967): 535-66; Walter Dean Burnham, *Critical Elections and the Mainsprings of American Politics* (New York: Norton, 1970).
3. Kristi Andersen, *The Creation of a Democratic Majority* (Chicago: University of Chicago Press, 1979); Aage Clausen et al., "Electoral Myth and Reality: The 1964 Election," *American Political Science Review* 59 (June 1965): 321-36.
4. These changes could be clearly seen in the 1970s, and were noted in Norman Nie et al., *The Changing American Voter* (Cambridge: Harvard University Press, 1976), chap. 13. The theoretical basis is provided by V.O. Key, "Secular Realignment and the Party System," *Journal of Politics* 21 (May 1959): 198-210.
5. See Pomper, *Voters' Choice* (New York: Harper, 1975), chap. 5; Helmut Norpoth and Jerrold Rusk, "Partisan Dealignment in the American Electorate," *American Political Science Review* 76 (September 1982): 522-37; Martin Wattenberg, *Decline of American Political Parties* (Cambridge: Harvard University Press, 1984), chaps. 3, 4.
6. The New York Times/CBS News poll, as reported by Adam Clymer in the *New York Times,* 11 November 1984, 30.
7. All data not otherwise cited are from the CBS News/New York Times poll, either derived from the original data made available by CBS News or as reported in the *New York Times,* 8 November 1984, A19.
8. Los Angeles Times exit poll, reported in *National Journal* 16 (10 November 1984): 2131.
9. "Campaign '84: The Inside Story," *Newsweek,* November/December 1984, 38.
10. Hedrick Smith, *New York Times,* 19 September 1984, A1.
11. The Republican television campaign is described in "Campaign '84," 87-90.
12. CBS News/New York Times polls of August, September, and twice in October. In the election day exit poll, a tenth of the voters said that the vice-presidential candidates were a major factor in their vote. Of these, the Democrats won six of ten votes. In the Los Angeles Times exit poll, however, only 4 percent cited the vice-presidential candidates. Of these, 56 percent preferred Bush.
13. See Jeffrey Smith, *American Presidential Elections: Trust and the Rational Voter* (New York: Praeger, 1980).
14. The opinion data are from William Schneider, in *National Journal* 16 (8 September 1984): 1690-91, and Adam Clymer, *New York Times,* 25 November 1984, IV: 2E.

The quotation is from Frank Holman, New Jersey Republican state chairman.

15. *Washington Post,* 31 October 1984.

16. Alan Abramowitz, "The Impact of a Presidential Debate on Voter Rationality," *American Journal of Political Science* 22 (August 1978): 680-90; Douglas Rose, "Citizen Uses of the Ford-Carter Debates," *Journal of Politics* 41 (February 1980): 214-21.

17. Texts of the debates may be found in the *New York Times,* 9 October 1984, A26-A29; 12 October 1984, B4-B6; 23 October 1984, B27-B29.

18. Los Angeles Times exit poll, 7 November 1984.

19. R. Brownstein, "Raising the Stakes," *National Journal* 16 (27 October 1984): 2040.

20. Los Angeles Times poll, 11 October 1984; CBS News/New York Times poll, 23-25 October 1984. The effect of the televised debates is strikingly similar to that reported for radio broadcasts in the first scientific study of voting: Paul Lazarsfeld et al., *The People's Choice* (New York: Columbia University Press, 1944).

21. William Safire, "Nobody's Perfect," *New York Times,* 5 November 1984, A19.

22. *National Journal* 16 (11 August 1984): 1542.

23. "The Democrats Need a Unifying Theme," *New York Times,* 5 October 1984, A31. V.O. Key made a similar point in refuting the earlier argument that Franklin Roosevelt's election victories were based on personality rather than policy performance. See *The Responsible Electorate* (Cambridge: Harvard University Press, 1966), 56.

24. CBS News/The New York Times poll, 12-16 September 1984, 3.

25. For example, see Gregory Markus, "Political Attitudes during an Election Year," *American Polticial Science Review* 76 (September 1982): 538-60.

26. The theoretical problems are discussed by Richard Brody and Benjamin Page, "Comment: The Assessment of Issue Voting," *American Political Science Review* 66 (June 1972): 450-58; and in Nie et al., chaps. 7-10.

27. Los Angeles Times exit poll, *National Journal* 16 (10 November 1984): 2131.

28. Adam Clymer, *New York Times,* 11 November 1984, 30. See Stanley Kelley, Jr., *Interpreting Elections* (Princeton: Princeton University Press, 1984), for an incisive discussion of the theory and methods employed in analyzing election mandates.

29. "Where's His Mandate?" *Washington Post,* 2 November 1984, A23.

30. This position is persuasively argued in the major work of Morris Fiorina, *Retrospective Voting in American National Elections* (New Haven: Yale University Press, 1981). Also see Anthony Downs, *An Economic Theory of Democracy* (New York: Harper, 1957).

31. CBS News/New York Times poll, 14 October 1984; Los Angeles Times poll, 16 October 1984.

32. William Schneider, "Performance Is the Big Campaign Issue, and That Gives Reagan a Big Edge," *National Journal* 16 (6 October 1984): 1894-95.

33. V.O. Key, "A Theory of Critical Elections," *Journal of Politics* 17 (February 1955): 3-18.

34. *New York Times,* 19 November 1984, B10.

35. *Washington Post,* 2 November 1984, A1; *National Journal* 16 (10 November 1984): 2132; Committee for Study of the American Electorate, *Non-Voter Study '84-'85,* 12 November 1984.

36. The metaphor is from Samuel Lubell, *The Future of American Politics* (Garden City, N.Y.: Doubleday, 1956).

37. Closing statement at the vice-presidential candidates' debate, reported in the *New York Times,* 12 October 1984, B6.

4

Public Opinion in 1984

Scott Keeter

Walter Mondale's problem was succinctly summarized in a cartoon that appeared during the campaign. It showed a sunbathing couple on a sandy beach, warmed by the rays of a bright sun with the face of President Ronald Reagan. Haranguing them was a donkey, clutching a heavy overcoat around him, saying, "I tell ya, there's a storm coming!" A storm may indeed be coming, but the electorate of 1984 did not want to hear about it.

The general mood of well-being seen during much of 1984 was an unaccustomed pleasure for the U.S. public. Ronald Reagan promoted the mood in his speeches and campaign advertising, and crowds of young supporters greeted and cheered him with the familiar "U.S.A." chant from the summer's Olympics.

One impressive indicator of the changed mood was a Gallup poll question that asked about satisfaction "with the way things are going in the United States at this time." For the first time in many years, more of the public in 1984 was satisfied than dissatisfied, a remarkable increase from July 1979 when just over 10 percent said they were satisfied (see figure 4.1 on page 92).

The upbeat mood would have helped any incumbent, but Reagan was at a special advantage because of his great personal popularity. The President's ability to project an image of warmth and sincerity while also exuding strength and fortitude as the nation's chief of state was a potent combination. Yet the Reagan of November 1984 was no different personally from the Reagan of late 1982 and early 1983. Then, a majority of the public disapproved of the job he was doing even while liking him as an individual.[1] The economy, of course, explains the difference, and its performance is the key to understanding the election of 1984.

In this chapter, we will argue that the public's view of the President's economic management overrode most other considerations, including the voters' own financial circumstances. While some noneconomic issues were important,

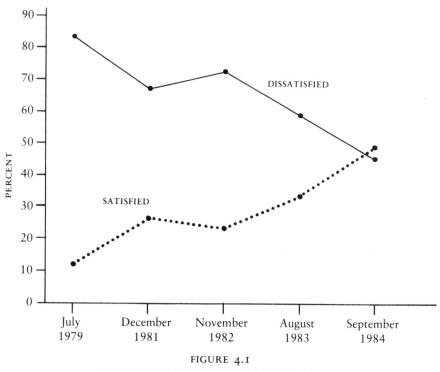

FIGURE 4.1

SATISFACTION WITHIN THE UNITED STATES

SOURCE: Gallup poll.

most of these simply reinforced voters' judgments about the economy. The elections also revealed a continuing divergence of the political preferences of men and women. The "gender gap," while not consequential in the presidential race, was important in many other races. Finally, the public continued to be largely pragmatic and nonideological in its expressions of electoral choice. Voters enthusiastically reelected a conservative President and at the same time supported many liberal politicians and propositions across the country.

Reagan's Popularity

Much was made of the public's affinity for Ronald Reagan, and of Reagan's skill in using television to communicate with voters. Even Mondale said he liked the President, and when asked on the day after the election, said that his own major liability was his failure to master the use of television. Democratic leaders characterized the outcome of the election as a personal rather than political victory for Reagan—a "mandate for the man."

Reagan *was* personally popular, though even this can be overstated. Sixty percent of voters said their general attitude toward him was favorable, the highest rating for any of the four candidates on the two national tickets.[2] However, 78 percent of Mondale's voters had an unfavorable opinion of Reagan, somewhat larger than the 72 percent of Reagan's voters with an unfavorable opinion of Mondale. Not everyone liked the President.

The personal quality most helpful to Reagan on election day was neither warmth nor affability but rather strength. His image as a strong leader was the one characteristic most frequently cited in two different election day polls. Four out of five voters who mentioned strong leadership as a reason for their choice were Reagan voters.[3]

Personal attacks on the President failed in 1984, just as they had in 1980. The Democrats tried unsuccessfully in 1980 to paint Reagan as radical and insensitive, a strategy that probably backfired when much of the public saw instead a reasonable man with a sense of humor in the televised debates that year. In 1984, the best opening for personal attack seemed to be Reagan's penchant for factual errors in public statements, and his relatively leisurely approach to the job of running the country. Yet the voters' frequent mention of Reagan's strong leadership shows that the charge of laziness did not stick. And on the issue of knowledgeability, Mondale did no better than the President among those voters who said that this mattered. When asked for the one item they most disliked about the candidate they voted against, 13 percent of voters checked "doesn't know the things a President should" (a phrase taken nearly verbatim from Mondale). Yet Reagan actually received a majority of these votes.[4]

The Economy

A majority of voters said the economy had improved since 1980, and a majority gave the President credit for it. Mr. Reagan could hardly have dreamed of better circumstances in which to seek reelection. Both of the most visible signs of the economy's health, inflation and unemployment, worked in the President's favor. Together, the rates of inflation and unemployment were called the "misery index" by Jimmy Carter in his 1976 campaign against Gerald Ford (the index was 12.5 percent in October 1976). Grown to monstrous proportions (20.2 percent) by October 1980, it returned to haunt Carter. By contrast, Ronald Reagan ran for reelection on an index of 11.5 percent. Inflation, which had been Carter's nemesis, was below 5 percent, down from over 12 percent at the time of Reagan's inauguration. It was truly a consumer's economy, as a plurality of voters said they were better off financially than they were four years before. The strength of the dollar abroad made imported goods and overseas vacations more affordable than ever. Record sales of (imported) video cassette recorders were emblematic of the consumerism wrought by recovery and the strong dollar.

While slaying the dragon of inflation was obviously important, the economic indicator most closely associated with Reagan's popularity was the one on which he had made the least overall progress since taking office. The unemployment rate in October 1984 was 7.3 percent, barely below the level inherited from Carter but greatly improved from the late 1982 figure of 10.7 percent, highest since the Great Depression. Figure 4.2 shows the dramatic parallel of unemployment (with the scale inverted) and the public's approval of Reagan's presidency. The match of the two lines is startling, and the political consequence is clear as well. The nadir of Reagan's popularity came near the time of the midterm congressional elections, with the President's party losing 26 seats in the House. The recovery of the economy brought him back almost to the level of popularity he enjoyed just after taking office in 1981.

Walter Mondale attempted to combat the President's advantage by raising the the salience of noneconomic matters such as nuclear weapons policy and the President's command of facts. Yet, aware of the historic centrality of

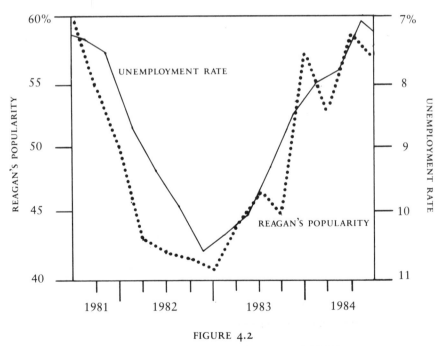

FIGURE 4.2

UNEMPLOYMENT AND APPROVAL OF REAGAN

SOURCE: *New York Times*, 26 October 1984. Data from Bureau of Labor Statistics does not include military.

the economy in U.S. presidential elections, Mondale had to confront that issue directly. He argued that the economy was not as healthy as it appeared (the overcoated donkey on a sunny beach), saying that the national government's budget deficit and the nation's trade deficit would prove catastrophic in the long run. At the same time, he appealed to the electorate's sense of fairness, charging that the President's policies rewarded the rich while demanding sacrifice from the poor.

Mondale made little headway convincing the public that the recovery was not what it appeared to be. In one election day poll, 57 percent of voters said the economy was better than four years ago.[5] In a different poll, a plurality of respondents said the nation's economy was beginning a long-term recovery, while another quarter acknowledged at least a temporary improvement.[6] Voters used criteria established by Democrats and Republicans alike and found the economy healthier than when the President took office. The central element of Mondale's warning on the economy, the long-term danger of the large deficit, was not particularly effective. If there was irony in a Republican President's use of deficit spending to stimulate the economy, Democratic protestations about it were doubly ironic.

Many voters *were* worried about the deficit and mentioned it on election day. Table 4.1 on page 96 shows voter responses to questions about issues in two different polls. In the ABC/Washington Post voter poll, 14 percent checked "the federal budget deficit," while 19 percent of those interviewed by the Los Angeles Times poll did so. In the CBS News/New York Times poll (not shown), one-fourth of voters said the deficit influenced their vote. Yet in all of these surveys, voters concerned about the deficit split nearly evenly between the two candidates.

Reagan was not hurt by the deficit because Mondale failed to pin the blame for it on him. Even though the deficit under Reagan was larger than that accumulated by any other President, half of the public blamed "the Democrats in Congress" rather than Reagan (30 percent blamed Reagan). When offered a choice of Reagan or "previous Presidents," an even larger portion of the public (60 percent) blamed Reagan's predecessors.[7] One can hardly find a better manifestation of the "Teflon presidency."

Beyond convincing the public of the seriousness of the deficit, Mondale had to propose a remedy. He presented a detailed list of spending cuts and promised a tax increase. Despite the President's denial that he too would seek a tax increase, the public in August believed overwhelmingly (75 percent) that the next President, whoever he was, would do so.[8]

Reagan campaigned enthusiastically on the issue of higher taxes, frequently saying of Mondale, "He never met a tax he didn't *hike*," and joking of dressing

TABLE 4.1

IMPORTANT ISSUES IN THE PRESIDENTIAL ELECTION

	Percent of voters	Percent for Reagan	Percent for Mondale
ABC/Washington Post poll			
The one issue where you most liked the stand of the presidential candidate you voted for:			
Military spending	14	75	25
Social Security	12	43	57
Unemployment	12	58	42
Federal budget deficit	14	47	52
Government spending	17	82	17
Problems of the poor	12	11	89
Tax increases	9	87	13
Foreign affairs	10	68	32
The one issue where you most disliked the stand of the candidate you did not vote for:			
Military spending	20	40	60
Social Security	6	33	67
Unemployment	5	30	69
Federal budget deficit	10	43	57
Government spending	13	84	15
Problems of the poor	10	24	75
Tax increases	26	92	8
Foreign affairs	10	59	41
Los Angeles Times poll			
Which issues—if any—were most important to you in deciding whom to vote for (check up to two):			
Government spending	22	69	31
Federal budget deficit	19	48	52
Foreign relations	19	67	33
Nuclear arms control	18	33	67
Inflation	17	83	17
Taxes	17	80	20
Unemployment	14	42	58
Civil rights	12	26	74
No issues really	11	75	25
Environmental protection	4	26	74
Farm problems	4	54	46

up for Halloween as Mondale's tax increase and scaring the neighbors. By election day, just over half the voters thought a tax increase would be necessary. But even among these voters, Reagan received 43 percent.[9] The degree of distaste for a tax increase was seen in the ABC/Washington Post question that asked voters for "the one issue where you most disliked the stand of the candidate you did not vote for" (see table 4.1). The most frequently checked item was "tax increases," selected by 26 percent; it is surely no surprise that over 90 percent of these voters went for the President.

Mondale was more successful with the issue of fairness, and it was clearly an important reason many voters chose him. When asked for "the one characteristic that best describes why you voted for your presidential candidate," 21 percent selected "He's fair to all income groups," and 90 percent of voters who said this voted for Mondale. Still, it was not enough. Since fairness was such a central theme of the Democrats, does their rejection suggest that the electorate was greedy? Voters did indeed know the effect of the administration's policies on the distribution of wealth. One particularly instructive survey item was a question asked several times since 1981 by the ABC/Washington Post poll. It read, "Would you say Reagan cares more about serving poor and lower-income people, middle-income people, upper-income people . . . or would you say he cares equally about serving all people?" In July 1984, only 6 percent said "middle-income people," while 56 percent said "upper-income people." One-third said he cared equally about serving all people. This perception was not simply a carryover of Reagan's image as a wealthy actor or corporate spokesman; when the question was first asked in February 1981, just after Reagan assumed the presidency, two-thirds said he cared about everyone equally.

If voters thought the rich were helped disproportionately by the administration's policies, one can hardly argue that votes for Reagan were based on greed. Most voters weren't rich. Far more anomalous was the extent of support for Reagan among voters whose incomes were *below* average. Amazingly, Ronald Reagan would have won the election even if the electorate had been restricted to voters with incomes below the median. Voters with incomes from $10,000 to $20,000 were one-fourth of the electorate and gave the President 56 percent of their votes (median family income in 1983 was around $24,000).[10] The poorest voters gave Mondale a small majority (55 percent of those making under $10,000), but they constituted only 16 percent of the electorate. Social class *was* related to the vote (as income rose, so did support for Reagan), but class issues were not sufficiently salient to deny the President a broad-based victory.[11]

The support given to politicians thought to favor the wealthy by U.S. voters of below-average means is an enduring source of puzzlement to foreign observers. The 1984 election was a remarkable demonstration once again of the power of "the American dream." Political scientist Robert Lane showed many years ago in his study of a small group of economically marginal men that the dream of becoming wealthy (or of one's children doing so) is a feature of the United States that, for many, makes one's unpleasant circumstances more tolerable.[12] "Don't soak the rich, I might be rich one day, too."

As usual, the public evidenced a great deal of ambivalence about how to treat those at the bottom. Most voters seemed to think that cuts in social programs had gone far enough. Nearly 80 percent said they favored no reduction in spending on the poor, and 40 percent favored increases.[13] However, other surveys during the fall revealed a great deal of resentment against welfare programs. One poll found that a plurality of respondents was concerned more about welfare recipients that didn't deserve assistance than about poor people who needed help but weren't getting it.[14] Similarly, CBS News/New York Times surveys over the past several years have found pluralities believing that most people on welfare could "get along without it if they tried."

The seeming contradiction in these findings reflects the tension between basic values held by the public. One set of values promotes compassion and a recognition that in the "game of life" some entrants have head starts and others have handicaps. Since the days of Franklin Roosevelt, the Democratic party has appealed to these values. A different set of values holds that the U.S. system is a meritocracy, in which favoritism by government dampens individual initiative and penalizes those who strive to succeed on their own. Reinforcing this notion is the Puritan adage that "the worst thing you can do for a man is to do him good," that handouts hurt the recipient by destroying character.[15] The President, with his sincere and warm persona, has been an especially effective spokesman for the latter set of values.

One final way to think about the role of economic self-interest in the election is in terms of Reagan's famous question to the public in the 1980 debate with Jimmy Carter: "Are you better off now than you were four years ago?" Exit polls in 1980 showed that this "retrospective finances" question was a fairly good predictor of the vote, as only one-fourth of those who felt worse off voted for the incumbent, Jimmy Carter. As the incumbent in 1984, Reagan won only 14 percent of voters who felt worse off, but this group was much smaller in 1984 than in 1980.[16]

Still, self-interest was not the whole story. While voters were concerned about their own pocketbooks, their assessment of how well the President had managed the economy was a more important determinant of their vote.[17] Table 4.2 shows Reagan's share of the vote divided according to both the voter's financial situation and the voter's judgment of whether the President was responsible

TABLE 4.2

ECONOMIC ASSESSMENTS AND SUPPORT FOR REAGAN

(in percent)

Family finances compared with four years ago:

Is Reagan responsible for improved economy?	Better off	About the same	Worse off
Yes	97	89	67
No	23	15	5
Not sure	70	44	24

NOTE: Entries are percentage voting for Reagan-Bush.

QUESTIONS: "In recent months, the nation's economy has improved. Do you think this is because of President Reagan's economic policies?" "Compared to four years ago, would you say your family is financially better off, worse off, about the same?"

SOURCE: NBC News election day voter poll, 1984.

for the improvement of the economy. Voters' opinions about Reagan's management of the economy were far more important than their personal financial condition. For example, those who were better off but said Reagan was not responsible for the improved economy gave him only 23 percent of their votes. Similarly, those whose finances were unchanged but who thought the President *had* helped the economy voted 9 to 1 for him.[18] Of course, the key to Reagan's success was the fact that these two survey items were strongly related to one another. Those who were better off were very likely to give the President credit, and those who were worse off usually blamed him.

In short, Reagan succeeded in accomplishing what most government heads try to do, and that is to have the cyclical upswing of the economy coincide with the latter part of an election year. The high level of public support for the President in 1984 provides an illuminating contrast with the relative unpopularity of Gerald Ford in 1976. The unemployment and inflation figures were similar, but the public reaction to each President was markedly different. Over the period, the public has come to tolerate levels of unemployment that are historically very high.[19]

Foreign and Military Affairs

Reagan was more vulnerable on foreign than domestic issues, but even in this arena he had a net advantage on election day. On two different questions, 10 percent of voters polled by ABC/Washington Post selected "foreign affairs" as a critical issue (see table 4.1); in each instance Reagan received a healthy majority of the votes. Similar results were seen in other exit polls. The 12 percent who selected "foreign relations" as the most important issue in the Los Angeles Times survey gave Reagan two-thirds of their votes. Eleven percent of voters checked "nuclear arms control," and two-thirds of these backed Mondale.

After four years of relative peace, most of the public no longer feared that a reckless Reagan would provoke a war. Over 60 percent of those interviewed by CBS News/New York Times in October said they weren't worried that, if reelected, the President might get us into war. While much of the public quarreled with specific elements of Reagan's foreign and military policy, it clearly liked the image of certitude and strength. Even if the United States couldn't control the world as it once did, many people liked a President who acted as if it could.

The issue of military spending divided voters, with 14 percent identifying it as an important issue on which they liked their candidate's stand. Three-fourths of these voted for Reagan (table 4.1). Twenty percent selected military spending when asked for the one issue on which they most *disliked* the stand of the candidate they did not vote for. Mondale won 60 percent of these.

Reagan's initiative in 1981 to build up the military had strong public backing, which had crystallized as a consequence of the hostage affair in Iran. By 1984, however, no consensus on continued military expansion was apparent. One July poll asked several questions on government spending priorities and found 48 percent of the public believing that Reagan's plans to increase military spending had gone too far; the remainder divided between saying the plans were "just right" or had not gone far enough. Similarly, another question found half the public agreeing that the United States could meet its national security obligations with a much smaller military budget.[20]

Despite public division over the necessity for continued increases in defense spending, the Democratic party acquired a clear—and negative—image on this issue. A CBS News/New York Times poll in late October found that even a plurality of *Democrats* (42 percent) thought the Republican party more likely to keep U.S. defenses strong. Two-thirds of all respondents said the Republicans would do a better job.

The public's greatest disagreement with the President concerned nuclear weapons policy. Over 60 percent of those interviewed in an October survey felt that the United States should do more to reach a weapons accord with the Soviet Union; even a plurality of Reagan supporters felt that not enough had been done.[21] Eleven percent of voters in the Los Angeles Times voter poll and 14 percent of those interviewed by ABC/Washington Post cited nuclear weapons as an important issue; two-thirds of these voters chose Mondale (table 4.1). Still, when given a choice on election day, 48 percent of voters felt we should build up our defenses before seeking to freeze nuclear weapons; 46 percent disagreed.[22]

Thus while Walter Mondale pointed to the administration's lack of progress on arms control, and its seemingly aimless policies in the Middle East and Central America, most voters were not greatly concerned with these issues, nor was there a consensus that the President could have done any better. Mondale differentiated himself from Reagan on nuclear weapons policy, but on many issues he tried to convince the public that he was just as tough as Reagan, an implicit "me too" stance. The public might have been willing to respond to a foreign policy based upon premises different from those of Reagan's first term, but it was not offered such a choice. No longer fearful that the President's policies might lead to war, the public had no compelling reason to abandon him.

The Role of Gender

THE GENDER GAP IN 1984 AND BEFORE

As in 1980, women gave the Democrats greater suport than men did. This was true not only in the presidential election but in nearly all the Senate races for which voter polls are available. A majority of women voted for Reagan, but in several other key races majorities of men and women supported different candidates. Table 4.3 on page 102 shows the size of the gap between men and women for several contests.

The "gender gap" in the 1984 presidential race ranged from four to nine percentage points, depending upon the poll. These findings are similar to those of 1980 when the range was six to nine points. During Reagan's first term in office, Gallup polls found gender differences in approval of the President's performance that ranged as high as 16 points, with women always less approving than men. But the data in table 4.3 show that gender differences are not simply a function of differential reaction to Ronald Reagan. Women provided the margin of victory for Democrats in several elections, including the Senate races in Illinois, Michigan, Massachusetts, and Iowa, and the gubernatorial race in Vermont. Had only women voted in North Carolina's rancorous and costly Senate race, Jesse Helms would have been defeated. Gender differences were evident at other levels, too. The national exit polls asked voters who they preferred in their local House of Representatives races; overall, a majority of women voted for Democratic candidates, while a majority of men voted for Republican candidates.

Consistent sex differences in response to candidates of the two parties is a new phenomenon in U.S. politics. Gender gaps have been seen before, but

TABLE 4.3

THE GENDER GAP IN THE 1984 ELECTIONS

(in percent)

		Reagan-Bush	Mondale-Ferraro
ABC/Washington Post	Men	62	38
	Women	54	46
CBS News/New York Times	Men	61	39
	Women	57	43
Los Angeles Times	Men	63	37
	Women	56	44
NBC News	Men	64	36
	Women	55	45

		Reagan	Carter	Anderson
1980 CBS News/New York Times	Men	54	37	7
	Women	46	45	7

		Ford		Carter
1976 CBS News/New York Times	Men	48		50
	Women	48		50

Other 1984 races	Democratic advantage among women (in percent)
Massachusetts Senate (NBC)	+14
North Carolina Senate (NBC)	+11
Vermont Governor (CBS News/New York Times)	+9
Minnesota Senate (NBC)	+9
New Hampshire Senate (CBS News/New York Times)	+6
Texas Senate (NBC)	+6
Oregon Senate (CBS News/New York Times)	+6
Virginia Senate (NBC)	+6
Illinois Senate (NBC)	+5
Michigan Senate	+5
Iowa Senate (ABC/Washington Post)	+4
New Jersey Senate (CBS News/New York Times)	+4
New Hampshire Governor (CBS News/New York Times)	+4

NOTE: Entries under "other 1984 races" were computed as percent support for Democratic candidate among women minus percent support for Democratic candidate among men.

never as large and as persistent as those observed in the past four years.[23] During the 1950s, women were slightly more likely than men to support Eisenhower and to identify with the Republican party. Even in 1960, John F. Kennedy did slightly better among men than among women. Men were much more likely than women to favor George Wallace in 1968. Beginning in 1972, a somewhat higher percentage of women than men have identified with the Democratic party, though polls disagreed on whether there were gender differences in the presidential vote that year. In 1976, some polls showed that Ford did a little better among women than Carter did.

Historically, polls have shown that women differ from men on issues of war and peace and social welfare, taking less militaristic or more liberal positions. This might account in part for the greater attraction of the Democratic party to women. But the past two decades have also seen an increase in the economic and psychological independence of women from men, and along with it the development of political interests different from, and at times in conflict with, those of men.[24]

Do such changes portend the rise of a political cleavage between the sexes? Much depends upon the direction taken by the Republican party in the coming years. In 1980, the party turned away from its long-standing commitment to the passage of the Equal Rights Amendment, and in 1984 "pro-life" elements obtained a platform plank that advocated a total prohibition of abortion. The party is also less willing now than in the past to seek legislative or judicial remedies for discrimination against women in hiring or pay. These issues become more important as women increasingly become independent economically, especially as heads of households.

The Mondale-Ferraro campaign was reluctant to address the particular interests of women in the 1984 campaign. While it is difficult to predict how successful such appeals might be in the future, common interests do not always develop spontaneously into group consciousness. Sometimes shared interests must be pointed out and appealed to. Consequently, the gender gaps observed so far are measures of "unmobilized sex differences," and might become much larger if candidates choose to appeal more directly to women voters.

Since 1980, Democratic party identification among men has declined from 42 percent to 33 percent, while among women the change has been only 1 point, from 47 percent to 46 percent.[25] Who, then, is responsible for the gap, men or women? Some Republicans argue that men are responsible, since they have responded to both the Reagan image of strength and the President's economic policies. Yet in resisting strong short-term political forces such as the economic recovery and the general mood of nationalism, the volition of women is also consequential.

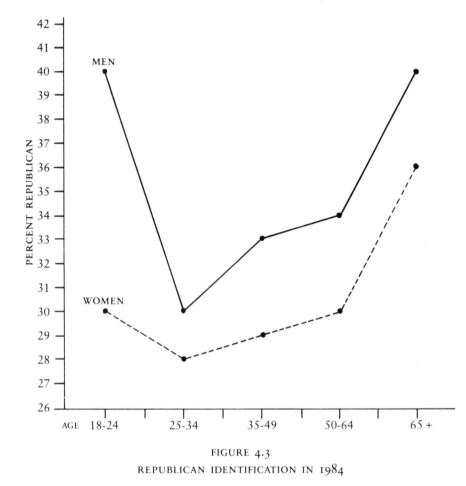

FIGURE 4.3

REPUBLICAN IDENTIFICATION IN 1984

Source: NBC News election day voter poll.

Gender differences in party identification among young voters in 1984 can be read as a harbinger of important political change. Figure 4.3 shows Republican identification for men and women across different age groups. The very large gap between men and women in the youngest age group may be a measure of the Zeitgeist—the "spirit of the times"—for the politics of gender. Women aged 18 to 24 are much like women aged 25 through 64. Young men, however, are much more Republican than the women and (with the exception of those over 64) their older male cohorts. If the forces that produced this pattern among the young persist, then we may well see an electorate increasingly polarized by gender in the coming years.

GERALDINE FERRARO'S IMPACT

On balance, Geraldine Ferraro's candidacy for the vice-presidency made little difference in how the public reacted to the two tickets. Her selection by Mondale provoked a great variety of predictions about her effect on the election. Some people hoped she would serve to mobilize many women who usually didn't vote, or would encourage Republican women to defect to the Democrats. While such hopes were not fulfilled, others who worried about public prejudice against female candidates found good news in the evidence that Ferraro's sex was of little consequence.

In fact, some voters said that the presence of Ferraro *did* matter to them. But among those who cared, the Democrats did about as well as the Republicans. For example, CBS News/New York Times asked voters which factors on a list mattered most to them; 10 percent checked "vice-presidential candidates" and over half of these voted for the Democrats. The ABC/Washington Post poll included a similar question with identical results. On that poll, 8 percent also checked "the Bush-Ferraro debate," and again the Democrats polled a slight majority of those voters.

The NBC election day poll asked voters whether or not Ferraro's presence on the ticket made them more or less likely to vote for it. Most voters said it made no difference, but for the rest, Ferraro hurt a little more than she helped. Of course, Ferraro's gender probably had little to do with some voters' negative reaction to her. Controversy over her financial disclosures, as well as her relative inexperience in foreign affairs, were cited by respondents in some fall polls. Still, one is hard pressed to argue that Ferraro was a drag on the ticket, since her overall image on election day was actually a little more favorable than that of Walter Mondale.[26]

Are voters prejudiced against women candidates? Polls that pose the question directly suggest that many voters — both male and female — are indeed biased against the idea of a female candidate. After Ferraro's selection for the Democratic ticket, the Los Angeles Times poll asked: "All other things being equal, would you be more likely to vote for a congressional candidate if he was a man or if she was a woman, or wouldn't that have any effect on your vote?" While three-fourths said it wouldn't matter, 19 percent preferred the male candidate and only 4 percent preferred the female. Almost half of the respondents agreed that "men are better at making decisions about war and peace than women are."[27]

Further evidence from the Los Angeles Times poll was provided by an experiment in which hypothetical candidates for governor were offered to the respondents. Candidate A was about 55 years old, raised in New York City, married with two children, and with a business background. Candidate B was

TABLE 4.4

THE EFFECT OF GENDER ON A HYPOTHETICAL ELECTION

	Voter group No. 1*	Voter group No. 2*
Candidate A: About 55 years old, born and reared in New York City, married with two children, and has a business background.	"Mr." A 48%	"Mrs." A 27%
Candidate B: About 50 years old, born and reared in the Middle West, married with three children, and is an attorney.	"Mrs." B 38%	"Mr." B 54%
	100%	100%

*Questions asked of two groups of registered voters. "Don't know" responses excluded.

SOURCE: Los Angeles Time poll, reported 2 September 1984.

about 50, raised in the Middle West, married with three children, and a career as an attorney. Two groups of respondents were asked to choose between candidates "A" and "B." For one group, "A" was a man and "B" was a woman; for the other group the sexes were reversed. The male candidate won each election by a comfortable margin (see table 4.4).

Yet the evidence from the presidential election in 1984, and from considerable research on congressional elections, indicates that in practice, the candidate's sex doesn't much matter.[28] Voters faced with hypothetical choices between male and female candidates may exhibit biases, but when confronted with real candidates, voters find other, more relevant bases of judgment.

The Winds of Change

YOUNG VOTERS

Is a new "generation gap" brewing? Many people thought so in the fall before the election. Republicans pointed with excitement to polls that showed the President strongest among young people. On election day however, age was unrelated to the vote. Reagan did equally well among all age groups.

Still, the pattern of the vote was encouraging to Republicans who look to the future. In 1980, Reagan was supported by only 43 percent of voters aged 18-29 while he won 54 percent of voters 30 and older. Thus, when comparing 1984 with 1980, Reagan's largest gains were among young people. Perhaps more consequential than the vote were figures for party affiliation which showed that the largest increase in Republican identification since 1980 occurred among voters aged 18-24.[29] As figure 4.3 suggests, much of this increase occurred among men.

What accounts for the attraction of young people to the Republicans? Ideology is not the answer, since voters aged 18-24 were more liberal than any other age group.[30] The simplest answer is that young people are good barometers of the current political climate because they are unencumbered by both the "political memory" and political experience that comes with age. Memory and experience help citizens to sort information and make sense of the present. For young people, the Democratic party is known mostly from the presidency of Jimmy Carter and the Republican party from the presidency of Ronald Reagan, a comparison the Republicans constantly made and the Democrats carefully avoided. The youngest cohort of voters today has no direct memory of Watergate; 10 years have passed since President Ford pardoned Richard Nixon. The Republicans did a better job of claiming the future as well; their optimism was appealing to young people facing an uncertain and often hostile job market.

IDEOLOGY

What do the elections of 1984 tell us about the ideological climate in the United States? Was the resounding reelection of a conservative politician evidence that the public is indeed moving to the right? Was the defeat of Mondale a defeat of the liberal approach to government?

During the campaign, the President spoke of ideology, charging that the Democratic ticket was "so far left they've left America." While the ticket was less balanced ideologically than usual, even Walter Mondale was not seen by the public as very far from the middle. A CBS News/New York Times poll following the Democratic convention found that only a third of the public identified him as a liberal.

TABLE 4.5

IDEOLOGY AND THE ELECTORATE

QUESTION: On most political matters, do you
consider yourself liberal, moderate, or conservative?

	November 1976	November 1980	November 1984
Liberal	20%	18%	17%
Moderate	48	51	44
Conservative	32	31	35

SOURCE: CBS News/New York Times election day polls.

Comparing voters' self-described ideology with earlier years, one finds only a glacial shift to the right. Table 4.5 on page 107 presents ideological self-identification since 1976. The portion of the public calling itself conservative has increased only 3 percentage points since 1976, while the proportion of liberals declined by the same amount. Other polls found more liberals and fewer conservatives than did CBS News/New York Times, but showed similarly little change over time.

Other ways of judging the ideological mood of the nation also yield mixed results. Viewed as a whole, the presidential and congressional elections appear to be a resounding vote of approval for incumbents of all stripes. Indeed, many Republican challengers grumbled that the President's "Dr. Feelgood" advertising campaign worked to their detriment with its implicit theme of "don't make any changes."

The anomalous character of many state-level verdicts suggests that ideology provides no consistent explanation for the behavior of the electorate. Consider three states—Tennessee, Iowa, and Illinois—that delivered healthy majorities to Reagan while electing new senators with clearly liberal credentials. Similarly, Delaware and New Jersey reelected liberal incumbents with huge majorities despite giving Reagan margins of 6 to 4 (see table 5.3 on page 117).

Voters directly expressed their sentiments on issues in a great variety of ballot propositions decided on election day, and here too no conservative trend was evident.[31] On issues of taxing and spending, state electorates were clearly *not* marching to a conservative drum. Voters in California, Michigan, Nevada, and Oregon rejected propositions that would have severely limited their states' ability to raise taxes (a similar measure passed only in South Carolina). In California, a measure that would have sharply reduced welfare payments was decisively rejected.

Conservatives did better on some social issues. In various states, voters approved prayer in public schools, a mandatory death penalty for certain crimes, and the right to "keep and bear arms." In South Dakota, a nuclear freeze measure was defeated, but one requiring voter approval for nuclear waste storage dumps succeeded. California voters endorsed by 7 to 3 the printing of federal election ballots only in English, and in Maine a state Equal Rights Amendment was rejected by a 6 to 4 margin. At the same time, voters in Washington rejected a measure that would have banned nearly all state-funded abortions, and Oregon voters defeated a "victim's bill of rights" that among other things would have eased restrictions on police in obtaining and using evidence in criminal cases.

Taken as a whole, the election results revealed no "prairie fire" burning in the heartland. Most voters cast a skeptical eye upon any candidate or proposition that would change things very much. Candidates endorsing the welfare state and referenda protecting it were supported enthusiastically even as Ronald Reagan was returned to the White House by the same voters.

Conclusion

The presidential election of 1984 provided a fair amount of support for the adage that the New Deal sowed the seeds of its own destruction. The success of so much collective enterprise, from agricultural research to federal support for medical education, ironically created a relatively affluent and empathetic following for Ronald Reagan, himself a liberal-turned-conservative. For their part, the Democrats faced a dilemma in how to appeal to this skeptical electorate. They felt that they had to remind the public of the continuing problems in society, problems that only government could address. Yet at the same time, this approach seemed to confirm Ronald Reagan's long-standing theme that the "policies of the past" had failed and ought to be discarded.

The election tells us less about Reagan's impact upon the political thinking of the U.S. public. The President has thus far succeeded in changing the images of the two parties. The Republicans are no longer seen primarily as the party of businessmen, and the Democrats (to their distress) are no longer the party of prosperity. But has he changed Americans' views of what approach is best? William Schneider has argued that ideological realignment proceeds in two stages: First, the President must demonstrate that his policies work; then the public may "convert to his vision of society."[32] But the conservative world view of Reagan—the individualist impulse—is already held by most Americans, coexisting with its opposite, the collectivist or communitarian impulse. Reagan has masterfully brought the former view to the fore, but he did not create it.

The individualist ideology is strongest when people believe that personal success—especially great success—is possible, and that failure will not lead to catastrophe. The welfare state has provided at least the illusion that even with the worst of luck, one can avoid starvation. At the other end, dreams play a role. Even though we must live in an era of limits, we prefer to believe in boundless upward mobility. Rather than lead to frustration and disillusionment, these beliefs have a pacifying effect for most people. In the campaign of 1984, Ronald Reagan was the lone merchant of such dreams.

NOTES

1. Gallup poll.
2. Los Angeles Times poll, 6 November 1984.
3. ABC/Washington Post election day poll; Los Angeles Times poll.
4. ABC/Washington Post election day poll.
5. CBS News/New York Times election day poll.
6. Los Angeles Times poll, 6 November 1984.
7. CBS News/New York Times August national survey.
8. ABC/Washington Post September national survey.
9. ABC/Washington Post election day poll.
10. Reported by William Schneider, "An Uncertain Consensus," *National Journal* 16 (10 November 1984): 2132.
11. A year before the election, many observers believed that the electorate in 1984 would be highly polarized along class lines. See, for example, David Broder, "America Appears Deeply Divided, Anxious to Vote," *Washington Post,* 1 January 1984.
12. Robert E. Lane, *Political Ideology: Why the American Common Man Believes What He Does* (New York: Free Press, 1962). See also Kay Lehman Schlozman and Sidney Verba, *Insult to Injury: Unemployment, Class, and Political Response* (Cambridge: Harvard University Press, 1979); and Jennifer L. Hochschild, *What's Fair: American Beliefs about Distributive Justice* (Cambridge: Harvard University Press, 1981).
13. CBS News/New York Times election day poll.
14. ABC/Washington Post national survey.
15. A good discussion of this is found in Garry Wills, *Nixon Agonistes: The Crisis of the Self-Made Man* (Boston: Houghton Mifflin, 1970). See also Karlyn H. Keene, "Who's the Fairest of Them All?" *Public Opinion* 7 (April /May 1984): 47-51.
16. Since poorer individuals are more likely to be worse off regardless of the movement of the economy, and are more likely to vote Democratic, a comparison of 1980 and 1984 is somewhat misleading, since the party of the incumbent was different in the two elections.
17. This supports the "sociotropic" explanation advanced by a number of scholars. See Donald R. Kinder and D. Roderick Kiewiet, "Economic Discontent and Political Behavior: The Role of Personal Grievances and Collective Economic Judgments in Congressional Voting," *American Journal of Political Science* 23 (August 1979): 495-517; D. Roderick Kiewiet, *Macroeconomics and Micropolitics: The Electoral Effects of Economic Issues* (Chicago: University of Chicago Press, 1983).
18. Analyses of other exit polls supported this conclusion. See William Schneider, "An Uncertain Consensus," 2130; David Treadwell, "Confidence in Economy Aided Reagan," *Los Angeles Times,* 7 November 1984.

    This table shows the proportion of respondents falling into each category of table 4.2. Entries in the table sum to 100 percent:

Is Reagan responsible for improved economy?		Better off (45)	About the same (38)	Worse off (17)	=	100
Yes	(53)	36	15	2		
No	(34)	5	16	13		
Not sure	(13)	4	7	2		
	100					

19. Edward R. Tufte, *Political Control of the Economy* (Princeton: Princeton University Press, 1978); Douglas A. Hibbs, "Political Parties and Macroeconomic Policy," *American Political Science Review* 71 (December 1977): 1467-87; Douglas A. Hibbs, "The Mass Public and Macroeconomic Performance: The Dynamics of Public Opinion Toward Unemployment and Inflation," *American Journal of Political Science* 23 (November 1979): 705-31.

20. ABC/Washington Post poll, July 1984.

21. CBS News/New York Times poll, 23-25 October 1984.

22. CBS News/New York Times election day poll.

23. See Sandra Baxter and Marjorie Lansing, *Women and Politics: The Visible Majority,* rev. ed. (Ann Arbor: University of Michigan Press, 1983), chap. 4; "The Gender Gap" fact sheet, Center for the American Woman and Politics, Eagleton Institute of Politics, Rutgers University.

24. See Susan Carroll, "Women's Autonomy and the Gender Gap," paper presented at the annual meeting of the American Psychological Association, Toronto, August 1984. For other explanations of the "gender gap," see John C. Blydenburgh and Roberta S. Sigel, "Key Factors in the 1982 Elections as Seen by Men and Women Voters: An Exploration into the Vulnerability Thesis," paper presented at the 1983 annual meeting of the American Political Science Association, Chicago, Illinois; Kathleen A. Frankovic, "Sex and Politics—New Alignments, Old Issues," *P.S.* 15 (Summer 1982): 439-48.

25. Adam Clymer, "Diverging Politics of Sexes Seen in Poll," *New York Times,* 30 September 1984, 28. Data were based on polls taken in September 1980 and 1984.

26. Los Angeles Times poll, 6 November 1984.

27. All data reported here were taken from Cathleen Decker, "Ferraro Fails to Boost Mondale's Propects," *Los Angeles Times,* 2 September 1984.

28. See, for example, R. Darcy and Sarah Slavin Schramm, "When Women Run Against Men," *Public Opinion Quarterly* 41 (Spring 1977): 1-12.

29. NBC News election day voter poll.

30. Los Angeles Times poll, 6 November 1984.

31. Much of the information in this discussion was drawn from Lynda V. Mapes, "Tax Revolt Stalls in Statewide Ballot Tests," *National Journal* 16 (11 November 1984): 2121, 2170.

32. William Schneider, "Half a Realignment," *New Republic* 191 (3 December 1984): 19-22.

5

The Congressional Elections

Overall, the 1984 congressional elections constitute a reinstatement of the status quo. Side by side with the triumphant reelection of Ronald Reagan to a second term in the presidency, Congress remains divided, with the numerical balance of power in each of the houses unchanged in any important way. This is in sharp contrast to the outcome four years earlier when Reagan was accompanied to power with the first Republican majority in the Senate since 1953 and a conservative majority in the House of Representatives. In 1984 Republicans lost two seats in the Senate and made a net gain of 14 seats in the House. When the 99th Congress assembled in January 1985, the partisan bicameral division that had begun in 1981 continued. The numbers were as follows:

> House: 253 Democrats, 182 Republicans
> Senate: 47 Democrats, 53 Republicans

American voters in 1984 did not extend their enthusiasm for President Reagan in his landslide victory to his partisan allies in the coordinate branch of American government. Indeed, recent history lends a broader perspective to this paradox. Republican Presidents have usually been bedeviled by mixed verdicts. In 1972, Richard Nixon was elected to a second term with an 18 million vote plurality, and on the same day his Republican legislative cohorts gained but 12 seats in the House and lost two Senate seats, an outcome nearly identical to that of 1984. Similarly, in 1956, Republican President Dwight Eisenhower was reinstated in a massive landslide of votes, but Republicans actually *lost* two House seats, and there was no net change in the Senate.

Elections and the New Congress

It is a truism that American political parties are coalitions of ideologically diverse groupings in the polity. Yet these coalitions have left-liberal (Democratic) and right-conservative centers of gravity, and the more numerical the weight of one over the other accentuates that center. Moreover, to a President, the force of the symbolic party tie of his political brethren is a natural and promising target of persuasion. Thus Presidents crave Congresses controlled by their partisan associates. During the past half century, the usual lack of legislative party control has frustrated Republican Presidents. Indeed, President Eisenhower was the last Republican to enjoy partisan congressional kinship in *both* houses for even a brief time (1953-55). To survey how Congresses have varied more recently, consider table 5.1

TABLE 5.1

CONGRESSIONAL PARTY CONTROL, 1965-87

Party Alignment

Congress	Years	House (D)	House (R)	Senate (D)	Senate (R)	President
99th	1985-87	253	182	47	53	Reagan (R)
98th	1983-85	267	168	45	55	Reagan (R)
97th	1981-83	243	192	47	53	Reagan (R)
96th	1979-81	276	159	59	41	Carter (D)
95th	1977-79	292	143	62	38	Carter (D)
94th	1975-77	291	144	61	39	Ford (R)
93rd	1973-75	243	192	57	43	Ford, Nixon (R)
92nd	1971-73	255	177	55	45	Nixon (R)
91st	1969-71	243	192	58	42	Nixon (R)
90th	1967-69	248	187	64	36	Johnson (D)
89th	1965-67	295	140	67	33	Johnson (D)

SOURCES: *Congressional Quarterly Weekly Report* 42 (10 November 1984): 2891; and *Congressional Quarterly Weekly Report* 40 (23 October 1982): 2742.

A number of observations can be made. First, the largest Democratic majorities in recent years coincided with the Johnson landslide election of 1964. The first Nixon election of 1968 brought with it slight increases in the Republican congressional contingent, but still a minority. The President's disappointment of 1972 has already been noted. The close Carter victory in 1976 coincided with only the slightest increase in congressional majorities. And the 1980 Reagan triumph was accompanied by a crucial strengthening in *both* houses of Republicans *and* conservative allies. On the other hand, attention to midterm election results (even-numbered Congresses) validates the conventional wisdom that the President's party can expect to lose seats at midterm. Nonetheless, an interesting variation in the size of these losses will be discussed when we later consider the future of the Republicans in Congress.

THE HOUSE

The 1984 legislative elections show stability rather than change. The first explanation of these results must be a tribute to the vitality of the familiar phenomenon of incumbent advantage. There are many factors that give powerful advantages to the sitting congressman over the "strangers" who emerge as competitors. Chief influences are the incumbent's visibility and familiarity in constituents' eyes along with his record of services to the district and its residents.[1] In 1984 this inertial force was exaggerated by a remarkably small number of open seats, where the absence of an incumbent permitted competition among newcomers.

All of Congress's 435 seats were up for election. But of that number, only 27 incumbents failed to run for reelection (nearly all of them retiring or running for other offices). Thus 408 incumbents contested, and of these 392 (94 percent) were reelected. The paltry contingent of 16 defeated incumbents included 13 Democrats and 3 Republicans. In consequence, the freshman class of 1984 (31 Republicans and 12 Democrats) was the smallest in decades. The qualitative consequences of the electoral switches are meager. A few of the defeated Democrats, particularly Clarence D. Long of Maryland and Joseph G. Minish of New Jersey, had accumulated considerable seniority in the House and headed subcommittees, but the overall losses included not a single full committee chairman or party leader.[2] This result, again, is in contrast to the 1980 outcome when eight major Democratic legislative leaders were dispatched.

In searching for a larger message in the congressional electorate's decisions, any notion of trend must be approached cautiously. To be sure, one notes that among the partisan switches, eight new seats went Republican in the South, and five in the East, both regions of historic Democratic strength. Also, three of the Republican gains in the East were in blue-collar districts of Democratic lineage.[3] Yet, there are many idiosyncratic (contest-specific) explanations for these turnovers. For example, undoubtedly the politically damaging reapportionment of Minish's New Jersey district left him vulnerable. Similarly, Congressmen Daniel Crane of Illinois and George Hansen of Idaho remained underdogs because of their taints of personal scandal. In the end, the small number of deviations from past party and population patterns makes the limited cases seem insignificant.

THE SENATE

Curiously, in 1984 the electoral outcome in the Senate mirrored that of the

House in two striking ways. An unusually large number of senatorial incumbents chose to run again for office, and 90 percent of them were victorious. The results are surprising, for modern experience with senatorial elections has accustomed us to expect much less of an incumbent advantage. (For example, in 1980, one-third of Senate incumbents who ran were defeated.) The reasons for greater senatorial vulnerability are the longer senatorial term, and subsequent visibility, as well as public awareness of the senator's position on issues of national controversy. In consequence, unlike their House counterparts, senatorial incumbents are frequently faced by challengers with some statewide visibility and repute.[4] Uncharacteristically, the freshman class of 1984 is the smallest in a presidential election year in the twentieth century.

Of 33 senators up for reelection, only four chose to retire, thus creating an unusually small number of open seats. Of the remaining 29 incumbents, only three were defeated (see table 5.2). Democrats experienced a net gain of two seats in the Senate, restoring the Republican majority to exactly the same size as at the beginning of President Reagan's first term There is evidence, however—to be examined later—that the orientation of that majority may differ significantly from that in 1981.

TABLE 5.2

CHANGE IN THE SENATE, 1984

State	Incumbent	Party	New member	Party
Illinois	Percy*	Republican	Simon	Democrat
Iowa	Jepsen*	Republican	Harkin	Democrat
Kentucky	Huddleston*	Democrat	McConnell	Republican
Massachusetts	Tsongas**	Democrat	Kerry	Democrat
Tennessee	Baker**	Republican	Gore	Democrat
Texas	Tower**	Republican	Gramm	Republican
West Virginia	Randolph**	Democrat	Rockefeller	Democrat

*Defeated.
**Retired.

SOURCE: *Congressional Quarterly Weekly Report* 42 (10 November 1984): 2905.

Why were these defeated incumbents exceptions to the general rule of reelection? Two of the three contests were so close as to easily have gone the other way. Percy lost to Simon by less than one percentage point, and the Huddleston-McConnell race was so near a draw as to provoke a call for a recount. Only Senator Roger W. Jepsen was defeated decisively (56-44). The reasons for Jepsen's loss seem the clearest. From the outset he was vulnerable as a result of his highly publicized and startling changes of position on national issues and numerous rhetorical blunders. Greater damage came with the disclosure that the senator had once applied for membership in a club that was subsequently closed because of prostitution.[5]

The victory of Republican challenger Mitch McConnell over Senator Walter D. Huddleston of Kentucky was one of the biggest surprises of the election. Huddleston had been considered safe up to the balloting. The challenger's campaign was energetic, but there seemed no outstanding, divisive issue. McConnell mainly caviled about Huddleston's attendance record (actually about average) and the fact that Huddleston had not been sufficiently supportive of the Reagan revolution.[6] On the other hand, Senator Charles Percy's defeat is more explicable. The Republican incumbent simply had not established a firm hold on his state constituency. During his incumbency he had shifted back and forth, right to left to right again with the shifting circumstances of the political environment. In past elections he was helped by lackluster Democratic opponents who failed to win necessary majorities in urban Illinois. Percy had added his suburban and rural strength to sufficient Chicago support to succeed. By 1984, the senator suffered from an image of remoteness—"Washingtonitis"— and uncertainty about his own *real* ideological commitment.[7] Faced with an estimable and experienced opponent in Congressman Paul Simon, Percy was unable to benefit sufficiently from President Reagan's coattails. This observation introduces a broader electoral theme.

COATTAILS AND TICKET-SPLITTING

When congressional elections coincide with presidential elections, political scientists and journalists search for "coattails." The theory rests in part on the strength of party identification. However, such identification has clearly declined in intensity in recent years. We have expected that a popular presidential candidate—being the main attraction and appearing at the top of the ballot in any constituency—would help candidates of his party farther down the list. That is, the partisan choice at the outset would be crucially important to subsequent voter choices. This could be particularly true in jurisdictions that provided for voting the "straight ticket" in one act.[8]

But there is an antithesis to the coattails thesis: the phenomenon of ticket-splitting, or voting for candidates of different parties in different offices. For present purposes, let us sample the relationship between presidential and congressional choices by looking more closely at the 33 senatorial elections that occurred across the country (see table 5.3 on page 117).

In striking contrast to Ronald Reagan's personal penetration of Democratic bastions across the nation in the presidential vote, the impact of his popularity on the senatorial outcomes in the aggregate was virtually nonexistent. We can

TABLE 5.3

SENATE AND PRESIDENTIAL VICTORY MARGINS, 1984

State	Winning party (Senate)	Percentage	Winning party (presidential)	Percentage
Alabama	Dem.	62	Rep.	60
Alaska	Rep.	71	Rep.	67
Arkansas	Dem.	58	Rep.	61
Colorado	Rep.	64	Rep.	63
Delaware	Dem.	60	Rep.	60
Georgia	Dem.	80	Rep.	60
Idaho	Rep.	72	Rep.	73
Illinois	Dem.	50	Rep.	57
Iowa	Dem.	56	Rep.	54
Kansas	Rep.	77	Rep.	67
Kentucky	Rep.	50	Rep.	60
Louisiana	Dem.	x	Rep.	61
Maine	Rep.	74	Rep.	61
Massachusetts	Dem.	55	Rep.	51
Michigan	Dem.	53	Rep.	59
Minnesota	Rep.	58	Dem.	51
Mississippi	Rep.	61	Rep.	62
Montana	Dem.	57	Rep.	60
Nebraska	Dem.	53	Rep.	71
New Hampshire	Rep.	59	Rep.	69
New Jersey	Dem.	65	Rep.	60
New Mexico	Rep.	72	Rep.	60
North Carolina	Rep.	52	Rep.	62
Oklahoma	Dem.	76	Rep.	68
Oregon	Rep.	66	Rep.	55
Rhode Island	Dem.	73	Rep.	52
South Carolina	Rep.	67	Rep.	64
South Dakota	Rep.	74	Rep.	63
Tennessee	Dem.	61	Rep.	63
Texas	Rep.	59	Rep.	64
Virginia	Rep.	70	Rep.	63
West Virginia	Dem.	52	Rep.	55
Wyoming	Rep.	78	Rep.	71

x = no opponent.

SOURCE: *Congressional Quarterly Weekly Report* 42 (10 November 1984): 2923-31.

see that 11 of the 17 Republican senators won by margins *greater* than the President's. Clearly, these candidates won in their own right. Of the remaining six Republican winners, four had sizable margins of safety, ranging from 59 percent to 72 percent, indicating, again, an absence of dependence on presidential popularity. In the end, only two Republican senators might be cited as beneficiaries of Reagan's coattails. Jesse Helms of North Carolina and Mitch McConnell of Kentucky each gave signs of latent political mortality. They achieved only narrow margins in states where Ronald Reagan at the head of the ticket won three of every five votes.

Another political scenario ought to be considered: defeat of opposition incumbents. An unusually popular presidential incumbent may run so strongly as to defeat marginal legislators. In 1984, particularly, Senators David Pryor of Arkansas and Carl Levin of Michigan were apparently in danger. Yet both managed to survive the Reagan onslaught. Finally, though the President's coattails may have helped a small number of House candidates of his party, the extraordinarily small number of contests and the massiveness of incumbent return suggest that presidential presence was insignificant in the aggregate. Indeed, the striking paradox of the elections of 1984 was the inability of a President, who gave hints of forging a new and durable majority coalition for his party at the presidential level (see chapter 3), to have a corresponding impact on legislative races that would be necessary to create a majority *governing* coalition.

MONEY, ELECTIONS, AND ACCESS

Money—its sources, amounts, and uses—has important effects on campaigns and elections. The fear of buying elections or unfairly weighting the scales of competition with gold has always been nettlesome to the democratic consciousness. And each new legislative mechanism designed to regulate (and thus make fair and accountable) the voting marketplace has spurred imaginative new alternative means of deploying dollars in the service of electoral influence.[9]

In 1984, the expected increase in total getting and spending stands out. Even before polling day, spending on congressional campaigns had risen 21 percent over 1982 levels to $213.4 million during the period January 1983 through June 1984.[10] Among the major sources of congressional campaign fund raising, political party organizations contribute only about 2 percent of the total, and Political Action Committees (PACs) about 23 percent. The remainder consists of loans and personal funding by candidates.[11] Between the two parties, total candidates' spending is nearly equal in the aggregate, with Democratic candidates spending about 6 percent more than Republicans.

Spending by PACs is growing especially fast. These contributors have increased their spending on candidacies by 46 percent to $50.7 million during this period. PACs have come to accept the advantage of incumbency, and behave accordingly. Thus, the PACs gave 80 percent of their funds to incumbents and about 60 percent of the funding went to Democrats, reflecting the larger number of Democratic incumbents. The ideology-based PACs, such as the National Conservative Political Action Committee, Fund for a Conservative Majority, and National Congressional Club (of Senator Jesse Helms), raise the largest amounts of money (the above three alone raising over $25 million) but spend most of their treasuries on organizational activities rather than direct payments to candidate campaigns. Thus, they work to help candidacies and groups advocating their approved causes up and down the line, serving as political infrastructure builders.

Unsurprisingly, the largest contributions in 1984 were made on behalf of the most competitive contests. Thus, the most expensive Senate campaigns were the Helms-Hunt contest in North Carolina (over $20 million), the Gramm-Doggett set-to in Texas ($10 million), the Rockefeller-Raese tilt in West Virginia ($8.5 million), the Percy-Simon contest in Illinois ($6.7 million), and Boschwitz-Growe fight in Minnesota ($5.8 million).[12] Three of these races were close, won by 52 percent or less. Apparently, the greater the uncertainty of a race, the stronger the enticement to invest in either potential winner—the gambling challenge. When the contest ends in a close call, the retrospective claim that money made the difference becomes more plausible.

Perhaps the greatest impact of money is in rewarding the perceived advantage of incumbency and, so, measurably helping to fulfill that same prophecy. Campaign contributions can also serve purposes other than winning elections. Considerable PAC money went to unquestionably secure senators. To cite a few illustrative cases, Senator Pete Domenici of New Mexico, who would win his election with 72 percent of the vote, was the fourth highest PAC recipient. Farther down the list, Senator Sam Nunn of Georgia garnered 80 percent of the vote in his contest, while receiving nearly $300,000 in PAC contributions. Senator Bill Bradley of New Jersey won 65 percent of the votes in his test (eighth on the list of recipients) and had been awarded nearly $500,000 in PAC monies.[13] In none of these contests, and many others like them, was there ever any serious question of electoral vulnerability. Unquestionably, the kind of investment being made in these cases was not directed to recruitment but to access. These senators (and in similar cases some of their House colleagues) are established, influential leaders in the legislative process. Election time provides an opportunity for groups that seek representation in routine legislative decision-making arenas to establish their bona fides, to court sympathetic attention to their causes. This is why four out of five PAC dollars went to incumbents.

The New Congress: Partisanship and Ideology

In examining the new Congress, we are interested in such things as its potential

effectiveness as a legislative body, the ideological tendencies likely to predomin-
ate, and the nature of its relationships with the President in the enactment of
public policies. Some relevant clues may help to forecast future directions.

EXPERIENCE

Particularly in recent decades, the Congress has become a body of political
professionals. That is, most of its members have moved into national legislative
office after a considerable apprenticeship in political and public office at state
and local levels. Moreover, upon arriving in Congress, members have tended
to stay on, and make a career on Capitol Hill. The style of work in Congress
has also taken on some of the qualities of a professional, bureaucratic organization. The geometric growth of congressional staff is symptomatic of such profes-
sionalism.[14] Stable tenure, along with other internal organizational factors, gave
rise to discussions about the institutionalization of the House of Representatives.[15] Then the upheavals of the 1970s, ranging from Watergate-related instability to a general disenchantment with a system seen as badly in need of reform,
led to volatility in both houses of Congress. One reflection of this upheaval
was in large biennial turnovers, so that by the beginning of the Reagan era half
the membership of the House had been renewed in the previous four years.

The experience of 1984 may well signal a resettling into stability and norms
of gradualism, and even institutional discipline. The incoming House freshmen
are typical of their predecessors in that most have held offices or had some
form of political experience. What is more significant, however, is the fact that
there are so few of them. The smallest freshman class in modern memory will
not constitute a large faction that must be newly socialized into the organizational norms and practices of the body. Moreover, as noted earlier, House turnovers have not resulted in yawning leadership gaps. There is a limiting case
here or there to prove the rule: For example, House Republicans will experience
some loss with the retirement of senior Ways and Means Committee minority
leader, Barber Conable. For the Democrats, the loss of Maryland's senior law-
maker, Clarence Long, has removed a longtime important presence on the Foreign Affairs Committee.[16] Nonetheless, these are minor blemishes on the broad
surface of continuity and stability.

We can render much the same verdict on the Senate. First, there is the min-
iaturization of the freshman class, seven in strength. But more important, fewer
than half of these freshmen are newcomers to national legislative life. Senators-
elect Paul Simon of Illinois, Tom Harkin of Iowa, Albert Gore of Tennessee,
and Phil Gramm of Texas are all former members of the House, seasoned in
the legislative process. In numerous instances, they have already occupied posi-

tions of responsibility and leadership in important substantive areas, such as the budget, education, and defense strategy.[17] Thus, inexperience will not be one of the problems of the new Congress.

LIBERALISM AND CONSERVATISM IN THE NEW SENATE

Positions on the great issues of American politics are conventionally polarized between traditional movements toward liberalism or conservatism. To be sure, these ideological labels are not exact. Philosophical debate about what really *is* the liberal or conservative position on particular issues is a commonplace of political dialogue. Yet the distinctions are useful; more important, most political figures think of themselves as predominately one or the other, and this self-designation has much to do with their actual behavior.

In Congress, granting the exceptions that always exist, liberals *tend* to be more open to social and political experimentation than their conservative counterparts. They *tend* to favor domestic social welfare and economically redistributive programs as against the normal conservative suspicion of such thrusts. Historically, liberals tend to tolerate a larger role for the federal government and freer government spending. Conservatives have an ingrained skepticism about big government and usually advocate a tighter rein on the public treasury.

To examine the ideology of representatives and senators, we can employ the evaluations of legislative behavior made by groups that define themselves as standard-bearers of ideological positions. Several such groups routinely monitor legislative voting records. Among them are the chief liberal groups: Americans for Democratic Action (ADA) and the Committee on Political Education of the American Federation of Labor-Congress of Industrial Organizations (COPE); and the chief conservative groups: Americans for Constitutional Action Research Institute (ACARI) and Chamber of Commerce of the United States (CCUS). Each year these groups select about 20 major issues before Congress, define the "correct" ideological position on the issue, and score the legislators on whether or not they conform to the liberal or conservative position.

Using the 1983 "liberalism" scores of the ADA enables us to assess the ideological change likely to follow from the advent of seven new senators. There is a difficulty in comparison, however. Some of the freshmen senators do not have ADA scores because they had not held positions rated by ADA before entering the Senate. As an alternative in these cases, we shall look at the support given to these candidates by the leading ideological interest groups.[18] Table 5.4 on page 122 reports the nature of support, liberal or conservative, and the number of groups supporting each freshman elected.

We can draw a clear conclusion from the table data. Not only did the Democrats increase the size of their partisan minority, but the freshman group

TABLE 5.4

IDEOLOGY AND SUCCESSION IN THE SENATE

State	Incumbent	ADA rating (percent)	Winner	ADA rating (percent)	Support groups
Illinois	Percy (R)*	40	Simon (D)	70	Lib, 3
Iowa	Jepsen (R)*	15	Harkin (D)	90	Lib, 3
Kentucky	Huddleston (D)*	60	McConnell (R)	—	Cons, 1
Massachusetts	Tsongas (D)**	95	Kerry (D)	—	Lib, 2
Tennessee	Baker (R)**	20	Gore (D)	70	Lib, 2
Texas	Tower (R)**	15	Gramm (R)	—	Cons, 3
West Virginia	Randolph (D)**	50	Rockefeller (D)	—	Lib, 2

*Defeated
**Retired

SOURCE: *Congressional Quarterly Weekly Report* 42 (14 July 1984): 1695 and (17 November 1984): 2971-76.

is also more moderate or liberal than the group it replaced. Senators Percy, Jepsen, and Baker were replaced by three former congressmen who brought with them liberal support and (since they had been House members with ADA assessments) liberal voting *behavior*. The 1983 ADA ratings for Simon, Harkin, and Gore were 70, 90, and 70 respectively. Democrats Tsongas and Randolph were succeeded by like-minded liberals. At the same time, Senator Tower's seat will be occupied by a staunch conservative successor, Phil Gramm. Undoubtedly freshman Republican McConnell will be more conservative than his Kentucky predecessor. In the aggregate, 1984 Senate freshmen add weight to the left in the 99th Congress.

If we look for a connection between electoral verdicts and political behavior among those other senators who kept their seats in 1984, we conclude that the votes for Republican senators in 1984, tilted in the direction of *moderate* Republicanism. As noted above, fully 11 of the 17 reelected Republican incumbents ran ahead of the President in their states. A large proportion of these (such as Senators William Cohen of Maine, Mark Hatfield of Oregon, Nancy Kassebaum of Kansas, Pete Domenici of New Mexico, and Larry Pressler of South Dakota) have established reputations for their independence of mind and casualness about conservative dogmas. Most of those whose voter support was considerably less than that of the President, on the other hand, were already staunch conservatives. Thus such senators as Jesse Helms, Thad Cochran, Phil Gramm, and James McClure are convinced believers in little need of presidential leverage for their support. A previous conclusion needs underlining. In 1984, the American electorate — across the regional and demographic range — restated its overwhelming confidence in the conservative President while refraining from that gesture in legislative voting.

LIBERALISM AND CONSERVATISM IN THE NEW HOUSE

Of the 43 incumbents of the House who either retired (27) or were defeated (16), almost half (21) supported the ADA position more than 50 percent of the time, and could reasonably be considered liberals. As might be expected, these were all Democrats.[19] The 99th Congress has 43 freshmen (31 Republicans, 12 Democrats), about whose ideological tendencies we can only speculate. Yet if we can once again apply the maxim that a person is known by the friends he keeps, campaign group support levels for these freshmen may be indicative. Table 5.5 reflects the sentiments of supportive groups in 1984.

TABLE 5.5

GROUP SUPPORT FOR HOUSE FRESHMEN, 1984

All candidates group support	N	%	Republican groups	N	%	Democratic groups	N	%
Three groups	9	21	Cons, 3	9	29	Lib, 3	0	0
Two groups	18	42	Cons, 2	13	42	Lib, 2	5	42
One group	13	30	Cons, 1	7	23	Lib, 1	6	50
No group	3	7	Cons, 0	2	6	Lib, 0	1	8
TOTAL	43	100		31	100		12	100

SOURCE: *Congressional Quarterly Weekly Report* 42 (17 November 1984): 2971-76.

In the case of House freshmen, 94 percent of Republicans elected had conservative group support, the average candidate having had the support of two such groups. Among freshmen Democrats, 92 percent had liberal group support, again about half of them winning the backing of two groups. There is no certainty that the endorsing groups will be proportionately rewarded by approved legislative ideological behavior. Yet ideological interest groups were unwilling to place their bets in only 8 percent of the candidacies.

One conclusion that seems plausible in terms of net effect rests upon the 4 to 3 superiority of freshmen Republican numbers. If group support is accurately targeted, then these freshmen will, as a group, tilt marginally in a conservative direction. While 1984 appears to have added an increment of strength to the conservative cause in the House, that strength shows up exclusively in the increased Republican contingent. And that contingent remains in the minority. The ability to use that minority as a base to build conservative dominance in the legislative arena is contingent on other factors in the governmental process.

The New Congress and the Reagan Agenda

Directions in the new Congress—whether it is effective or ineffective, whether its work is dominated by conservative or liberal impulses, whether it strengthens or weakens support for the entire political system—will be shaped in large measure by the body's symbiotic relationship with the President. Modern Congresses demand legislative leadership from Presidents, and Presidents must work for support from Congress. A productive relationship depends upon the skill of the President in applying the arts of persuasion[20] and the ability and will of the legislators to respond. The interplay of partisan support, legislative institutional arrangements, and issue priorities on both sides is crucial to a rewarding consummation of public policy.

THE LEGISLATIVE PARTIES

A major measure of the stature of any presidency is the extent to which the chief executive succeeds in convincing Congress to enact his policy preferences. In the attempt, Presidents must rely primarily on legislative support from among their partisans and secondarily on support from the opposition party. The greater the size of the majority of the President's party in Congress, the better are his chances of success. Reciprocally, when the President's party is in the minority in Congress, his programs will suffer. Success is determined by the extent to which Congress agrees with the presidential position on policy matters coming before the lawmakers.[21]

If we look back on the record of the post-World War II administrations, Congress by Congress, the most striking conclusion is that even when the President is beleaguered by the minority status of his party in Congress, he will always succeed more than half the time, and generally will win support for two out of every three of his policy preferences. When the President's party controls Congress—even narrowly, as in the first Eisenhower term—he can anticipate legislative support more than four times out of five.

The size of congressional majorities also affects presidential success. Thus, when the size of the Democratic majority shrank significantly in 1967, Lyndon Johnson's success rate declined. On the other hand, when the President's party is already in the minority, modest shifts in size do not seem to affect presidential success greatly, as in the Nixon years. Cataclysmic events seem to have an impact on presidential success that transcends partisan majorities. Lyndon Johnson's low point (1967-68) coincided with the agony of Vietnam; Richard Nixon's low point (1973-74) reflected the crisis of Watergate.[22]

In the House of Representatives, in particular, an additional factor that influences the ideological direction of the chamber's work beyond the partisan differences is the phenomenon known as the "conservative coalition." Indeed, it throws into bold relief the distinction between partisan polarities and ideological polarities. Since the early days of the Roosevelt New Deal, conservative northern Republicans and conservative southern Democrats have made common cause in opposing the policy direction of the generally liberal, northern Democratic leadership and its supporters. In truth, this has often resulted in a virtual three-party system in Congress.

The conservative coalition comes together only on votes that clearly pose conservative principles at odds with liberal principles, but these constitute most *major* issues.[23] In any given year, the conservative coalition may appear on about one-fourth of the votes, and, on average, will win on two of three such roll calls. It is clear that a large part of President Reagan's legislative success rate during the first two years of his administration rested on the faithful support of the coalition. Thus, in 1981, the coalition materialized on 21 percent of congressional votes. But the coalition was victorious in 92 percent of those contests — an all-time high since such records have been kept.[24] The chronic obstacle to achievement for Democratic Presidents had perforce become the prescription for legislative success for this conservative Republican President.

STRUCTURES OF POWER

In his relations with Congress, the President must influence and treat with two foci of internal power: the party legislative leadership and a decentralized collectivity of chairmen of the standing committees.[25] At the beginning of the 99th Congress, it appears that this dual challenge will be shaped by different circumstances in the House and Senate.

In the House, the most obvious — and also most important — condition is the Democratic majority. This means that setting the agenda, the procedural repertoire, the management of the institution, and publicity on the issues will be dominated, if not monopolized, by the Democrats. In 1985 the already established principal issue on the agenda will surely engender high conflict and the strong possibility of deadlock. For on the one point there *is* bipartisan consensus: taxes, spending, and the deficit command immediate attention.

Aside from ideological differences, the White House and Capitol Hill will clash for two reasons. First, the disposition of these issues is managed by the most powerful and prestigious committees on the Hill: Ways and Means, Appropriations, and to a lesser extent, Budget. Representative Dan Rostenkowski, chairman of Ways and Means, is a 13-term senior legislator who will not be reluctant to exercise the independent judgment and personal power that accord with his position. Nor will the Appropriations committee lightly accede to the administration's call for still further and drastic reductions in domestic program allotments. Second, the most regular recurrent policy confrontations and deadlocks during the first Reagan term were produced by these issues, and the election of 1984 has wrought no institutional change in Congress that would lead us to expect a different atmosphere under Reagan II.

At the White House, the President's advisers have misgivings about the outlook in Congress because of its organizational instability. In an attempt to strengthen the institution's capacity to resist presidential dominance, Congress, over the past decade, engaged in a series of internal institutional reforms and self-evaluations. Was it undemocratic? It proceeded to make assaults on the seniority system in the House, and in 1975 the Democratic caucus actually deposed three committee chairmen. Was it overly secretive? It opened up its committee hearings to public scrutiny and introduced recorded teller voting in the House. Was it inefficient (most egregiously in handling its most important responsibility, money matters)? It responded in 1974 by establishing congressional budget committees with the power to present a systematic *congressional* budget. These are among the major items in a catalogue of reform that was characterized, more than anything else, by a rage to bring a greater and greater measure of democratic individualism to the legislative process.

By 1984, it was clear to many that one of the unintended consequences of the reform agenda was to make rational planning, programmatic discipline, and procedural effectiveness weaker and weaker. So, the 99th Congress opened with proposals in the House to overhaul congressional budget procedures; limit speech-making under certain circumstances; and merge tax changes, appropriations, and changes in entitlement programs into one comprehensive, omnibus work of legislative craftsmanship.[26] Such internal machinations introduce uncertainty and potential new obstacles to White House leadership of the legislative process.

A final kind of instability in the environment of the House in 1985 is the uncertainty about future leadership. Speaker "Tip" O'Neill has announced his intention of retiring at the end of the 99th Congress. This announcement, of course, opens the often agonizing process of leadership succession. Some obvious successor-candidates have appeared (Majority Leader Jim Wright, Chairman Rostenkowski) and still others will emerge. Careerist coalition-building will occupy the energies of some members; evaluating substantive position-taking on issues in light of the leadership candidates will occupy the attention of many. And, above all, there will be the enduring preparation for the midterm election of 1986 and consideration of issues in the light of their implications for partisan advantage.

If the President faces automatic opposition in the House, he might have expected cooperation and support from his co-partisans who control the Senate. Yet the circumstances of 1984 will disappoint any hopes of smooth compliance in the upper house. Two factors constituted immediate caveats to presidential calculation about future White House influence in the Senate as the 99th session commenced: changed leadership and instincts for institutional reform.

Consider the paradox of November. In the first week the President won a triumphant reelection, having consistently and enthusiastically advocated conservative principles and policies. In the last week of November, the President's partisan brethren selected as their leaders a corps marked by political moderation to an extent greater than any Republican establishment in modern memory. Clearly, the new Republican leadership does not constitute some kind of liberal Trojan horse! Yet, its constitution is marked by legislators whose past records suggest possible deviation from the White House line and whose present statements take friendly exception to some current presidential priorities.

Senator Robert Dole, the new Majority Leader, is known for legislative effectiveness, presumptive party loyalty, and a healthy individualism that permits him critically to confront even partisan allies. What was surprising about the Senate leadership changes however, was that the entire weight of the collective leadership shifted toward the center. In the top position, just below that of Majority Leader, Senator John Chafee of Rhode Island, a moderate within Republican ranks, became Republican Conference chairman and Senator John Heinz of Pennsylvania, of the Chafee stripe, took over the Republican Senatorial Committee. Nor are Senators William Armstrong (Colorado), Policy Committee chairman; and Alan Simpson (Wyoming), the Assistant Leader (Whip); among the hard-right majority of their colleagues. Senator Thad Cochran of Mississippi, who occupies the less influential position of Secretary of the Republican Conference, seems the only gesture to the far right that the Republicans were willing to make in 1984.[27]

The spirit of dissatisfaction, bred among congressmen out of a sense of institutional ineffectiveness, was shared by many in the new Senate. Thus the Senate put forward its new reform agenda designed to tilt the balance away from freedom (which many senators were beginning to refer to as "anarchy") toward responsibility. Thus, committee assignments were to be reduced (favoring specialization over dilettantism), abuses of filbustering tactics restricted, and procedural mechanism crafted to expedite the lawmaking process.[28] The focus was on giving leadership more authority. To the extent that an independent senatorial leadership can more effectively compete with executive leadership, a Senate less in disarray might also be a body less weakly compliant.

PRESIDENT, CONGRESS, AND THE FUTURE

Presidential leadership over Congress, coming on the heels of a massive electoral landslide, provides opportunities of consolidation, and of fulfillment. If Ronald Reagan is able to prolong his hold on the allegiance of the articulate majority of his fellow citizens, success may match his ambitions. That proposition must be undeniable after the revolution of 1981-82. Yet, one need not be imprisoned by historical determinism to find lessons in the recent past and recall unexpected aftermaths of similar electoral successes. Lyndon Johnson's triumph of 1964 was even more baroque than 1984; presidential purpose was supported by majorities exceeding two-thirds of his partisans in both houses of Congress. Before the end of that presidential term, his reputation was destroyed, his political gestures rebuffed, his hold on the presidency lost. In 1972, Richard Nixon's reelection was assured by a larger proportion of the popular vote than in 1984. Ambitious schemes of governmental reorganization, transformation of the welfare system, assertions of extraordinary executive prerogatives — these and many other pretensions dissolved within two years, along with the presidency. The litany does not foretell political disaster for Reagan II, though other political scientists and historians have done so.[29] Rather, it directs attention to constraints that could frustrate presidential ambitions in the coming years.

The political atmosphere of 1985 is importantly different from 1981. The ideological momentum of new beginnings has given way to many sober second thoughts. Hopeful curiosity about the future of the attractive crusader of 1980 is tempered by the experience of the intervening years. The recent electoral verdict may have been a retrospective approval *on balance.* Yet memories of the recession and unemployment levels of 1981-82, as well as the haunting specter of those unprecedented deficits, must leave room for tentativeness in commitment. The writ on experimentation may not run as long as in the heady days of yesteryear.

More basic is the simple fact that the administration does not have the numerical strength of support in Congress that it had four years ago. To review the facts tersely, the midterm elections of 1982 resulted in a loss of 26 Republican seats in the House, and with that loss, the inability to forge conservative coalitions for votes on major administration projects.[30] In order to duplicate the legislative successes of 1981-82, it was unanimously agreed in advance by Republican and Democratic leaders that the party would have to recapture those midterm losses in 1984. That, of course, did not happen. The only possible way of compensating for Republican deficiencies would be a complementary *increase* in the strength of numbers of conservative Democrats who would regularly carry water for the President.

The extraordinarily limited personnel shifts in Congress in 1984 give no evidence of having produced that feat. Indeed, the evidence is quite opposite. In 1981, 48 Democratic congressmen defected and voted for the administration's major tax bill, and 40 also defected and voted for Reagan's domestic spending cuts. These were the legislators who were collectively referred to as the "boll weevils."[31] Legislators on that list who are present in the 99th Congress are 12 fewer than in 1981, providing fewer political allies in the new Congress.

In the Senate, Republican majority cohesion accomplished for the President in the 1981 economic battles what the conservative coalition provided in the House. For example, on seven days in July 1981, 27 votes were taken in the Senate on amendments offered to the administration's tax package. In only one of those tests was an amendment adopted that ran counter to the leadership's position and split the Republicans badly. In every other instance, crushing majorities of Republicans were responsible for the adoption of favorable, or rejection of hostile, amendments. A large number of these votes recorded unanimity among the President's partisans. On only a small handful did more than one or two Republicans deviate. On the crucial amendment that assured adoption of the President's package, the Republican vote was 52-1.[32]

It is most unlikely that Republicans in the Senate will show similar steadfastness in the 99th Congress. The major reason for this caution is fear of the electoral consequences of supporting policies—which the administration has already forecast—that further reduce public benefits or do not address widespread concerns about growing deficits. Both Congressman Robert Michel, the House Minority Leader, and Senator Robert Dole have put the administration on notice that their concern looks first to the electoral viability of their followers. In the Senate that viability is more tenuous in the next election than it has been in the past. The grim memory of Republican losses of 12 seats in the Senate and 43 in the House two years after the Nixon landslide of 1972 wonderfully concentrates the minds of responsible leaders on the path to survival. The path is likely not infrequently to branch away from the presidential policy road.

ON TO 1986

In an inquiry devoted primarily to an understanding of elections and their consequences, it seems fitting to conclude with a consideration of future elections. To be sure this is a matter already weighing on the minds of the lawmakers. At this early stage what can be said about the prospects for 1986? Two harbingers may be called into account, dealing respectively with the Senate and House.

The 1986 Senate election shows a disadvantage for the Republicans, the arithmetical disadvantage that comes from the staggered nature of Senate officeholding. The contest will challenge the seats of 34 Senate incumbents, but only 12 of them will be Democrats. Thus nearly twice as many Republican as Democratic Senate incumbents will be called upon to surmount the challenge of reelection. In terms of the odds, Republicans are at considerable risk.

A different prospect affects the House midterm election of 1986, resting partly on empirical data and partly on the faith that there is regularity in political behavior. It too is of little comfort to the Republicans. We return to the experience that proclaims that the party of the presidential incumbent loses seats in the House in midterm elections. To justify this judgment, let us consider the national elections of the past quarter century (see table 5.6).

TABLE 5.6
LOSSES OF SEATS IN THE HOUSE IN MIDTERM ELECTIONS, 1962-82

Date	Presidential winning margin (percent)	Date	Net loss of House seats succeeding election
1960	0.1 (D)	1962	5 (D)
1964	23.0 (D)	1966	47 (D)
1968	0.7 (R)	1970	12 (R)
1972	23.0 (R)	1974	48 (R)
1976	2.0 (D)	1978	16 (D)
1980	10.0 (R)	1982	26 (R)
1984	19.0 (R)	1986	? (R)

SOURCE: *Congressional Quarterly Weekly Report* 40 (6 November 1982): 2780.

At least in recent decades, the larger the winning margin of the presidential victor, the larger the number of House seats lost in the midterm congressional elections two years later. Should this tendency continue into 1986, Republicans might expect to lose 30 to 40 seats, other things being equal.

Of course, other things are not always equal.

NOTES

1. See especially David R. Mayhew, *Congressional Electoral Connection* (New Haven: Yale University Press, 1974); Morris P. Fiorina, *Congress: The Keystone of the Washington Establishment* (New Haven: Yale University Press, 1977); and Richard F. Fenno, Jr., *Home Style: House Members in Their Districts* (Boston: Little, Brown, 1978).
2. *Congressional Quarterly Weekly Report* 42 (10 November 1984): 2897.
3. Ibid., 2899.
4. See, for example, Barbara Hinckley, *Congressional Elections* (Washington, D.C.: Congressional Quarterly, 1981), 47-57. See also Gary C. Jacobson, *The Politics of Congressional Elections* (Boston: Little, Brown, 1983), 29-30.
5. *Congressional Quarterly Weekly Report* 42 (13 October 1984): 2537.
6. Ibid., 2541.
7. *National Journal* 16 (13 October 1984): 1911-12.
8. See V.O. Key, *Politics, Parties, and Pressure Groups,* 4th ed. (New York: Crowell, 1958), 615-16; and Warren E. Miller, "Presidential Coattails: A Study of Political Myth and Methodology," *Public Opinion Quarterly* 19 (Winter 1955-56): 26-39.
9. See F. Christopher Arterton, Gary C. Jacobson, Xandra Kayden, and Gary Orren, "An Analysis of the Impact of the Federal Election Campaign Act, 1972-78," in *Report by the Campaign Finance Study Group to the Committee on House Administration* (Washington, D.C.: U.S. House of Representatives, May 1979).
10. Federal Election Commission press release, 21 October 1984, 8.
11. Ibid., 3.
12. *Congressional Quarterly Weekly Report* 442 (27 October 1984): 2777.
13. Federal Election Commission press release, 21 October 1984, 8.
14. See, for example, Harrison W. Fox, Jr., and Susan Webb Hammond, *Congressional Staffs: The Invisible Force in American Law Making* (New York: Free Press, 1977); and Michael J. Malbin, *Unelected Representatives: Congressional Staff and the Future of Representative Government* (New York: Basic Books, 1980).
15. The seminal study is Nelson W. Polsby, "The Institutionalization of the House of Representatives," *American Political Science Review* 62 (March 1958): 144-68.
16. *National Journal* 16 (10 November 1984): 2142-50.
17. *Congressional Quarterly Weekly Report* 42 (10 November 1984): 2902-3.
18. There are a half dozen such groups that we will examine, three liberal and three conservative. ADA and COPE are represented among the three liberal groups, and ACA (Americans for Constitutional Action) is represented among conservative support groups. In addition, on the liberal side, the National Committee for an Effective Congress (NCEC) was active. On the conservative side, the two additional rating groups were the Business-Industry Political Action Committee (BIPAC) and the National Conservative Political Action Committee (NCPAC). See *Congressional Quarterly Weekly Report* 42 (17 November 1984): 2970-76.
19. *Congressional Quarterly Weekly Report* 42 (14 July 1984): 1696-97.
20. See Richard Neustadt, *Presidential Power: The Politics of Leadership* (New York: Wiley, 1980).
21. The Congressional Quarterly Service analyzes presidential messages, remarks at press conferences, and other presidential documents and statements to isolate the

presidential position on issues before Congress. Congressional votes are then tabulated in terms of whether the President's position has been sustained or defeated. At the end of the year a percentage score reflecting the proportion of presidential victories is posted. See *Congressional Quarterly Weekly Report* 42 (27 October 1984): 2802.

22. Ibid., 2802-3.
23. Ibid., 2820.
24. Ibid., 2821.
25. The best analysis of legislative party leadership in the House is Robert L. Peabody, *Leadership in Congress* (Boston: Little, Brown, 1973), chaps. 1 and 2.
26. *Congressional Quarterly Weekly Report* 42 (24 November 1984): 2983.
27. *New York Times,* 29 November 1984, 1, B14.
28. *New York Times,* 30 November 1984, A14. See also a series of articles on the ferment in the Senate in the *New York Times,* 25, 26, 27, and 28 November 1984.
29. See *New York Review of Books,* 16 August 1984, 33-34.
30. *Congressional Quarterly Weekly Report* 40 (6 November 1982): 2780.
31. *Congressional Quarterly Weekly Report* 39 (1 August 1981): 1375.
32. Ibid., 1416-19.

6

The Second Reagan Term

Ross K. Baker

Presidents riding the crest of a great electoral tide are usually tempted to place their personal imprint on the future. In recent history, the record of second presidential terms, especially, have been marked by a desire to influence posterity. The means used to achieve that end, however, have sometimes been impulsive and ill-starred.

The second term of Franklin D. Roosevelt saw his most conspicuous act of executive overreaching in the plan to "pack" the U.S. Supreme Court with six extra justices to dilute the power of the conservative bloc. It was also the occasion for Roosevelt's effort to "purge" the party of uncooperative southern Democrats in Congress. Both efforts misfired, and their long-term consequences gave birth to an enduring coalition of southern Democrats and conservative Republicans. The second Roosevelt term also saw the nation slide back into recession, and by the midterm election, in 1938, the Republicans came back strongly, gaining 71 House seats and six new senators.

Harry Truman's second term was marred by the inconclusive Korean War and the failure of his ambitious domestic program, the Fair Deal. Eisenhower's second term saw a major business recession in 1958. It ended on a note of confusion and fecklessness over the U-2 incident in which Eisenhower asserted, in effect, the unilateral right to spy on the Soviet Union with overflights of its territory.

Lyndon Johnson's second term was marked in its earlier period by the triumphs of his Great Society. It ended bogged down in the Vietnam War—the product of an open-ended commitment from Congress to fight a war in an inauspicious place under unfavorable circumstances.

But while it appears that the prospects for second-term Presidents are not very bright, it was in Franklin Roosevelt's second term that the groundwork was laid for American military preparedness for World War II. Truman's second term was crowned by the establishment of the Atlantic Community and Eisenhower's by the first enforcement of the Supreme Court's antisegregation decision in the *Brown* case. What does the future hold for Reagan?

Again, the Mandate Question

The disposition of a newly elected second-term President to be bold (or perhaps, impulsive) seems to depend in large measure on his own and others' perception of a mandate for his policies. Looking back on the 1980 election, something of a scholarly consensus has emerged. Supporters of the newly elected President moved quickly to assert the existence of a conservative mandate in the face of rather persuasive evidence that the election was more nearly a rejection of Jimmy Carter.[1] The dispositive statement about the 1980 mandate or lack of it was by House Speaker Thomas P. O'Neill who said, "The record *shows* there was no mandate. But Congress thinks there was and it's reacting in that manner."[2]

Unlike 1980, no bold claim on a mandate was asserted with any force or consistency this time. The conventional opinion, even among Republicans, was that it was more a personal triumph than either a partisan or an ideological one.[3] At least part of this reluctance to claim a mandate derives from Reagan's reticence in setting forth his vision for a second term with any clarity or precision. Reagan's use of the old Al Jolson teaser, "You ain't seen nothin' yet," can either mean more of the same or a radical departure. Will the second Reagan term be crowded with accomplishments of an enduring quality, or will it be merely an effort to consolidate the gains of the first administration? The outcome depends on a number of factors.

The first is the reelected President himself and whether he can sustain the remarkable vigor and determination he showed in his first term. The second set of influential factors is the nature of the issues that he will either broach or will have thrust upon him. Will it be a four-year period given over largely to preoccupations with the economy—as many suggest—or will foreign policy matters intrude on the agenda of the second Reagan term? The third group of shaping forces stems from the nature of Ronald Reagan's closest associates and his political opposition—most notably the newly strengthened Democratic contingent in the Senate and the House Democrats who managed to ride out the landslide with a solid majority intact. But there is more than Democratic opposition to consider. Even so conspicuous a conservative as President Reagan may find danger to his political right in a combative group of younger Republicans, mostly in the House, who have styled themselves as "populist" conservatives and aligned themselves with some outspoken ideologues outside government to watch over the conservative flame that was ignited by Reagan. In the words of one of them — former Secretary of the Interior James Watt — they urge, "Let Reagan be Reagan." By this injunction, they hope to inoculate him against the toxins of pragmatism and to keep his conservatism uncontaminated and pure.

We do not know precisely how the major issues will present themselves in the course of this administration, but we do have a sense of what they are at the outset. So we will turn first to the issues, holding for subsequent consideration the likely conduct of the political opposition and the President's own partisan and ideological allies. We will pay special attention to the cabinet and the man in our nation's second-highest office, George Bush, and his prospects as Reagan's successor. Finally, we will turn to Ronald Reagan, the man and President.

Issues in the Offing: The Economy

A consensus exists on the number-one problem facing the economy. It is the federal deficit, standing at $174 billion last year, and projected by the Congressional Budget Office to reach $263 billion by 1989.

A deficit is the product of government spending in excess of revenues. It can be produced by a burst of spending while taxes remain constant, by cutting taxes while spending rises, or by a combination of spending increases and tax cuts. Activities that produce a deficit are generally those that stimulate the economy. Spending by the government for anything from social programs and public works projects to a buildup for the military will create jobs and increase the purchasing power that comes with a paycheck or a bigger paycheck. Cutting taxes causes more of a paycheck to be left over for spending on goods and services. In either case, purchasing power — what economists call "aggregate demand"— gets a boost.

A few annual deficts are not considered a problem; indeed, government spending in excess of revenues or tax cuts without equivalent cuts in spending are regarded as proper responses to deal with a recession. The United States, however, has had deficits of unprecedented size, which means that the government has had to borrow and will continue to borrow to pay its bills. The larger and longer the deficit, the more the national debt increases as the government scrambles to get people to lend it money and finds that it must attract them by paying higher rates of interest. What is stimulative in the short run can lead to great problems in the long run.

Prolonged and successive deficits produce a number of very undesirable effects.

Trouble develops with the economy when savings are persistently diverted into financing a government deficit; it has to make up the shortfall by borrowing in the financial markets. The money it borrows in this way would otherwise have been available for investment in business plants and equipment and housing. Although deficits start reducing the level of investment immediately, it may take several years before the cumulative effect of lower investment in depressing growth is generally recognized.[4]

The massive diversion of money away from the foundations of economic growth to merely servicing a huge debt spells trouble down the road for the American economy. But what is required to stave off the worst eventuality is not necessarily the message the President wants to hear. He cannot merely repeat his budget cutting performance of 1981 when he prevailed upon Congress to cut $36 billion from the fiscal 1982 budget. Cuts of that magnitude would be resisted by the Democrats in Congress or accepted by them only if the President capitulated on tax increases. Even if Mr. Reagan were willing to cut the military budget significantly—something that he has sworn steadfastly he will not do—it will be several years before any impact on the deficit will be detectable.[5]

The deficit-cutting corollary of budget reductions is, of course, increasing taxes. Reagan swore that taxes would be raised "only as a last resort." He could safely retreat behind the old show business injunction, "never say never" and not suffer any damage in the campaign because of Walter Mondale's early and oft-repeated vow to raise taxes. The fear of a President Mondale removing his hand from the inaugural Bible and immediately inserting it into their pockets was enough to persuade taxpayers that their fortunes were more secure in Reagan's hands.

But, of course, Reagan will have to raise taxes, even though he will probably try to put off the inevitable as long as possible and disguise it artfully when he embraces the proposal. He would be better advised to be done with the grim matter as early as possible so as to take advantage of the brief honeymoon accorded second-term Presidents.

What emerged first from the administration, however, was not a tax bill but a plan for tax simplification. Its purpose was not merely to liberate taxpayers from the labyrinthine complexity of Form 1040 but to close major tax loopholes and thus broaden the tax base. The plan, proposed in late November 1984 by Donald T. Regan when he was Treasury Secretary, was billed as "revenue-neutral"; that is, it was expected to produce neither significant new revenues nor create any outflow of revenues. The proposal, then, was not introduced with deficit reduction in mind, but with adding to the number of those who pay taxes.

Anyone familiar with the federal tax code would agree with Regan's characterization of it as a "swamp." Still, there are a number of fearsome reptiles who have made it their home. Favorite corporate loopholes such as the investment tax credit were on Regan's hit list along with a curtailment of the accelerated depreciation allowance for factory equipment. Pushing such a reform "will put Congress up against every interest group in the country," according to House Ways and Means Committee Chairman Dan Rostenkowski. His former Senate counterpart, Robert Dole, admitted, "When all those lobbyists arrive at the Senate Finance Committee, I don't want to be there."[6]

If dealing with the deficit is what the President really wants to do in his second term, it seems unlikely that he would expend much political capital on a highly controversial simplification plan that leaves the deficit largely untouched. To make any serious assault on the deficit there must be new or increased taxes or more budget cuts.

The gap between revenues and expenditures will be compounded in the second Reagan term by the onset of indexing—a device to prevent inflation from pushing people into higher tax brackets. Basically, indexing provides that a taxpayer will be moved into a higher bracket only when an increase in his income warrants such a move. In the past this occurred when a salary in inflation-bloated dollars pushed him into a bracket in which he paid a larger percentage of his income in taxes.

Indexing, a provision of the 1981 tax bill, will take effect in 1985 and will cut off the federal government from what many consider a form of unjust enrichment. While the effect of indexing on federal revenues is not expected to be significant, because inflation is low, "bracket creep" is one revenue-raising device (albeit a deceitful one) that might have helped to cut the deficit. President Reagan has been emphatic in his assertions that he will maintain indexing, and this does not seem a likely candidate for repeal.

The question for President Reagan is how he will be able, simultaneously, to maintain his pledge of no tax increases, honor his commitment to deficit reduction, reaffirm his support for increased military spending, and not trifle with major entitlement programs such as Social Security. Put more bluntly, how can he deal responsibly with the deficit without reneging on a series of very well-publicized and oft-reiterated pledges?

The most direct answer is, of course, that he will try to do both and that this attempt will test the limits of the ingratiating Reagan personality and his vaunted skill as a communicator. A new kind of tax—as opposed to increases in existing taxes—would technically vindicate the pledge of no increases. Such an approach might involve the proposal of a Value Added Tax, or VAT, such as is used in some countries in Western Europe, or a national sales or purchase tax. What is so beguiling about the VAT in the form that has been discussed is that it is a tax that can be hidden from the ultimate consumer and not appear on the register tape in the supermarket. One feature it does share with more conventional sales taxes is that it is regressive—it falls most heavily on those who spend the largest portion of their incomes, as opposed to those who invest the largest portion. Never a lover of the progressive federal income tax, where the greater amount of money you make the larger the percentage in taxes you pay, President Reagan may be drawn to a VAT, which lacks the progressivity feature altogether.

Other revenue-raising possibilities, aside from the VAT or a sales tax, might be some kind of surtax that would leave the present income tax basically intact but erect a new revenue-raising structure alongside it. There might even be a new tax of limited duration sold as an emergency deficit-reduction measure but designed to be phased out on the achievement of a certain level of deficit reduction.

Spending cuts offer even less room for presidential creativity, especially if Reagan asks no more than Secretary Caspar Weinberger's token cuts in the Pentagon budget. The $34 billion in spending reductions proposed by Reagan in December 1984 consisted of a package of reductions in such programs as child nutrition, veterans' pensions, farm price supports, and agricultural research. He proposed outright elimination of subsidies for Amtrak, small business administration loans, and loans by the Export-Import Bank. In order to avoid the accusation that such a budget is palpably unfair, Congress will go well beyond the White House and the Pentagon in limiting spending. Retirees will probably be spared cuts or deferrals in Social Security benefits, but Medicare may be fair game for the budget axe.[7]

The most novel idea for dealing with spending came from House Minority Whip Trent Lott, who proposed a freeze on all federal spending—a step that Senate Majority Leader Dole estimated as saving about $50 billion, but only if the freeze included defense spending and entitlement programs. Such an approach treats the worthy programs the same as the unworthy ones. However, it has the added virtue of simplicity—a characteristic now in vogue and one that prevents such ideas from being dismissed out of hand. The President hastened to endorse the freeze concept but insisted that the freeze not apply to the Pentagon budget.

On the revenue side, the odds are strongly against either a sweeping simplification of the tax system or of an increase in individual or corporate income taxes. The way out, if it is found, will be typically incremental and one that allows all parties a maximum of political cover, especially Republican senators up for reelection in 1986 (see page 129). Finding a plan with those characteristics that also closes the fiscal gap more than just a hair's breadth will be the preeminent political challenge of the second Reagan administration.

A NEW, NEW FEDERALISM?

When Ronald Reagan dusted off the ancient phrase "New Federalism" in 1981, many people thought that it was just another incarnation of a concept that had historically received much lip service but little real enthusiasm. Ironically, the phrase itself had been coined in the New Deal, which began the trend toward centralization of governmental powers at the federal level. It became an axiom of politics and public administration that powers once assumed by Washington could never again be recaptured by the states.

Ronald Reagan had been preaching for years that the federal government had reached, and exceeded, its capacity to absorb new governmental functions. This was neither startling nor original, but rather part of traditional Republican suspicion of big government. Eisenhower issued ritualistic condemnations of centralized power but left New Deal federal programs intact. Nixon hit upon the concept of revenue-sharing to reinvigorate the states and used block grants to localities to circumvent the federal bureaucracy. More basically, the first four Reagan years saw a profound change in the nature of federal-state relations.

By 1981 there was a climate of opinion congenial to Reagan's view that the federal government had become too intrusive and burdensome. There was broad support for the idea that states ought to assume more functions but an accompanying fear that Reagan could more easily strip the federal government of functions than hard-pressed states could assume them — a case of the ship deserting the sinking rats.

The states, however, proved more resilient than many had believed. They were particularly resourceful in reducing deficits created by reduced federal funds. Almost all states have constitutional requirements for balanced budgets and so enacted 113 tax increases between 1981 and 1984. Most impressive, however, was the resoluteness with which state spending was cut: While federal spending increased by 10 percent between 1981 and 1984, state spending actually declined by 2 percent.[8]

The future of federal-state relations in the second Reagan term will hinge, in large measure, on the final form of the President's efforts to close the fiscal deficit and simplify federal taxes. To mention but one implication of a "flat tax" approach there is the provision common to most flat tax plans that would disallow tax deductions at the federal level for state and local property taxes. States with relatively high taxes have much to lose under the simplified tax scheme; it is less clear who the winners are. In general terms, however, what seems abundantly clear is that, the fundamental expression of Reagan's views on federalism [will] be his tax and budget policy. A federal government that faces almost insuperable deficits . . . cannot realistically contemplate the absorption of expensive responsibilities from other levels of government. A national government that permanently indexes its income tax revenues will . . . have to struggle to justify each marginal expansion in federal functions. The restrictiveness of the federal budget constraint is likely to force state and local governments to retain at least their present allocation of service and financing responsibilities, and provides a recurring impetus to further devolution.[9]

It may be jarring or unsettling to think of it this way, but now and for some years to come the states and cities of this country will be very much on their own. We will see the gap in state services between the most affluent and least wealthy states widen, and we will likely see an unprecedented degree of heterogeneity in what the various states can or will provide to their citizens. The massive denationalization of governmental functions will accelerate during the second term. Only calamitous events will reverse that trend.

American Foreign Policy in the Second Reagan Term

Given his preoccupation with the domestic economy, one might wonder how President Reagan would have much time or energy to pursue a very active course in foreign policy. The first Reagan term, while hardly tranquil in the field of foreign relations, was not characterized by the degree of innovation and programmatic change that was seen domestically. Yet, if President Reagan had one conspicuous weak spot in the campaign of 1984, it was his unsettling truculence toward the Soviet Union and unabating hostility to the Sandinista government in Nicaragua. However, neither they nor his ill-starred deployment of U.S. Marines to Lebanon caused him much trouble with the voters.

Those looking for reassurance that Reagan will pursue a more low-keyed and centrist foreign policy in his second term could take heart in Secretary George Shultz's meeting with Soviet Foreign Minister Andrei Gromyko in Geneva. Despite Reagan's history as a hardliner, it must be said on his behalf that even a less ideologically rooted President would find it difficult to deal with a Soviet leadership that seems to be going through continuous transition. An enfeebled Konstantin Chernenko succeeded a Yuri Andropov who was, at best, a fleeting figure. One senior member of the ruling Politburo has suffered a stroke. This is hardly an environment for tackling major problems. The preoccupation on the part of the White House with the 1984 election did little to create conditions for discussion. But even before the election was over, the Soviets had signaled their recognition that Reagan was likely to be reelected, even though they remained scrupulously neutral.

There is probably good reason to believe that President Reagan really does want some kind of arms control with the Soviets. His proposal for "umbrella talks" on a broad range of strategic weapons showed a disposition to be bold, as did his "START" proposals to reduce nuclear weapons rather than simply limit them. In a news conference and an interview immediately after the election, the President asserted categorically that "we are going to devote whatever time it takes to [arms reductions] . . . I just happen to believe that we cannot go into another generation with the world living under those weapons. . . ." He also vowed, "We are prepared to go forward with the arms control talks, and I have to believe that the Soviet Union is going to join us. . . ."[10]

Talks there may be, but a significant arms control agreement in the second term seems unlikely. First, it will take time simply to rebuild a climate of trust and for the negotiators to get accustomed to negotiating again. A second obstacle is that important figures in the administration simply do not want an arms control agreement. Defense Secretary Weinberger does not want one and has thrown his support behind efforts to derail any agreement. Despite the desire of Secretary of State Shultz to crown his period of stewardship of American diplomacy with a major arms control agreement, his path will be strewn with snares placed there by Weinberger and his associates. Part of this feud over arms control is ideological, part of it is personal. But the greatest part of it is simply bureaucratic rivalry between departments with very different views of the world. If the President is indeed in earnest over arms control, he must discipline the warring factions.[11]

Barring any unforeseen snares in U.S.-Soviet relations, we are unlikely to hear another "evil empire" speech, although the President will never let go of the opportunity to hold Moscow's feet to the fire. Reagan is no less the ardent anticommunist that he was when savaging the USSR as "the focus of evil in the modern world," but he feels that his military buildup has placed the United States in a position where it can afford to be more conciliatory. The President seems satisfied with his ability to install Pershing II and Cruise missiles in Western Europe over local objections and threats by the Soviets to abandon arms control talks, to ride out a brief storm of protest by Western European peace groups and a walkout by the Soviets, and to find his hand strengthened considerably. The protests have, for the time being, abated; the Soviets and Americans have resumed arms talks, and the missiles are exactly where the administration wanted them to be. Having made his point, the President feels he can negotiate from a position of strength. That the Soviets are willing to talk, however, is not the same as having an agreement close at hand.

It should be pointed out that so far as the Soviet Union is concerned, it was Ronald Reagan's rhetoric rather than his policies that constituted a stark departure from previous administrations. Every postwar President had pursued the policy of containment of the Soviet Union. As Ronald Steel observed perceptively, Reagan "differs from Jimmy Carter only in trying to do it first class instead of on the cheap."[12] After the arms buildup and tough talk of his first four years, the President can be more relaxed in his relations with the USSR as he enters his second term.

The same degree of relaxation, however, is not evident in President Reagan's attitudes toward leftist governments and movements in the Western hemisphere. The most reliable guide to his likely course in Latin America is captured in a phrase used often by the chief executive, but never so passionately or emphatically as in his acceptance speech before the Republican national convention in Dallas: "In the four years before we took office, country after country fell under the Soviet yoke. Since 20 January 1981, not one inch of soil has fallen to the communists." What this means, quite simply, is that the pressure on the Marxist government of Nicaragua will be unremitting. Just how effective this pressure can be was seen in the invasion scare that took place shortly after the U.S. election. Intelligence reports, which turned out to be false, suggested that the Soviets had sent the Nicaraguans high-performance MIG fighters, and the alleged presence of these planes was labeled a threat by the State Department. So unnerved were the Nicaraguans by the report and the ominous interpretation placed on it by the Americans that they began to prepare for an invasion. In doing so, they weakened an already crippled economy by diverting manpower and resources to the army and away from the civilian sector.

We can confidently expect more invasion scares and more efforts to undercut the Sandinistas. It does not matter a great deal whether the U.S.-supported government in neighboring El Salvador comes to terms with its own leftist rebels. The administration is also not particularly in earnest about the Contadora negotiations to end bloodshed in Central America. As James Chace recently observed, "By so quickly dismissing Nicaragua's willingness to sign the [Contadora] treaty, the Reagan administration exposed what appears to be its true position—a refusal to accept the Sandinistas in power no matter what security guarantees they might be willing to provide."[13]

Efforts by President Reagan to have a showdown with Nicaragua might run afoul of the new lineup of committee chairmen in the Republican-controlled Senate where he once enjoyed strong support. The new chairman of the Senate Intelligence Committee, Senator Dave Durenberger of Minnesota, is opposed to the use of the CIA against the Sandinistas. Barry Goldwater, the new chairman of the Armed Services Committee, is skeptical of secret aid to the Nicaraguan rebels, but is said to feel Central America is the one place in the world where the dispatch of U.S. troops would be warranted. Richard Lugar, new chairman of the Foreign Relations Committee, seems to believe that the use of force against Nicaragua should be ruled out unless it is clear that the country has become a Soviet base. In terms of covert aid, at least, it appears that further official U.S. help for the anti-Sandinista rebels looks bleak.

A seriously weakened Sandinista government might succumb to serious American military pressure, but no one in Washington has given any indication of what kind of government would replace the Sandinistas. This is at least one symptom of a policy that has not been very clearly thought out and seems to reflect a position based more upon sheer animus than on reasoned opposition. Having gone far in the direction of dismantling the New Deal, the second Reagan administration probably has in mind the same fate for the Good Neighbor Policy.

It there was a common denominator in the domestic and foreign policies of the first Reagan administration, it was luck. As the economy benefited adventitiously from an oil glut and good growing weather for farmers, so did Mr. Reagan's foreign policy profit from matters over which he had little control.

The Middle East provides the best example of the President's good fortune. He managed with no serious political damage to extricate the American forces from a disastrous involvement in Lebanon. The Palestine Liberation Organization, which the White House had regarded as a major irritant in the region, split apart. Diplomatic relations were reestablished with Iraq, after an interval of 17 years, and the so-called moderate group of Arab states that includes Egypt, Jordan, and the Persian Gulf states seemed more self-confident and cohesive. These three developments occurred with minimal American involvement. The two radical states of the region — Libya and Iran — seemed increasingly isolated and frustrated, and Syria seemed to have taken a moderate turn.

The brightness of the international picture is particularly impressive for the fact that the United States really has no comprehensive national security policy other than a massive military buildup, no Middle East policy worthy of the name, and no hemispheric policy other than a determined opposition to leftist movements and regimes. The response to acts of international terrorism has typically been a pugnacious threat followed by inaction. Luck can take the United States so far, but as Bret Harte reminded us, "The only thing sure about luck is that it will change."

There are some leading international candidates for areas where American luck may go sour. In our own hemisphere is Chile, the grim exception to the rule of resurgent democracy in South America. Chilled by memories of a leftist government deposed by a military coup in 1971, the United States has given uncritical support to General Pinochet. Democratic alternatives to the military government may erode as the political opposition to the general becomes radicalized. We may then be faced with the self-fulfilling prophecy that the choice all along was between the military and the extreme leftists. A parallel to Chile exists in the Philippines where a strong communist insurgent movement waits for the democratic opposition to President Ferdinand Marcos to fail.

A real prospect for constructive developments does exist in the negotiations over the fate of Namibia (South-West Africa). There, Assistant Secretary of State Chester Crocker has been acting as a middleman in negotiations between Namibia's current ruler, the Republic of South Africa, and Angola, the country that has been the haven for rebels who want independence from South Africa. The complicating factor has been the presence of Cuban troops who have been helping the Marxist Angolan government combat its own internal opposition.

Progress in those negotiations will probably take place when South Africa realizes that the Reagan administration's time is running out and that no successor would be as friendly to that government.

While it is better to be lucky than hapless in international politics, good fortune is no substitute for a clear vision of the world to guide diplomacy. This the Reagan administration has lacked. The consequences of that absence of a guiding vision were obvious in the first Reagan term, most notably in the almost casual deployment of those ill-fated marines to Lebanon. What saved the situation there, paradoxically, was the blithe and breezy reationale for withdrawing them. The spontaneous, ad hoc, and sometimes even petulant reactions of the first four Reagan years to developments in the world seem likely to persist. They will persist because of personal, bureaucratic, and ideological feuds that the easygoing President is unwilling or unable to quell.

This is a pattern that developed in the first administration, and it is one that is likely to intensify in the second as preoccupation grows as to the nature of the world after Reagan. Lame-duck Presidents—even the most engaging and energetic ones—lose their ability to control events as their ability to mete out future rewards and punishments begins to expire. Accordingly, much of what President Reagan hopes to accomplish will be shaped by the opposition party and, of equal significance, the forces now contending for influence within the Reagan administration.

Lying in Wait: The Democrats

If there is one thing that the President cannot count upon in his efforts to close the fiscal gap is that the Democrats in Congress will pull his chestnuts out of the fire. Congressional Democrats believed that they acted responsibly in helping to pass the 1984 tax bill during the 98th Congress that provided for tax increases of $50 billion and budget cuts of $13 billion and received for their troubles the withering partisan scorn of the President. His repeated paraphrase of Will Rogers—that they never met a tax they didn't like, or hike—rankled Democrats who went out on a limb for President Reagan. They were stung by what they considered his demagoguery over the shutdown of the federal government on 4 October 1984. Reagan blamed House Democrats for the problem because of their failure to pass appropriations bills, while it was the Republican-controlled Senate that should properly have shouldered a greater share of the blame. The Democrats were aggrieved when the President refused to compromise on the military spending portion of the federal budgets for a period of six months after the House had passed the document. His voice dripping with scorn, Majority Leader Jim Wright said of the President, "I don't know whether he deliberately mistates the facts or he just does not know any better," while Speaker O'Neill accused Reagan of "embarrassing his office by using the presidency to engage in a Hollywood publicity stunt."[14]

During the 98th Congress, House Democrats fought the President on aid to the Contras in Nicaragua and frustrated his efforts to fund the MX missile. Democrats also managed to defeat an administration bill to permit organized prayer in the nation's public schools. Bad blood was created when the President sought to embarrass Democrats over his anticrime bill, and the House Democrats tried some public humiliation of their own when they passed a bill requiring the President to submit a balanced budget.

The Democrats in the House to whom Mr. Reagan most often appealed in his first term—the group of conservatives known as the "boll weevils"—are not so likely to be reliable allies in the 99th Congress. Even before the November 1984 election in which Republicans gained a disappointing 14 House seats, boll weevil chairman Charles W. Stenholm (D-Texas) was predicting that 1985 would be a very contentious legislative year. He added, somewhat ominously, that he foresaw no honeymoon period for Mr. Reagan.[15]

One thing that experience has taught both Democrats and Republicans is that the deficit as an issue is not one that has been very successful in election campaigns. For years, Republicans railed against deficits run up by Democratic Presidents and got the backs of the voters' hands for their fiscal prudence. Walter Mondale pounded away on the issue in 1984, and made dire predictions about the future effect of the deficit, and his warnings were discounted. Now Reagan must make the case to Congress—Republicans and Democrats alike—that some calamity is in prospect without action on the deficit, yet it is likely that few senators or members of Congress will hear anything from their constituents on the subject until some very tangible by-product of the deficit begins to affect their lives. People feel the shock of unemployment when they discover the pink slip in their pay envelopes. They experience inflation when there is too much of the month left over after the paycheck has been spent. The deficit is nothing more than an abstraction until its effects begin to have their impact on people, and it will not begin to move Congress in anything like a unified direction until members begin to hear the cries of outraged constituents.

Congress does little of importance in the absence of a consensus. The welter of November and December surprises that emanated from the Treasury Department and the Office of Management and Budget will take some time to be digested by Congress. Once digested, however, it will take considerably more time for a plan of action to emerge. Congress will not be stampeded into action on the deficit or any other matter by the gloomy forecasts of economists or the eloquent pleas of cabinet officers unless Hannibal is truly at the gates. Refusal to be stampeded in the absence of demonstrable danger is a conviction shared by both parties in Congress. If the President finds that his appeals for cooperation evoke no immediate response in once-burned moderate-to-liberal Democrats and are treated standoffishly by boll weevils, may he then assume that his own partisans in Congress will hark eagerly to this most popular of Republican Presidents in a quarter century? Here, too, the prospects look far from bright.

The Prags vs. the Wingers

Many observers predicted that the radical right wing within his own party would be a source of trouble for President Reagan in his first term. That threat never materialized. After issuing a number of threats to George Bush to comport himself in proper conservative style, the ultraconservatives were either coopted or else contented themselves with ineffectual sniping at White House Chief of Staff James A. Baker III, the leading pragmatist, or "prag" in the White House. The Republican right wing, or "wingers" as they are sometimes called by the White House staff, were in no position to challenge Reagan at the zenith of his influence. They concentrated their fire on members of his staff or on Republicans in Congress, who seemed in danger of straying toward the center. So, a leading conservative fund raiser, Richard A. Viguerie, called on Illinois Republicans to support a Libertarian for the Senate over Charles H. Percy. Also, he accused James Baker of masterminding one of the "all-time greatest blunders in American politics" by emphasizing Reagan's reelection to the virtual exclusion of Republican congressional candidates.[16] "Populist" conservatives, as members of the new right-wing style themselves, were criticizing House Republican Floor Leader Robert Michel for being too cozy with Speaker Tip O'Neill.

The zealots of the populist right tend to be relatively junior Republican House members, such as Robert S. Walker of Pennsylvania, Vin Weber of Minnesota, and Newt Gingrich of Georgia. The latter attained a reputation for cheekiness unparalleled even in Congress by condescendingly referring to President Reagan as "a transitional figure." These callow but vocal House members threaten President Reagan less than their own leadership in Congress. Indeed, the second Reagan term may see a growing split between "wingers" and "prags" in Congress that may prevent any repetition of the remarkable party unity among congressional Republicans that characterized the early part of the first term.

The election of Robert Dole to the post of Senate Majority Leader and Alan K. Simpson as Majority Whip would, by themselves, be seen as signal victories for Republican pragmatists. The moderates, however, also found themselves in control of strategic committees. The only identifiable right-wing senators in leadership posts in the Senate are Jesse Helms of North Carolina on Agriculture and James A. McClure of Idaho on Energy. Even Barry Goldwater is too free a spirit to be counted a consistent ultraconservative stalwart.

The pragmatists in Congress who, on the whole, gave very strong support to the President's legislative agenda in the first term may be the people he calls on to keep his conservative program in trim during the second. The cooperation between White House pragmatists and their counterparts on Capitol Hill may be a red flag to the populist conservatives but, as A. James Reichley has noted, "The trick is to keep the program sufficiently wide and inclusive to maintain general social harmony and achieve enduring political success."[17]

The one group of Reagan followers who actually fared the worst in terms of tangible legislative achievement during the first term was the religious right. Mr. Reagan tempted them with large helpings of rhetorical red meat but after he was finished, their plates were essentially empty. They received no school prayer, no significant new limitations on abortion, or no more than a chain of teenage chastity centers and a cutoff of federal aid on American population programs overseas that recommend or perform abortions. It is entirely possible that the preachers will present their due bill in the second term. If the inexorable passage of years takes its toll on the U.S. Supreme Court, they may well have their payoff.

The legislative agenda of the religious right may fare even more poorly in the second term, but if the fundamentalists were given several new justices of the likes of Associate Justice Sandra Day O'Connor, they might then mark the bill "paid." Table 6.1 on page 148 lists the justices of the U.S. Supreme Court along with their date of birth and the names of the Presidents who nominated them.

TABLE 6.1

THE UNITED STATES SUPREME COURT

Justice	Year of birth	Nominated by President
Warren Earl Burger	1907	Nixon
William J. Brennan, Jr.	1906	Eisenhower
Byron R. White	1917	Kennedy
Thurgood Marshall	1908	Johnson
Harry A. Blackmun	1908	Nixon
Lewis F. Powell, Jr.	1907	Nixon
William H. Rehnquist	1924	Nixon
John Paul Stevens	1920	Ford
Sandra Day O'Connor	1930	Reagan

With five justices nearing the age of eighty, death or retirement might present Mr. Reagan with the broadest opportunity to shape the Court since the last twice-elected President, Richard M. Nixon. While every justice except Thurgood Marshall took his seat on the Court during the first term of the President who nominated him or her, the average age of the members of the tribunal is slightly more than seventy. Figuring the survival odds on a President who himself takes office at the age of seventy-four is difficult enough. Forecasting the mark that he will leave on the high court is even more conjectural. One thing is certain, however, and that is whatever opportunities he has will be exercised with an eye toward placing a conservative imprint on major legal decisions for many years to come. The President may be disinclined or unable to deliver socially conservative public policy to his fundamentalist supporters, but if he can shape the Supreme Court, he will leave them a bequest of enduring value.

The Reagan Cabinet

Ronald Reagan never seriously challenged Franklin Pierce's record for stability in a presidential cabinet. Pierce left office in 1857 with the same cabinet he appointed in 1853. There was considerable reshuffling of Reagan's principal advisers shortly after the election. The policy implications of these changes are probably less significant than simple restlessness. Jobs lose their challenge, opportunities beckon to the private sector, and even access to the President loses its luster.

Reagan's use of the cabinet is a fairly accurate reflection of his attitude toward the federal government: The parts of it he considers important he uses; the parts he considers superfluous he ignores. If you believe, as the President does, that the core responsibilities of the federal government are national defense, macroeconomic concerns, and diplomacy, you rely heavily on the secretaries of Defense, State, and Treasury and, of course, your budget director. The Reagan second term will again be government in 3-D: *Defense, Diplomacy,* and *Deficit.*

The mediocrity of the rest of the Reagan cabinet is of little consequence to him because he basically does not believe that what their cabinet departments do is very important and is inclined to let them languish in what Grover Cleveland called "innocuous desuetude." So if Judge Pierce (Housing) resigns in disgust or John Block (Agriculture) returns to the family farm, Ronald Reagan will spend no sleepless nights. Even Malcolm Baldrige, who was expected to play a prominent role in the Reagan cabinet, has found that the President prefers to foster business through the tax laws than through the kinds of constituency services that his Commerce department provides.

The two outcast departments created during the Carter years—Energy and Education—will probably not even receive a decent Christian burial because that might involve Reagan in a battle he would just as soon avoid. His replacement for Ambassador Jeane Kirkpatrick at the UN, Vernon Walters, is capable of administering a sound verbal thrashing to the Soviets when the occasion warrants it, and he can hold the Third World's feet to the fire. Reagan reposes little faith in the UN as a peacekeeping body.

The Man with the Fantastic Credentials: George Herbert Walker Bush

The turn-of-the century sage of Archey Road, Mr. Dooley, said of the Vice-President, "Every morning it is his business to call at the White House and inquire after the President's health. When told that the President was never better he gives three cheers and departs with a heavy heart."[18] Given the robust good health of President Reagan, this fate probably awaits George Bush. History has not been kind to sitting Vice-Presidents who seek the presidency; only three have ever been elected to the highest office after completing their vice-presidential terms. The last serving Vice-President to win the presidency in an election was Martin Van Buren in 1836, although 12 have ascended to the presidency as a result of the death of the chief executive.

One source of the political difficulties faced by Vice-Presidents is that they are sometimes chosen because they possess personal characteristics different from those of the head of the ticket. A presidential candidate who is a westerner may want an easterner, and a Protestant might want to balance the ticket with a Catholic. At other times they are chosen because they represent a defeated wing of the party that needs to be placated. Occasionally, people are placed on the ticket as a gesture of reassurance to a group of voters that has reservations about the presidential candidate. In any case, their different traits can cause them political problems.

Bush's personal characteristics are very close to Reagan's, and the conservative wing of the party is so dominant that Bush's placement on the ticket in 1980 cannot be seen as an effort to mollify the party's anemic liberal wing. We must look to the third rationale for the presence of Bush on the ticket in 1980. He was seen as a reassuring "establishment" figure to offset the uncertainty of the doctrinaire former actor who headed the ticket. This very comforting respectability is also the most imposing barrier to his aspiration to be Ronald Reagan's successor in 1988. Indeed, in light of the antipathy that conservatives harbor toward him, it would be difficult to imagine George Bush's receiving a Republican presidential nomination. One is tempted to say that George Bush will be President of the United States only if Ronald Reagan dies in office. And even if that melancholy event should take place, Bush's efforts to win a full four years on his own will be fought every step of the way by his party's right wing. They will never be reconciled to his leadership of the party or country.

This is ironic in view of the manner in which the Vice-President conducted himself in the first term and during the campaign of 1984. Bush displayed the zeal of a born-again Reaganite, even to the extent that he appeared almost fawning and slavish at times. Aside from one public disagreement over abortion, it was impossible to see where he and the President differed on any important policy. But despite Bush's impeccable fidelity, the party's right wing regards him as a counterfeit conservative who will desert Reagan's principles at the first occasion upon assuming the presidency.

The ill-concealed animus of the Republican right for George Bush casts a pall on the long-term prospects of the party. It suggests an equally chilly reception for Howard Baker, who has left the Senate to dwell in the bosom of the Washington establishment while he bides his time until 1988.

There are perhaps two individuals who would be seen by conservatives as legitimate guardians of the Reagan flame: Representative Jack Kemp of New York and Senator Jesse Helms of North Carolina. Kemp may be a sufficiently ecumenical figure, who would also gain acceptance by party moderates, but a serious bid by Helms would energize the party's somnolent moderate and liberal wings.

In many ways Bush would be the ideal successor to Reagan—a Republican of moderate stripe who served loyally in a conservative administration. It is not just loyalty that Bush would bring to the presidency but a wealth of experience in a half-dozen major governmental posts before 1980 and as a major supporting player in the first Reagan administration. Bush was instrumental in selling our NATO allies on the stationing of Pershing II and Cruise missiles on their soil and in heading the task force on red tape and paperwork. He has been a peripatetic Vice-President who has visited nearly 60 countries. And, unlike his boss, he has held talks with Konstantin Chernenko and his predecessor.

If Bush did not evoke such hostile reactions from within his own party, his prominent presence in a second Reagan administration would be a perfect launching pad for the presidency. As matters stand, however, he will have to fight for his party's nomination even from within the Oval Office itself.

Ronald Reagan: A Man and His Mission

Defying the conventional wisdom of generations of political scientists and journalists who proclaimed that an ideologue could win a major party nomination but not the presidency, Ronald Reagan did both in 1980 and duplicated the feat in 1984. President Reagan must be mindful of the possibility that his successor may not worship with such fervor at the conservative altar. This realization would surely prompt him not merely to consolidate the Reagan revolution but, simultaneously, to spread and entrench it and to ensure that it is not easily undone.

In the aftermath of the 1984 election, conservatives in and out of government moved with a sense of purpose to shape and influence that most visible and refractory symbol of big government—the federal bureaucracy. One conservative group, the Leadership Institute, is actually training "a whole new generation of conservative activists" with the purpose, literally, of infiltrating them into the bureaucracy to dilute what many conservatives see as the liberal bias of the federal civil service. Political appointees in the agencies are leaving no doubt in the minds of the bureaucrats they command that they must support the President's programs.[19]

What we are likely to see, then, is an accelerated effort on the part of conservatives at the policy levels of government to tame the federal bureaucracy and make it conform to a conservative agenda. Some of the more passionate conservatives would like to so cripple and discredit the federal bureaucracy that people can no longer turn automatically to Washington for help. Certainly, Reagan's proposal to cut executive branch salaries by 5 percent in 1985 would, if adopted by Congress, make the bureaucracy a less attractive place for able people to work. We can assume that the efforts to shrink and domesticate the bureaucracy have the President's blessings.

As in the first term, Reagan will be used selectively to lobby on television for the major parts of the administration's economic programs. It is an open

TABLE 6.2

Position	Name	Age	Residence
President	Ronald W. Reagan	73	California
Vice-President	George W. Bush	60	Texas
Secretary of State	George P. Shultz	65	California
Secretary of Defense	Caspar W. Weinberger	67	California
Secretary of the Treasury	James A. Baker III	54	Texas
Attorney-General	Edwin Meese III	59	California
Secretary of the Interior	Donald P. Hodel	50	Oregon
Secretary of Agriculture	John R. Block	49	Illinois
Secretary of Commerce	Malcolm Baldrige	62	Connecticut
Secretary of Education	William J. Bennett	42	District of Columbia
Secretary of Health and Human Services	Margaret M. Heckler	54	Massachusetts
Secretary of Labor	Raymond J. Donovan	54	New Jersey
Secretary of Housing and Urban Development	Samuel R. Pierce	62	New York
Secretary of Transportation	Elizabeth H. Dole	49	Kansas
Secretary of Energy	John S. Harrington	45	California
Director, Office of Management and Budget	David A. Stockman	38	Michigan
Ambassador to the UN	Vernon A. Walters	68	Florida
Special Assistant to the President for National Security Affairs	Robert C. McFarlane	48	Maryland
Director of Central Intelligence	William J. Casey	71	New York

THE REAGAN ADMINISTRATION

Religion	Previous Experience	Education
Christian Church	Governor of California	B.S., Eureka College
Episcopalian	Oilman; Congressman; Chairman, Republican National Committee; Ambassador to United Nations; Director, CIA	B.A., Yale
Episcopalian	Professor, industrial relations; Director, OMB; Secretary of Treasury	B.A., Princeton; Ph.D., MIT
Episcopalian	State legislator; Republican state chairman; Chairman, FTC; Director, OMB; Secretary of HEW	B.A., Harvard
Protestant	White House Chief of Staff	B.A., Princeton; LL.B., Texas
Lutheran	Counselor to President	A.B., Yale; J.D., Berkeley
Lutheran	Administrator, Bonneville Power Authority; Under-Secretary, Interior	B.A., Harvard; J.D., Oregon
Lutheran	Farmer; Director, Illinois Department of Agriculture	B.S., U.S. Military Academy
Congregational	Business executive; Republican state finance chairman	B.A., Yale
Roman Catholic	Chairman, National Endowment for the Humanities	B.A., Williams; Ph.D., Texas; LL.B., Harvard
Roman Catholic	Member of Congress	B.A., Albertus Magnus; LL.B., Boston College
Roman Catholic	Republican fundraiser; Construction company executive	B.A., Notre Dame Seminary, New Orleans
Methodist	Judge; General Counsel to U.S. Treasury	A.B., LL.B., Cornell
Methodist	Member, FTC; Assistant to President for Public Liaison	B.A., Duke; M.Ed., LL.B., Harvard
Protestant	Assistant Secretary, Energy; White House Personnel Director	B.A., Stanford; LL.B., Hastings College
Methodist	Member of Congress	B.A., Michigan State
Roman Catholic	Ambassador-at-large; Deputy Director, CIA; General, U.S. Army	St. Louis Gonzaga University (Paris); Stonyhurst College (England)
Protestant	Officer, U.S. Marine Corps; Military Assistant to Henry Kissinger	B.S., U.S. Naval Academy; M.S., Institut des Hautes Etudes, Geneva
Roman Catholic	Attorney; Chairman, SEC; Under-Secretary of State	B.A., Fordham; LL.B., St. John's, New York

question whether he can be used to as good effect in 1985 and beyond as in 1981, when he performed brilliantly on behalf of his tax and budget cuts. Without his resident media genius, Michael Deaver, the selling of Reagan's programs falls into less-experienced hands. As successor to the smooth and diplomatic James Baker in the post of Chief of Staff is the cantankerous and free-wheeling former Treasury Secretary, Donald T. Regan, who will run a tighter but possibly more rigid and timid group of personal advisers.

While many people tend to equate Reagan with the idol of his liberal days, Franklin Delano Roosevelt, Reagan, in personality, actually resembles more William McKinley, of whom Margaret Leech wrote:

> [He] was more than popular—and he was beloved. Scores of his associates were his friends, and many of them held him in worshipful admiration. Even his political opponents were attracted by the peculiar sweetness of his personality. . . .

But, at the same time, "He had few intellectual resources. . . . In literature and music he looked for an obvious sentimental, patriotic or religious content."[20]

Comparing President Reagan to President McKinley is not an unflattering gesture. McKinley was the perfect instrument of one of the best political minds of the era, Mark Hanna, as Mr. Reagan was used to exquisite advantage by a surpassingly gifted James Baker. McKinley, we should recall, presided over one of the few great partisan realignments in American politics. Mr. Reagan may also have the opportunity to look upon the elections of 1980 and 1984 as a hinge of history, but whether these elections are earthquakes or just mudslides will depend upon his performance.

As governor of California and as President, Ronald Reagan went forth to do political battle clad in the chain mail of a crusader and bearing aloft the banner of sacred conservative principles. Taking the high road enabled Reagan to portray his adversaries as wicked, sleazy, or both. The starkness and acerbity of some of his depictions of his foes are somewhat startling in a man universally praised for his decency. Those who attempted to play roughly with Reagan, however, found that most Americans rejected attempts to portray him in dismal hues.

THE REAGAN LEGACY AND A LOOK AHEAD

If Ronald Reagan were to pass from the scene today and be judged solely by the accomplishments of his first term, he would be recorded as one of our more successful Presidents. By his own lights and by the vision that he brought to the office in January 1981, Ronald Reagan can claim a niche in that compact pantheon of Presidents who achieved more or less what they set out to accomplish. This was true of Roosevelt in 1936, but it was also true of Nixon in 1972.

Having sought and won a second term, Reagan puts on the line a track record of success, and he wagers that the next four years will, at the least, not vitiate the accomplishments of the first four. One may aspire to crown the achievements of the first term with greater accomplishments in the second. The ebbing influence of a President at the end of his constitutional cycle does not point in that direction.

President Reagan will not disgrace himself in the manner of Richard Nixon; he has too much self-confidence and integrity. The principal peril that faces him is not scandal so much as it is a kind of disarray—a sort of collective undiscipline that comes when too many people are calculating future political options and maneuvering themselves into advantageous positions. The greatest accomplishments, then, are likely to be in consolidation rather than in innovation; in shoring up rather in than pushing forward.

But given the enormity of the changes that he has wrought, Ronald Reagan can take comfort in the fact that any revolution that hopes to endure must pass through this indispensable phase.

NOTES

1. Gerald M. Pomper, ed., *The Election of 1980* (Chatham, N.J.: Chatham House, 1981), 85-89; and Fred I. Greenstein, ed., *The Reagan Presidency* (Baltimore: Johns Hopkins University Press, 1983), 15-16.
2. *Wall Street Journal,* 27 April 1984.
3. See Adam Clymer, "Long-Range Hope for Republicans Is Found in Poll," *New York Times,* 11 November 1984.
4. Martin Feldstein and Kathleen Feldstein, "Why Worry about the Deficits?" *Washington Post,* 30 September 1984.
5. Leonard Silk, "Deficit's Impact on the Campaign," *New York Times,* 12 October 1984.
6. Ann Reilly, "Business Will Bear the Brunt," *Fortune* 110 (26 November 1984): 30.
7. Steven R. Weisman, "Back to Reality, Stockman's Data Collide with Boss's Promises," *New York Times,* 18 November 1984.
8. *Time,* 17 December 1984.
9. George E. Peterson, "Federalism and the States: An Experiment in Decentralization," in *The Reagan Record,* ed. John L. Palmer and Isabel V. Sawhill (Cambridge: Ballinger, 1984), 258.
10. *Time,* 19 November 1984; and "Transcript of President's News Conference on Foreign and Domestic Issues," *New York Times,* 8 November 1984.
11. Robert G. Kaiser, "Arms Control? Probably Not," *Washington Post,* 25 November 1984; and Henry A. Kissinger, "Ronald Reagan's Great Opportunity," *Washington Post,* 20 November 1984.
12. Ronald Steel, "Minding Our Business," *Vanity Fair,* March 1983, 238.
13. James Chace, "In Search of a Central American Policy," *New York Times Magazine,* 25 November 1984, 62.

14. David Hoffman and Keith B. Richburg, "Government Shut Down by Reagan," *Washington Post,* 5 October 1984.

15. Steven Pressman, "President's Leadership Style and Split in GOP Ranks Are Keys to Second-Term Success," *Congressional Quarterly Weekly Report* 42 (27 October 1984): 2784.

16. Richard A. Viguerie, "Reagan's Campaign Double-Crossed the GOP," *New York Times,* 8 November 1984.

17. A. James Reichley, "The Reagan Coalition," *Brookings Review,* Winter 1982, 9.

18. *Dissertations by Mr. Dooley* (New York: Harper & Bros., 1906), 118.

19. See Robert Pear, "Reading, Writing, Roping Liberals," *New York Times,* 4 December 1984; and Jane Mayer, "New Right Tends a New Generation," *Wall Street Journal,* 4 December 1984.

20. Margaret Leech, *In the Days of McKinley* (New York: Harper & Bros., 1959), 23-24.

7

The Meaning of the Election

WILSON CAREY MCWILLIAMS

The election of 1984 was not a season for heroes; it was won by summer soldiers and sunshine patriots. Mr. Reagan was pleased to have it so; repeatedly, his campaign assured Americans that the long night of crisis was over, giving way to a new morning. Reagan proclaimed that America is "back," the republic of our fonder memories, affluent and powerful, a "shining city" and an Opportunity Society, built of alabaster and free from tears.

American voters recognized the hyperbole in the President's rhetoric. They knew that some Americans are poor—in fact, there are more poor people in every section of the country than there were when Ronald Reagan took office—and a good many Americans worried, fitfully, about the "fairness" of the President's policies, but the great majority did not allow such concerns to be decisive. Unemployment, the great Democratic issue, worried voters more than inflation, but relatively few Americans were disturbed about either. Ronald Reagan was credited with curing inflation and restoring a modest economic confidence, allowing Americans to anticipate well-being even if they did not enjoy it. For many voters, foreign affairs were the area of greatest concern, but the country was at peace, and the things Americans feared, however troubling in prospect, were at least not at hand.[1]

Most Americans knew, or suspected, that the good times would not always be with us.[2] For a considerable number, in fact, the Reagan recovery probably represented not springtime but Indian summer. Nevertheless, the Americans who gave Ronald Reagan his great victory wanted at least a respite from the politics of crisis and thought they could expect it. Immediately after the election, when the President's forecasts turned bleak and the administration began to speak of tightening belts, Congressman Newt Gingrich (R-Georgia), a leader of the New Right, observed that "the American people have to feel a little like they thought they were walking into the office of a cruise ship and found out they were in a cancer clinic." Conservative Senator James McClure (R-Idaho), summed it up: "There is nothing you can read in the election that says the American people are ready for sacrifice."[3]

There is more than self-interest in the mood of the majority. Tocqueville wrote that American democracy could endure political conflict and the ordeal of change because of the security Americans found in social and moral life. The health of democracy presumes, Tocqueville declared, that moral ties grow stronger as political bonds are relaxed; in America, the political world was "agitated, uncertain and disputed," but the moral world was "classed, adapted, directed and foreseen."[4] The America Tocqueville was describing, of course, was simpler and more uniform, a republic by, if not only for, Protestant white Anglo-Saxons. Uneasily, the United States has been growing more pluralistic ever since. Nevertheless, Americans could rely, until recently, on certain social and moral decencies as stable standards of right, the sources of direction and meaning. "Our common difficulties," Franklin Roosevelt declared in 1933, "concern, thank God, only material things."[5]

No more: Americans are troubled by social disorganization and moral *dissensus*. The spiritual foundations of the New Deal are at least as eroded as its politics. In 1984, Americans embraced material prosperity, hoping that *it* would provide the basis for social and moral renewal. Like every presidential contest since 1972, the election of 1984 involved a modest mandate to rebuild the private foundations of public life. Some of Ronald Reagan's militant supporters favored an outright counterrevolution to overthrow the legacy of the '60s, if not the New Deal. More generally, however, Americans were concerned to recover some sense of social and moral order without surrendering any of their material gains or their individual liberties. The majority of Americans are ambivalent, unready to make great social and moral commitments. In the moral and social as well as in the economic world, Americans wanted a moment of relaxation, and Ronald Reagan, campaigning as "Dr. Feelgood," knew better than to prescribe any bitter medicine.

Reagan's victory was so one-sided as to suggest a shift in the balance and composition of American political parties, but here, too, Americans were hesitant. The Republican presidential coalition does seem to have acquired considerable stability, and in some locales—especially in the South and among younger voters—there were shifts away from the Democrats. But the Democrats held the House and gained in the Senate. The theory of critical elections presumes that our party loyalties and our political identities are reasonably coherent, consistent, and stable; in this respect, the theory may have become obsolete.[6] The election of 1984 does not indicate a stable change of allegiance so much as the unsettling, for a considerable number of Americans, of *all* political allegiances, a weakening of the bonds between voters and the political system. A new political era is coming to birth, but not necessarily an attractive or a happy one.[7]

Reagan and the Politics of the Electronic Age

The personality and presidency of Ronald Reagan dominate the politics of the '80s. Reagan has been a more skillful and successful President than most of us expected. In the role of Chief of State, Reagan has been the ablest President since Kennedy, carrying out the ceremonial functions of the presidency with considerable grace. He has proved, as we are often reminded, to be a "great communicator," a master of the public presidency in the media age.

From the standpoint of popularity, the Reagan administration had matchless timing. Its worst years were its first, and the very depth of the early recession made the recovery seem even brighter. Jimmy Carter probably finished off his chances for reelection by setting out, in an election year, to cure inflation by means of draconian monetarism; Reagan's administration avoided hard decisions in 1984, until the election was over. He offered us the easy life, not blood and toil, and the results speak for themselves.

Yet Reagan's landslide victory was a mixed blessing for his party. Reagan ran as a moderate candidate, a fact that helped to move the Republicans—in popular perception—closer to the center of American politics. But Reagan virtually portrayed himself as a mainstream Democrat: At the Republican convention, the band played the New Deal anthem, "Happy Days Are Here Again"; Reagan quoted Roosevelt, Truman, and Kennedy to the exclusion of Republicans; his campaign even traveled on Truman's whistle-stop train.

Reagan went beyond simple symbols: He embraced programs and policies that, until recently, were considered left of center; he justified mountainous deficits, pledged not to cut present or future entitlements to Social Security, and voiced support for Medicare.[8] It helped that Walter Mondale, encumbered by honor and honesty, was forced to the fiscal right. Mondale felt compelled to offer a plan for reducing the deficit, and even with a tax increase, he was barely able to hold the line on social programs. Mondale had no room for exciting new programs and policies; the deficit, and his attempts to combat it, would have made Mondale seem uninspiring even if he had the tongue of angels.[9]

Moreover, it fell to Mondale to emphasize the limits of federal power on social issues and in foreign policy. The combination of fiscal responsibility and political restraint made Mondale sound vaguely like an old-line Taft Republican.[10] That fact probably enhanced Mondale's appeal to Anderson Republicans, but those voters are too few in number to add more than moral tone. With Walter Mondale's assistance, Ronald Reagan blurred the old lines.

At the same time, the Republican party became even more dominated by its conservative wing. At the Republican convention, the key victories were won by the right; during the campaign, Republican moderates suffered notable defeats—Elliot Richardson, for example, lost a senatorial primary in Massachusetts, and Charles Percy was denied reelection—while the most visible champion of the right, Jesse Helms, survived. The Republicans, as a party, were bent on drawing the line between left and right, though, admittedly, a line of a new sort.

The President's strategists smoothly ditched his party. Reagan made campaign appearances to support Republican candidates, especially at the end, but this formal support could not eliminate the disparity between the style of the President's campaign and the stance of Republican candidates. Ronald Reagan, in other words, gave the voters no real reason—much less a sense of urgency—to defeat Democratic candidates for Congress. "Why would somebody vote for President Reagan and then vote for John Kerry?" asked Ray Shamie, the defeated Republican nominee for the Senate in Massachusetts. "It doesn't make any sense."[11] But a great deal of Mr. Reagan's campaign was devoted to telling voters, implicitly, that it did make *sense,* even if it was not the choice the President would *prefer.* Had his strategists charted a more partisan campaign, Reagan might have lost another half dozen states, but he might also have won a working majority in Congress. In the end, the public voted for Ronald Reagan for the same reason that it voted the Democrats back into control of the House and strengthened their position in the Senate: It desires no great change.[12]

All through the campaign, the Democrats were daunted by Reagan's mastery of television, as they had been ever since he took office. The President reads a speech extremely well, and his humor—especially, his gift for good-spirited self-deprecation—covers many faults. Even the President's intellectual limitations help: Nixon was too shrewd not to *know* when he was being evasive, distorting the facts or contradicting some earlier position, and it showed; Reagan reads his lines innocently and with evident sincerity. The Democratic candidates were not in Reagan's league; only Jesse Jackson had forensic talent, and Jackson's rhetoric is suited more to the pulpit than the screen.

The Democrats' disdvantage, however, was due only in part to the idiosyncrasies of their candidates; it has something to do with their party. The Democratic party in 1984 was still rooted in an older political science and political practice, the pluralistic doctrine that formed the basis of "interest group liberalism."[13] Too many of the leaders of the party—and most notably, its intellectual leaders—failed to recognize the new shape of political society. In 1984, the

Democrats were brought face to face with the inadequacy of the public philosophy that succeeded the era of the New Deal.

Pluralistic doctrine plays down the importance of public speech. In line with the traditional assumptions of American political practice, pluralistic political science assumes that speech is *mediated*—that what candidates say passes to voters through "gatekeepers" such as interest groups, local party organizations and the press, in a "two-step flow of communication."[14] In this view, the public is insulated against the media and against public speech, trusting its gatekeepers enough to let them interpret words and events.

What matters, in this view, is not eloquence but the ability to *do*, and especially the ability to persuade the gatekeepers of one's ability, competence, and force. Adlai Stevenson, consequently, was damned as a "talker," too inclined to play Hamlet, and Humphrey tried vainly to live down his reputation for being "gabby." One's public qualities as a leader, Patrick Caddell observes, are "discounted in Washington, where conviction is less important than the ability to get results."[15] As Caddell implies, Washington insiders are especially likely to esteem leaders who show a mastery of fact, persuasiveness in small and expert groups, and skill in hammering out agreements. Lyndon Johnson and Walter Mondale passed those tests with high marks, and Jimmy Carter—though he failed in many respects—at least aspired to do well.

Ronald Reagan, on the other hand, is not highly regarded—to put it mildly—by the insiders, who tend to be contemptuous of Reagan's superficiality, his administrative weakness, and his too frequent ignorance.[16] Yet the antipathy of the insiders has failed to shake Reagan's appeal to ordinary voters.

In fact, the contemporary public is increasingly without gatekeepers. Local party organizations are in disarray. Even when voters are members of interest groups, they are apt to feel distant and disaffected, as so many trade unionists do. The print media, the citadel of interpretation, have declined in favor of television and other forms of direct access to the public. The shattering of the old structures of mediation confronts the Democrats—and political scientists—with a truth they should not have forgotten: Politics is fundamentally a matter of speech, and in democracies, of public speech. But it also confronts America with a public that more and more lacks both the arts of listening and the friendship of critics and guides.

Reagan's staff knows the secrets of campaigning in our mass society. It recognizes, in the first place, that there are no terrors in the press. Reagan's campaign provided good "logistical support" for reporters, but it denied them any real access to the candidate, just as the White House staff kept news conferences to a minimum. Mondale, by contrast, appeared to enjoy give-and-take with reporters, holding a news conference almost every day.[17]

Despite his age, Ronald Reagan is more contemporary than his rivals because he was shaped by movies and by his career as host of "Death Valley Days": Reagan, in fact, is the first candidate who is genuinely the product of the era of the visual media. All previous candidates — and certainly Walter Mondale — grew up and were formed in the years before television dominated the American scene. Ronald Reagan is part of a *New* Right in precisely this sense. The Old Right was tied to a structure of mediation, the business and professional leaders, the editors and the Republican officials of small city, small-town America; the New Right relies on television, as Jerry Falwell does, or on direct mail.

Moreover, Ronald Reagan's staff realizes that television can be *dominated*. Since what matters in politics is so often invisible, subtle, and substantive, it will never be well covered by a medium whose hallmarks are visibility, simplification, and a concern with style.[18] Television can be managed because of its limitations: Reporters can comment only in the context of a picture; the medium is impotent without "photo opportunities" and cannot easily resist a story with good visual possibilities. Reagan's strategists exploited those weaknesses with few scruples and great skill. The President's campaign assertions went largely untested and unchallenged; and the candidate was portrayed, pretty much, in the way his managers desired.

In one respect, the election of 1984 approximated George Orwell's imagined totalitarianism. Orwell feared that in the future, political regimes would find it possible to manipulate our memory of the past and thereby control the future. Things have not reached that pass, but the possibility is frighteningly foreseeable.[19] Ronald Reagan and his advisers recognize, intuitively at least, that the public has less and less memory, less ability to organize and to recall the past. The old, organic sources of political remembrance in families and communities are breaking up and are being replaced by television's presentation of time as a series of disjointed moments, each a discrete unit, available for reordering at will.[20]

Illustratively, Ronald Reagan maintained that, in 1981, he inherited a "mess" that was the work, over many years, of his Democratic oponents. Yet Republican Presidents held office from 1969 to 1977; just as Reagan attempted to enlist Roosevelt, Truman, and Kennedy, he created the sense that Nixon and Ford somehow counted among the Democrats.[21] One might pass this off as campaign cunning were it not clear that Reagan's own version of history is strikingly disordered; his memories are intertwined with odd fantasies and with bits drawn from old movies, all recalled and related as *fact*. This is an old pattern with Reagan, not a sign of age. He is, in this as in other things, a very modern man, one for whom history is not an objective past but an existential creation, the product of will.[22]

LEADERSHIP: OLD VALUES AND NEW AMERICA

Ronald Reagan's reputation as a "strong leader" is his greatest political asset, and the quality of his leadership—so generally admired by the electorate—reveals a good deal about the state of America as a political society.

In speech, Reagan is almost invariably firm and decisive, certain of his values and his direction, and inclined to strong language and striking expression. In action, Reagan often wavers and vacillates. In relation to Lebanon, for example, Reagan denounced those who were ready to "cut and run" and proclaimed his own unwillingness to "surrender"—only to order the withdrawal of American forces. William V. Shannon was led to write that, in foreign affairs, there is "no knowledge, no understanding and no commitment in anything that Reagan does."[23] Yet at each muddled stage of the imbroglio in Lebanon, including our eventual retreat—the President called it a "redeployment" —Reagan exuded confidence and proclaimed success. In domestic affairs, the President's defeats have been less dramatic and less frequent, but his pragmatic flexibility has been just as evident.

Reagan suits our mood. Americans, for the most part, want a leader who gives us a sense of direction and moral purpose, but not one who really *does* dangerous or demanding things. It is significant that Reagan flatters us outrageously; in his rhetoric, the American people are sinned against but never sinners. Following Reagan's lead, George Bush denounced Jimmy Carter's famous reference to a national "crisis of confidence" because Carter had "blamed the American people." In 1984, at least, Reagan's leadership combined the language of moral purpose with the practice of social and moral complacency.

The President's vulnerabilities, which his critics expect to bring disaster, only endear him to his audience. Americans know that Reagan is not brilliant, that his command of facts is uncertain, and that he is prone to "gaffes," but they excuse and indulge such evidences of fallibility. As Philip Rieff pointed out, in the symbolism of modern politics, political leaders—especially in mass democratic states—cannot afford to be too superior to their constituents. A leader must be one of us, an ordinary citizen glorified, and consequently must have faults. Reagan's mistakes, in fact, enable citizens to feel protective toward the President.[24]

Reagan's particular weaknesses, however, say something about our times. Franklin Roosevelt's weaknesses were physical, like the material problems of the country he governed. Spiritually, Roosevelt seemed to tower; even those, like Justice Holmes, who found his intellect second-rate, conceded that FDR had a first-class temperament. Roosevelt was great-spirited in a way that Ronald Reagan is not. Reagan, on the other hand, vaunts his physical vitalities; in 1984, he delighted in his prowess at arm wrestling. By contrast, he shies away from the political "brain wrestling" with the press at which Roosevelt was a past master. Reagan's vulnerabilities, as the voters have every reason to know, are defects of mind and spirit, suited to a country that is troubled in its soul.

The President celebrates traditional values and symbols, but he understands American ambivalence. As a people, Americans suffer from moral uncertainty and spiritual hunger, and they feel and show considerable nostalgia for the old verities and social landmarks. But most Americans do not want to return to the old order; they prefer life in the cities or suburbs, they have grown accustomed to a second income in the family, and they enjoy a certain amount of liberation and latitude in their personal lives. The public has its moments of guilt and regret, but it is unwilling to live by the old ways.

A television commercial portrays a young man returning for a celebration at the family farm, intoning that "America's coming home to the good taste of butter," but we know that whatever eating habits the young man takes away, he will not *stay* on the farm. A second commercial shows a farm mother gratified because a son who did *not* return for the family get-together sent a van full of appliances in his stead. These and similar commercials almost exactly parallel the "upbeat" advertising of Reagan's campaign, with its suggestion that economic growth is sufficient homage to the old virtues.

Reagan recognizes that Americans want standards set and meanings affirmed, and that they expect traditional beliefs to be shown respect. At the same time, the President realizes that this creed, like his own, is a *civil* religion, devoted to America as a political society rather than to the God of judgment.[25] Reagan gave his evangelical and socially conservative allies little more than symbolic support during his first term, allowing their legislative program to languish, and he is not apt to do more in his second four years.

In relation to moral values and social institutions, Walter Mondale was again the victim of his own virtues. Mondale is visibly a man of the old order. His ideas and programs may look to the future — and a surprisingly large number of voters saw Mondale as a man of vision — but his relationships and affects seem to point to the past. His marriage, for example, is apparently stable and happy and, hence, is one with which few contemporary Americans can identify. Gary Hart's marriage, by contrast, amounted to a contemporary soap opera, full of storm, stress, and separation leading to a happy ending. Similarly, Ronald Reagan's family troubles — his divorce and remarriage, his estrangement from his older son, even his failure to meet his infant grandchild — all make him someone we imagine to be like ourselves, able to understand our hopes and pains. Mondale's undisturbed monogamy was, symbolically, at least as out of date as the brand of politics Tip O'Neill seemed to personify. And to make matters worse, Mondale told us that we had to choose between our decencies and our comforts; most Americans preferred the President's happy discovery that it is possible, after all, to serve both God and mammon.

Reagan also understands the ordinary citizen's sense of grievance against the federal government, the conviction that complex government works to the advantage of the powerful and clever, who understand the loopholes of law and the workings of power. Reagan has usurped the Democrats' role as spokesman for many of America's outsiders. In an important sense, Reagan has reaped where the liberals and the New Left sowed.[26] The critique of American policy in Vietnam and the exposures surrounding Watergate worked, for a time, to the advantage of the liberals and the left, discomfiting their immediate enemies. But the attack on public authority also had the effect of undermining confidence in the federal government as a whole, calling its benevolence into question as much as its competence.

The mood to which Reagan appeals is alienated rather than conservative, more suspicious than committed. A great many voters, obviously, have responded to Reagan's pledge to "get the government off the backs of the American people." That response, however, is not born out of confidence in one's ability to go it alone—Americans know their private indignities too well for that— but out of distrust of the federal government as a champion.

In 1984, Ronald Reagan claimed to have restored America's belief in progress, her secular faith in the future. For Reagan, the old sense of possibility is very much alive, and he speaks of extending prosperity to the poor and developing a "Star Wars" defense against nuclear attack. Reagan remains convinced human beings can master nature and, in the President's favorite quotation from Tom Paine, "We have it in our power to begin the world over again."[27]

The public's response was overwhelmingly positive, but it was also cautious and restrained. Despite the vogue of optimism, only 23 percent of Reagan's voters cited his "vision of the future" as a reason for their support.[28] The public seems wary of high hopes; Reagan received a vote of thanks for the present more than a mandate for the future. The great majority of Americans voted for Reagan because, with the country at peace, they were ready to answer "Yes" to the question, "Are you better off now than you were four years ago?"

Most Americans appear to be moved by the President's words, but they are content in practice with a scaled-down prosperity and patriotism, tailored to an age of lowered expectations. The experience of the '70s taught us something about America's limitations and vulnerabilities. In 1984, the majority of Americans were content to overlook the poor and happy to settle for Grenada— a small-scale victory won at low cost. The prevailing opinion is satisfied with an America that is neither heroic nor beautiful, but one that preserves—for most of us—our private comforts and decencies. Reagan has not drawn us together; he has assured us that public life is unnecessary and that we can, safely and in good conscience, confine ourselves to our separate private interests and existences.

Reagan and America are likely to need less anemic loyalties. Looming economic problems are all around us. The federal deficit is now growing faster than the rate of growth in the Gross National Product, and the increased interest on the federal debt exceeds all of the cuts in domestic spending effected during Reagan's first term. Even that well-publicized public indebtedness pales when compared with our *private* debt, now growing at about $300 billion a year.[29] Debt has become an economic way of life. When, during his debate with Geraldine Ferraro, Vice-President Bush sought to dramatize inflation under Carter, he did not refer to the high price of goods but to the high cost of *borrowing* ("twenty-one percent interest rates!"). In fact, Americans are outspending their earnings at the rate of about 10 percent a year, an inflationary pressure held in check so far only by an overvalued dollar and cheap imported goods. In the 1960s, the United States borrowed abroad to finance investment; in the 1980s, we have been borrowing to finance consumption.[30]

In the workplace, Americans who were reemployed after the recession now work, on the whole, for smaller paychecks. Moreover, the growing sector of the job market offers only low-status work, often temporary, requiring little skill and offering low pay and benefits.[31]

Economically, the administration and the country have been living on borrowed time as well as borrowed money. Threats in foreign policy and the erosion of our social institutions only reinforce the moral that a government devoted to private comforts and dedicated to leaving us alone is not adequate to the problems we face. In that truth, the Democrats may find their opportunity, if they are equal to it.

The Democratic Prospect

For the Democrats in 1984, the primary process—as usual—was divisive, exhausting, and inclined to emphasize the role of ideological activists, organized interests, and, in states with open primaries, voters from outside the party's ranks. Mondale, the winner, was as disgusted as the losers. Nevertheless, the Democrats are not likely to make any major changes for the better; the "Fairness Commission," promised to placate Senator Hart, Jesse Jackson, and their supporters, easily could make matters worse. Modest improvements are possible, but the voters have grown accustomed to the system and the Democrats will have to make the best of it, enjoying what promises to be a Republican donnybrook in 1988. In any case, the Democrats have more fundamental problems.

THE NEW DEAL COALITION AND THE NEW DEAL STRATEGY

After the election, the *New York Times,* while urging a new Democratic agenda, observed that Mondale had won substantial majorities among racial minorities, Jews, trade unionists, big-city residents, and the unemployed, and concluded that "the old New Deal coalition . . . remains very much alive."[32] The *Times'* prescription for the Democrats makes sense, but its political history is in error, and that mistake says a great deal about the failure of the Democrats in presidential politics.

The New Deal *coalition*—the majorities that four times elected FDR—began with the Democratic party that Roosevelt inherited, a party built around southern whites and northern Catholics, the latter providing the crucial base of the urban Democratic organizations. The New Deal *strategy* took both groups more or less for granted, and it set out to add enough votes to create a national majority. New Deal tacticians, consequently, courted liberals (in those days, more likely to call themselves "Progressives"), Jews, the unions and—half-incidentally—blacks and racial minorities.

Like any such strategy, the New Deal's political design gave special attention to the groups it aimed to win. In the event, the New Deal strategy attuned Democrats to the values and sensibilities of the target groups and made the party increasingly tone deaf, if not hostile, to the sensitivities of Catholics and southern whites. In order to hold the New Deal coalition together, Democratic strategists relied on historic loyalties, on the power of the urban party organizations, and on an appeal to the economic interests of all those who benefited from New Deal programs—the poor and the working class, of course, but also protected groups like subsidized southern farmers.

Loyalties and memories erode with time. Even while Roosevelt was alive, southern conservatives grew restive. In 1944, an anti-Roosevelt ticket, the "Regulars," ran unsuccessfully in Texas, and in 1948 the growing conflict over racial policy erupted in the Dixiecrat revolt that eventually took Strom Thurmond, among others, out of the Democratic party. Similarly, party organizations grew weaker, partly because of secular changes in American life, but also because of the hostility of liberals, who promoted legislation and party rules designed to weaken or break up the "machines."[33] Today, party organizations are no more than an interest group—and not always a strong one—in local party politics, much too confined to their own supporters to be able to deliver votes to the national party.[34]

By 1972, Democrats were left, in relation to southern whites and northern Catholics, with a kind of pseudo-Marxism, the hope that an appeal to economic interests would prove sufficient to hold voter loyalties. "If we don't have an economic issue for those people," Robert Squier declared in 1984, speaking of "born-again" Christians, "we don't seem to have any issues."[35] As Democrats are acutely aware, the success of their own policies has lifted the majority of such voters at least marginally out of poverty; as a result, Democrats often feel reduced to waiting for a recession. In any case, Democrats know that economic interests are not a sufficient guarantee of party loyalty. No party leader imagines that the economic ties between lower-class blacks and the Democrats would long survive racial insensitivity, and economic interest in the narrow sense would probably lead liberals to support the Republicans. Political allegiance involves our deepest feelings and our highest aspirations as much as our prosaic needs; in the last analysis, political loyalties are a matter for the soul.

The New Deal strategy has played out, whatever we may think of the prospects for the New Deal coalition. It is exhausted because it has succeeded; the groups the New Dealers courted and cultivated have been *won*. The periphery of the New Deal coalition has become the heart of the Democratic party and the historic Democratic party—northern Catholics and southern whites—has moved to the periphery, if it has not been lost to the Democrats altogether. The Democrats need a new strategy—whether they hope to restore the old coalition or to build a new one.

The heart of the new Democratic party—the liberals, the racial minorities, and the trade unions—so accustomed to being wooed, will have to learn how to do the courting, attending to the values, affects, and dignities of others. And correspondingly, the core Democratic groups will have to adjust to their own position. The unions, the minorities, and the liberals will have to ask which items on their respective agendas they are willing to give up in order to win. It is not easy to break a pattern of institutional sensitivity, especially one a half century old, associated with great names and triumphs and buttressed by ideology. The Democrats may find it impossible. Nevertheless, the electoral logic is obvious.

Liberals, for example, have no place else to go. Given the nature of American national politics, they can choose between the Democrats and the irrelevance of third-party candidacies. It is not even clear that such third parties hurt the Democrats very much: Henry Wallace's Progressive party in 1948 helped establish Truman as the candidate of the center and freed the Democrats from association with the "extreme left," and while John Anderson's candidacy in 1980 certainly cost the Democrats some votes, it may also have helped to hold some southern and moderate Democrats behind President Carter. Organized liberal groups, moreover, seemed relatively ineffective in the electoral politics of 1984. Feminists—having applied pressure heavy-handedly, making Mondale's selection of Geraldine Ferraro look weaker and less daring than it was—failed to deliver a vote sufficient to suport their pretensions. Eastern women did give

Mondale and Ferraro a majority, and the Democratic ticket did well among younger, unmarried women, but the majority of women voted for the Republican ticket.[36] In any case, it is not credible that organized feminists, or other groups on the liberal-left, will be able to support a Republican candidate in the foreseeable future. Such voters need the Democratic party at least as much, and possibly more, than it needs them.

Trade unions, similarly, no longer have any serious leverage between the political parties. In 1980, Mr. Reagan advertised his terms as president of the Screen Actors' Guild as proof of his sympathy for unions; that argument did not surface in 1984. In fact, Reagan set his administration, and the Republicans, on a firmly antiunion course.[37] The image of organized labor has become undeservedly negative among voters in general; labor's position of power *within* the Democratic party is one of its few remaining political assets. Walter Mondale would not have won the nomination without the unions, but the embrace of the AFL-CIO helped tag him as a servant of "special interests." Whether it plays its cards foolishly or well, organized labor will continue to be a major power in the internal politics of the Democratic party, but given its external vulnerabilities, labor will have to walk more carefully and speak more softly.

Of all the elements of the Democratic core, Jewish voters—at least, those who are not identifiable liberals—may be the most likely to defect to the Republicans. Democrats will certainly need, consequently, to continue to support Israel, and they have every reason to censure anti-Semitism. Yet the increasing role of right-wing Christians within the Republican party seems likely to tie Jews more closely to the Democrats. "The group that Jews love to hate most," Milton Himmelfarb remarked, "is the Moral Majority."[38] Even Jewish Democrats, in other words, can probably expect somewhat less solicitude than they have learned to take as their due.

Blacks and Hispanics may find it hardest to accept the restraints entailed by their position at the heart of the Democratic party. Both groups, after all, still have a long agenda of demands and resentments; poverty and social injustice aside, they have overcome political exclusion only recently, if at all. It is not surprising, consequently, that Jesse Jackson campaigned in 1984 on the premise that blacks should approach the Democrats as outsiders, a pressure group that cannot be "taken for granted." But black officeholders, and a surprisingly large majority of black voters, recognize a stronger commitment and obligation to the party.

In inner cities, the Democratic party is increasingly dominated by blacks; it is becoming as much "theirs" as it was the preserve of the Irish during their glory days, and blacks have every interest in preserving or building the party's ties to whites. Black voters supported Jackson in the primaries on symbolic grounds but appear to have preferred, on pragmatic grounds, that the eventual Democratic nominee be a candidate with a chance to win. Even more striking, only 4 percent of those who supported Jackson indicated that they would be less likely to vote for Mondale—or less likely to vote—if Jackson did not endorse the Democratic ticket.[39] Democrats, of course, would be unwise to underrate Jackson's strength or the mood of assertiveness among new and younger black voters. By and large, however, blacks are straight-ticket regulars; it is that fact which entitles them to greater representation at the highest levels of the Democratic party and may, conceivably, make them willing to share the party's burdens.

There are compensations for the hard-core Democrats that may encourage them to make the programmatic and affective sacrifices necessary to build a new presidential coalition. They have become the party's establishment, and for practical purposes, the party is their instrument. It is a sign of the times that Walter Mondale, not so long ago regarded as a left-liberal, was identified in 1984 as a "mainstream" Democrat. Yet just as it is hard to change from being cared for to caring for others, it is difficult to accept responsibility for a political institution. Political adulthood, like personal adulthood, is bittersweet. Whatever their regrets, however, the core Democrats have no alternative if they hope to reestablish a national majority.

OLD FRIENDS: THE HISTORIC DEMOCRATS

The most obvious strategy for the Democrats lies in attempting to win back the estranged elements of the old coalition, voters who, for the most part, still think of themselves as Democrats and vote for the party's local candidates. Since Franklin Roosevelt died, this has amounted to the Democrats' only recipe for success. In the elections since the Second World War, the Democrats have nominated one Catholic, Kennedy, two candidates from the South, Johnson and Carter, and one, Truman, who came from a border state with southern associations. With the exception of Carter's second try in 1980, all were elected. During the same period, the Democrats five times nominated northern Protestants (Stevenson twice, Humphrey, McGovern, and Mondale); all of them have been defeated. Other factors were at work, of course—no candidate, for example, could have beaten Eisenhower—but the pattern is too suggestive to be ignored.[40]

Nevertheless, Democrats should not underestimate the difficulty of reestablishing the old coalition. Even the historic loyalties that still tie so many Catholic and southern voters to the Democrats are a mixed blessing. There is no quarrel more bitter than a family argument. A great many Democrats who grew up thinking of the party as their political home have never recovered from the shock they received in 1972, when they found the national convention filled with strangers and themselves—or people with whom they identified—treated as unwelcome guests. And others have been embittered by what they experience as abandonment and years of neglect.

In 1984, Democrats rested much of their hope on the "fairness issue," the recognition that the burden of Reagan's policies falls disproportionately on poor and low-income Americans. Even more than in 1980, however, the Republicans benefited from their own, half-covert, "fairness issue"—the conviction that women, blacks, and Hispanics are receiving more than their "fair share," measured by the standard of equality of opportunity. Affirmative action objectifies the resentment of traditional Democrats who feel they have been shouldered aside by the party and ignored by its policies.[41]

On the whole, Democrats of this persuasion are not defending old-style racism or sexism. The many southern whites who voted for Carter in 1976 and 1980, defecting to Reagan in 1984, have adjusted to a considerable measure of formal equality, as their votes for Carter attest. And while Jerry Falwell may call on women to return to their status as "weaker vessels," Ronald Reagan suggests that a woman soon will, on her "merits," win a place on the Republican ticket. Walter Mondale recognized the strength of this resentment against the felt inequalities of opportunity. He emphasized his own commitment to "opening doors," and he suggested that American success at the Olympics was due to policies promoting racial and sexual equality. It was, however, too little and too late for 1984.

In any case, the Democrats cannot possibly abandon affirmative action. If they hope to conciliate traditional Democrats, they will have to seek new and better remedies. And the Democrats may need new sensitivities even more than a new agenda.

John Kennedy's nomination helped reaffirm the bond between Catholics and Democrats, which dates from the nomination of Al Smith in 1928, and a Catholic at the head of the ticket would certainly help to reconcile defecting Catholic voters to the Democratic party. Yet it seems unlikely that so simple a solution will be enough. In 1960, making allowance for Protestant fears and hostilities, Catholic leaders did not object when Kennedy declared that, in public life, he would follow his conscience rather than his church. In 1984, Geraldine Ferraro took a position more conservative than Kennedy's only to become embroiled in a long, lacerating argument with Archbishop John O'Connor and other members of the hierarchy over the question of abortion.

In 1960, of course, abortion was not an issue in national politics.[42] It is more important, however, that changes within the church—and in the place of the church in American society—have unsettled many of the old anchors of American Catholicism. Public anti-Catholicism has virtually disappeared.[43] Catholic leaders, on the other hand, have become more anxious and more assertive about the orthodoxy of the flock. At the same time, lay Catholics have developed a new touchiness about their identity as Catholics because commitment to the church has become problematic and personal.[44] Catholics, more likely to disregard the church's teachings in private life, are also protective about the church and inclined to resent any disrespect, in public life, for its leaders and its teachings. Walter Mondale's decision to cancel his appearance at the Al Smith dinner, for example, was probably a political error; a considerable number of Catholics surely recognized that Mondale's decision sprang, at least unconsciously, from anger at Archbishop O'Connor, and many must have suspected that Mondale—even if exhausted, as he surely was—would not have missed a dinner in honor of Golda Meir or Dr. Martin Luther King.

The effect of religiously charged issues on Catholic voting is not easy to assess. Catholic teaching argues that political decisions must be made holistically, not on the basis of discrete, absolute principles. A prochoice position on abortion, consequently, is not a fatal liability by itself.[45] Ferraro's views, for example, were familiar to her socially conservative, 70 percent Catholic congressional district. In her district, Ferraro was able to balance her position on abortion by support for tuition tax credits and for an antibusing amendment designed to protect neighborhood schools.[46] The national platform allowed no such flexibility. It seems clear that any Democratic effort to win back Catholic voters will have to offer some concessions to Catholic values and social concerns.

The Catholic hierarchy emphasized the possibilities of such a rapprochement immediately after the election. The Bishops' Pastoral Letter on poverty and economic life presented a trenchant critique of the Reagan administration's policies and a call for a national commitment to alleviate economic misery.[47] During the campaign, the hierarchy spoke almost exclusively about issues like abortion; now, Father Paul Steidl-Meier writes, "The other shoe has dropped."[48] Catholic doctrine is sympathetic to economic regulation for the same reason that it often supports social regulation: It sees the law as magisterial, necessarily and rightly involved in teaching morals and shaping character as well as controlling conduct.[49] The hierarchy's campaign role, combined with the Pastoral Letter, amounted, whether by accident or design, to a message to the Democrats: Catholic teaching cannot be opposed without cost, but if accommodated, it can also be a powerful ally. It remains to be seen if the Democrats heard, or if they will respond in the same spirit.

In 1984, after all, the Democrats sent a mixed message to white ethnic communities, their old strongholds. For some time, sparked by the self-assertion of racial minorities, ethnic consciousness has been revivified in communities of east and south European extraction.[50] Governor Mario Cuomo addressed that sensibility when he spoke of the "blood of immigrants," and in the last two weeks of the campaign, Mondale grew eloquent when he spoke of pluralistic political community.

Yet while Democratic party rules mandate representation of women, racial minorities, Hispanics, and young people in state delegations to the national convention, they do not call for inclusion of Poles, Greeks, Italians, or other, still relatively disadvantaged nationalities. Perhaps, in this respect, the Democrats do not suffer from recognizing too many constituencies, but too few.

In fact, the Democratic party's rules reflect an individualistic liberalism that implicitly disdains community. In the tradition of philosophic liberalism, human beings by nature are separate bodies whose merit is measured by their work. The only natural communities are defined by biological likeness—age, sex, and race—but these communities have no *moral* status. Inequalities based simply on physical differences demand special attention and correction because they breach the wall between *nature* and *political society.* Democratic party rules, in other words, recognize women, racial minorities. and young people in order to free them from the burden of classifications that are "suspect" because they are based on qualities that were not chosen and that do not reflect achievement.

Cultural communities differ because they are based on convention, custom, and choice. To be part of an ethnic community suggests, in the individualistic view, either that one *chose* not to pursue assimilation into the middle-class mainstream or that one *failed* in the attempt, and hence any discrimination or disadvantage is, to some degree, one's own fault. Ethnic voters do not need to spell out the philosophic principles of this argument to feel and recognize its effects.[51]

It is probably impractical and unnecessary for Democrats to mandate formal representation of white ethnic communities. Any Democratic appeal to such voters, however, must make clear that the party respects ethnic traditions and dignities, and is devoted to the values that, broadly speaking, characterize ethnic voters: "patriotism, a strengthening of families and neighborhoods and the work ethic."[52] Jimmy Carter's campaign in 1976 profited because it seemed to promise such devotion; Carter suffered in 1980 because he failed to deliver. In 1984, the Democratic candidates said many of the right words, but they failed to develop the Democrats' one great advantage over the Republicans, the willingness to use public power to support their verbal commitments. For ethnic voters, who tend to be economically and socially marginal and whose communities are ordinarily embattled, it is not enough to be decent; one must at least appear to be strong.

THE SOUTH AND SOCIAL VALUES

In the white South, Democratic losses are far more serious and difficult to reverse because they have carried over to the local level, suggesting a thoroughgoing change of party identification.[53] Moreover, southern white defections in 1984 were complicated by the contemporary political problem of race. The South today is hardly an egalitarian society, but memories of Jim Crow are fading; moderate southerners are less likely to feel guilt for the past and more likely to be anxious about the future. Already worried about the increasing black presence in the Democratic party—and especially, the Democratic parties of the South—white voters were alarmed by Jesse Jackson's demand for the abolition of runoff primaries, a policy calculated to insure black domination of state Democratic politics. Voters who would have been ashamed of the simpler forms of racism found it easy to rationalize hostility to Jackson. To white voters, Jackson suggests an inner-city hustler with an aura of financial sleaziness, self-promoting and injudicious, while Jackson's ventures into foreign policy were at least leftist and arguably unpatriotic.

It did not help that the extreme sensitivity with which Democratic leaders approached Jackson was coupled with an almost brutal disregard for the white South. Mondale selected Bert Lance to be national chairman and then abandoned him, under fire, a disloyalty made worse by the fact that the revolt against Lance centered on his connection to Jimmy Carter, not on his alleged financial peculations. To a great many voters, it must have seemed clear that Lance was subjected to public humiliation because of his connection to the South. The 1984 Democratic convention was apparently all too eager to ignore southern whites and to repudiate their leaders.[54]

Across the nation, evangelical religion deepened the revolt against the Democrats, but it was felt in the South with particular force. The members of the theologically conservative churches have traditionally been people of low income, likely to be and vote Democratic. But greater personal involvement in such churches tends to imply a greater commitment to the conservative emphasis on personal virtue and self-reliance and an increased likelihood that this conservatism will be expressed in political behavior.[55] Consequently, the "born-again" movement, with its tendency to heighten zeal and devotion, has been a time bomb for the Democrats, somewhat held in check by Jimmy Carter's very visible Christianity.[56] In 1984, evangelical Christians, North and South, were less likely than any other religious communion to express concern for the fairness of Reagan's policies and the most likely to cite abortion as a reason for their vote.

It is also no accident that the religious right is so deeply associated with television. Television has increased national awareness of moral and social

change. It has made any number of traditionally religious people more cogni-
zant of their embattled status, so that the claims of the religious right to speak
for a "Moral Majority" amount to desperate morale-building. It is part of Ronald Reagan's appeal, as *Commonweal* observed, that he understands this "sense
of grievance" among the religious, the feeling of disadvantage in relation to
secular culture. Reagan's apocryphal anecdotes about "court decisions" banning voluntary school prayer speak to the fear that religion is losing its place
in American public life, and the President seems to offer religious Americans
a chance to reclaim their "fair share" in the nation's *civil* religion.[57]

Even with all these disadvantages, however, the Democrats' position in
the white South is not hopeless. Jimmy Carter's relative success in the South,
even in 1980, suggests that recognition of the region—especially when combined with responsiveness to its religiosity—can go a long way toward holding
enough white voters to tip the balance. The new Republican strength, moreover, is unstable to say the least; the GOP made similar gains in the election
of 1980, only to see them disappear in 1982.[58]

The old Democratic coalition is not quite Humpty Dumpty. Any chance
of reassembling it, however, presumes that the Democrats can understand and
respond to the "social issue," that touchstone of discontent among erstwhile
Democrats. More and more Americans are aware of and disturbed by the growing fragmentation and disorder of American social life, our increasing tendency to privatism and our escalating indifference. They recognize, even if inartic-
ulately, that social institutions—especially the family and the school—are not
simply a "private" sphere separate from politics but the foundations of political
life, the places where citizens are first and fundamentally educated and shaped.
The health of society is necessarily the concern of any democratic regime.

Democrats recognize this, perhaps better than Republicans. They have been
willing to help families, especially among the disadvantaged, and they have
been deeply concerned about growing crimes against children. In 1984, the
Democratic candidates invoked and campaigned on the basis of "family values."
Yet Democrats have also been unwilling to set a *standard* for policy. They spoke
of "family values" without affirming that a social unit including two hetero-
sexual parents is the *norm* for family life on which public policy should be
based. To set such a standard does not entail cruelty to single-parent families;
quite the contrary, it calls attention to the difficulties under which such parents
labor, and it implies the need for special public support—stronger federal laws,
for example, enforcing the payment of child support. In the same sense Democrats cannot abandon their concern for the rights of gay Americans, even though
that support entails political costs, but they need not maintain that homosexuality is anything but an exception to the social rule.

Liberals have been unwilling to set such a standard, fearing its punitive potential, but the lack of regulating norms makes Democratic policies seem directionless, so much formless sentimentality. Democrats will find it impossible to address the social issue successfully unless they are willing to affirm *some* moral center for social life; the fear that we are coming to lack such a foundation is what all the fuss is about. Certainly, the Democrats must accept the fact that the troubling aspects of the social issue will not, as so many liberals have hoped, simply fade away, at least not in the near future.

Finally, the Democrats would be well-advised to reconsider their commitments on the vexing issue of abortion. In a sense, the abortion issue is similar to Prohibition, which split the Democrats into "wets" and "drys," except that the argument over abortion concerns first principles, the very definition of human life, and the argument is correspondingly more serious. The moral rights and wrongs aside, it is arguable that the "great experiment" in national abortion policy has failed, as Prohibition did, because it involves unacceptable political costs. Even the relatively small number of voters who cite abortion as a reason for their vote can hold the balance in a national election and the figures overlook those voters for whom abortion is not decisive but contributes to their final choice. Americans appear to be divided into three almost equal camps: Only 29 percent would ban all abortions, but only 35 percent are in favor of "free choice"; the rest would permit abortion only in specified cases.[59] Roughly 60 percent of Americans, in these terms, regard abortion as at best an exception to the rule; support for unqualified "free choice" not only costs the Democrats strategic support, it aligns them against a conditional majority.

Of course, the Democratic party cannot endorse any constitutional amendment that would ban abortions. It may be possible, however, to explore alternatives. Abortion could, for example, be returned to state jurisdiction, or the Democrats could accept the principle that abortion should be permitted only in some defined set of cases.[60] In any case, the Democrats will need to do some hard thinking about the principles that should govern social life.

Over the years, social conservatives have imagined, foolishly, that self-seeking and unrestrained liberty in economic life will not carry over into public life and moral conduct. They are wrong. We commit ourselves to communities, to people, or to the future only to the extent that we are confident of our knowledge of what is and will be. Instability and change make our knowledge of one another more superficial and the future more unpredictable. Since the free market implies an economy open to unregulated change, it weakens our commitments and promotes social decay.[61]

The liberal-left, on the other hand, has been devoted to the decencies of sympathy and generosity, but liberals have also defended a permissive private morality, confident that it would end repression but leave compassion intact. Confronted by so many new cruelties and the insouciant selfishness reflected in Reaganism, liberalism ought to recognize its own complicity: A doctrine that defends self-expression and self-gratification lays the foundations of selfishness and self-interest and may even point to enormities. George Orwell spoke to the point:

> For two hundred years we have sawed and sawed and sawed at the branch we were sitting on. And in the end . . . our efforts were rewarded and down we came. But unfortunately, there had been a little mistake. The thing at the bottom was not a bed of roses after all, it was a cesspool full of barbed wire.[62]

Even amid Reagan's jerry-built recovery, Americans are rightly worried about the moral foundations of the country. Walter Mondale did the Democrats good service for the future by championing decency. It remains to be seen if the Democrats — and, especially, the party's liberals — can learn that decency is an exacting creed, premised on self-denial. Caring for others presumes that we make their need prevail over our desire, and even a modest civility requires that private feeling yield to public form.

After 1984

The nation's moral and political future certainly lies with its youth. Today's younger voters lack a sense of their ability to change the world. Their relative conservatism, as Bernice Buresh writes, is "personal, not political," rooted in their sense of vulnerability, their desire to be reassured against the threats of a world that seems too much out of control.[63]

It makes matters worse that young Americans feel the weight of their elders so heavily. Social Security, of course, is increasingly costly, but it matters even more that older Americans clog the routes to employment, opportunity, and power. Increasingly healthy, older Americans want to work longer and, on the whole, have been able to make good their claims. Buttressed by seniority clauses and tenure provisions, older Americans are relatively protected against unemployment and economic insecurity; of workers laid off between 1979 and 1984, 40 percent were under thirty-five.[64] White youth, in fact, has its special reasons for resenting affirmative action: Since the Supreme Court has held that seniority clauses *do* outweigh the claims of women and minorities, the burden of racial and sexual equality falls almost entirely on the young.[65] Senator Hart's hints that he might consider limiting increases in Social Security did not hurt him with younger voters, and Democratic charges that Reagan cannot be trusted to protect Social Security entitlements may, in this respect, have helped the President. Social Security and collective bargaining, those pillars of the New Deal, are no great assets for the Democrats among the young.

At the same time, however, younger voters have no real commitment to the GOP. They seem fond of Reagan, but it is a soft sentiment, not a strong devotion; Hart's neoliberalism attracted young voters, many of whom voted for Reagan in November, at one point giving Hart a lead over the President in the polls. Younger voters are decisively *not* ideological conservatives. They voted for Reagan on pragmatic grounds, giving him credit for strong leadership and for the recovery, but they rarely cited traditional values or conservatism as reasons for their choice. Roger Stone, a Reagan strategist, worries that too close an identification with social conservatism and the religious right may shake the fragile bond between the Republicans and the young.[66]

Shaped by change and uncertainty, younger Americans are inclined to be self-protective and fearful of deep commitments. Loyalty—especially loyalty to institutions—does not rank high on their list of virtues and disciplines. A generation shaped by television, they are more likely to judge on the basis of images and styles; as in Johnny Carson's version of Hart's campaign, "Vote for me, I have Kennedy hair," the young are more likely to be guided by the shifting externalities of appearance than the inward bonds of soul.

Democrats can hope to recover lost ground among the young, and it is that possibility which inspires much of the Democrats' recent concern for toning up the party's image, with its vulgar fixation on Tip O'Neill's weight and rumpled appearance and its neglect of his legislative craft. Within limits, however, there is room and reason for Democrats to think about new images and new ideas. There is, however, a conflict between wooing traditional Democrats, who tend toward social conservatism, and pursuing younger voters who do not. The problem is not insuperable—Democrats have coped with a radically diverse coalition in the past—but it is a challenge to political art. The Democrats will need, in Theodore White's phrase, "to make new friends without losing old ones."[67] That exacting task demands new ideas and more; in 1988 and beyond, the Democrats will need to combine statesmanship and party government.

Some directions offer obvious possibilities. Work is the great theme uniting any prospective Democratic majority, and while there are tensions between old and young, whites and minorities, men and women, a policy of full employment aims to keep those conflicts within civil bounds by guaranteeing decent jobs for all Americans. In our society, as the New Dealers knew, employment is a virtual prerequisite of social dignity. As Robert Kuttner remarks, "American liberals went off the track when they opted for income transfers rather than full employment as the centerpiece of their economic strategy. Means-test income transfers are very destructive. You create a separate welfare class, which is encouraged to become dependent."[68] The Democrats may very well want to phase down welfare in favor of some forms of "workfare," through public service employment—as in proposals for a national Police Corps or a revived Conservation Corps—or through programs—such as wage subsidies, following the Swedish example—that stimulate employment in the private sector.

There are also good reasons for the Democrats to continue Walter Mondale's late campaign theme, developing programs that support community. For some time, social disintegration has sparked somewhat sporadic efforts to preserve or create community.[69] By the 1980s, almost half the country, according to Daniel Yankelovich, at least *claimed* to be deeply involved in the quest for community.[70] The Democrats have at least a chance to become the champions of community, and theory as well as practice may encourage them to make the attempt. Small, reasonably autonomous, and stable communities and neighborhoods are still our best schools of citizenship, and we all pay a cost for their decline.[71]

In general, the Democrats will need to reclaim their old position as the party of those who are outsiders in the labyrinths of bureaucracy. Wherever possible, the Democrats should embrace simplification and decentralization, but they can and should argue that to dismantle the federal government would only leave citizens at the mercy of private power. With good reason, voters want to simplify the *process* of government, but that does not necessarily mean that they want *weak* government. Quite the contrary, it may mean that they want a government that has discretion. There is considerable evidence that the suspicions of the '70s are waning. The Reagan administration demonstrates, rather paradoxically, that Americans want a government that at least appears strong, direct, and decisive; and in 1984, state referenda suggest that the "tax revolt" is ebbing. It may be that the electorate wants a government that is checked, not by denying it power, but by holding it accountable before the law and in political life.

The election of 1984 symbolized the beginning of the politics of the electronic age. The coming political era has its bright possibilities, but it is full of dangers as alarming as those of Orwell's imagining. Citizenship and statecraft will be more necessary than ever, but they will have to rest on new foundations. Ronald Reagan has presided over the demolition of the old politics; in the years after 1984, it will be necessary for Americans to see if they can build anew.

NOTES

1. *New York Times,* 4 November 1984, E5.
2. For example, about 70 percent of Americans were convinced, despite the President's protestations, that taxes would have to be raised.
3. Hedrick Smith, "Political Memo," *New York Times,* 7 December 1984, B18.
4. Alexis de Tocqueville, *Democracy in America* (New York: Schocken, 1961), 1: 33, 364.
5. *The Public Papers and Addresses of Franklin D. Roosevelt* (New York: Random House, 1983), 2: 11.
6. Dennis Hale and Marc Landy, "Are Critical Elections Extinct?" *Boston College Biweekly* 5 (15 November 1984): 8.
7. I find it suggestive that James Monroe, running in 1820 as the architect of the Era of Good Feeling, won a victory even more one-sided than Reagan's, and his triumph resulted in the death of the old party system and the rise of mass political parties.
8. Even after the election, the administration balanced its sharp cuts in domestic welfare programs—including Medicare—with a surprisingly liberal plan for tax reform.
9. Tom Wicker, "The Other Fritz," *New York Times,* 3 February 1984, A29.
10. On abortion, after all, Mondale was arguing that "you can't legislate morality."
11. Hale and Landy, "Are Critical Elections Extinct?"
12. Tom Wicker, "After 1984, What?" *New York Times,* 23 November 1984, A35.
13. Theodore J. Lowi, *The End of Liberalism* (New York: Norton, 1969).
14. For example, see Paul F. Lazarsfeld et al., *The People's Choice* (New York: Columbia University Press, 1944).
15. *New York Times,* 8 November 1984, A19.
16. James Reston, "Insiders and Outsiders," *New York Times,* 19 August 1984, E19.
17. Walter Robinson, "Accessibility and Excessibility," *Boston Globe,* 14 October 1984, A17ff; James Reston, "Reagan Beats the Press," *New York Times,* 4 November 1984, E25.
18. Television reporters, despite their array of technological supports, are often embarrassingly bad at covering politics: During an interview intended to introduce Gary Hart to the voters, for example, Roger Mudd seemed fixated on the stylistic question whether Hart was imitating Kennedy. See John Corry, "TV: Coverage of Hart," *New York Times,* 16 March 1984, C24.
19. David Burnham, "Experts Fear Computers' Use Imperils Government History," *New York Times,* 16 August 1984, 1ff.
20. We are, after all, on the political eve of TV's second generation—children raised by parents who themselves grew up in the era of television.
21. By contrast, when Roosevelt spoke of "inheriting a mess" in 1933, the Republicans had held office for 24 of the 32 preceding years; in the 32 years before Reagan took office, Republicans and Democrats had each held office for 16.
22. Michael Rogin's Gauss lecture, "Reagan, the Movie," at Princeton University in 1984 develops this theme in a matchless way. See also Gwinn Owens, "Reagan's Confusion of Fact and Fantasy Raises Doubts about Future Competency," *New Brunswick Home News,* 26 March 1984, B7.
23. William V. Shannon, "The Actor Comes Out in the President," *Easton Express,* 8 June 1984, A4; see the similar criticism in the *Wall Street Journal,* 16 February 1984, 62.
24. Philip Rieff, "Aesthetic Functions in Modern Politics," *World Politics* 5 (1953): 478-502;

this protectiveness extends, with better reason, to the President's staff. Given Reagan's disinterest in policy analysis or administrative detail, his staff—by insulating the President and controlling the information he gets—has a more than usual ability to maneuver Reagan, provided they respect his traditional beliefs, since Reagan is unlikely to seek additional information on his own. David Broder, "Shielding Reagan," *Boston Globe,* 14 October 1984, A23.

25. "Mr. Reagan's Civil Religion," *Commonweal* III (21 September 1984): 483-85; despite his evangelical support, Reagan's own theological comments are likely to be remarkably latitudinarian: "Everyone can make his own interpretation of the Bible," Reagan observed, "and many individuals have been making different interpretations for a long time," cited in Leo P. Ribuffo, *The Old Christian Right* (Philadelphia: Temple University Press, 1983), 268.

26. Richard Reeves, "The Ideological Election," *New York Times Magazine,* 19 February 1984, 26ff.

27. This assertion of Paine's is part of an argument that is radically hostile to the teachings of revealed religion; that Reagan uses it so often is an indication of his own civil religion.

28. *New York Times,* 11 November 1984, 30.

29. Ashby Bladen, "The Acid Test," *Forbes* 134 (17 December 1984): 245; *New York Times,* 2 February 1984, B9, and 5 February 1984, 1ff.

30. Bladen, "The Acid Test"; in fact, taking into account the stabilization of oil prices, there has been little decline in inflation under Reagan; see Robert Levine's letter to the *New York Times,* 17 September 1984, A18.

31. William Serrin, "White Men Discover It's a Shrinking Market," *New York Times,* 9 December 1984, E2.

32. "New Ideas," *New York Times,* 11 November 1984, E20.

33. See, for example, James Reichley, *The Art of Government* (New York: Fund for the Republic, 1959), or Everett C. Ladd, *Where Have All the Voters Gone? The Fracturing of Political Parties* (New York: Norton, 1978).

34. Gerald M. Pomper, "The Decline of the Party in American Elections," *Political Science Quarterly* 92 (1977): 21-41. In 1984, for example, white Democratic leaders in Chicago made relatively little effort to dissuade their constituents from supporting Reagan; instead, they offered to forgive their friends for such defections and hence to preserve social harmony and local community, if they would vote for Paul Simon, the successful Democratic candidate for the Senate. In doing so, they were probably making the best available bargain, but it indicates the diminished role of the "regulars."

35. *New York Times,* 25 November 1984, E2.

36. *New York Times,* 8 November 1984, A19.

37. The Teamsters Union did endorse Reagan, following its usual Republican habits, but the support probably embarrassed the President, since it was suggested that the Teamsters expected in return a less-than-zealous prosecution of their president, Jackie Presser.

38. *New York Times,* 18 December 1984, B14.

39. David Rosenbaum, "Blacks in Poll Prefer Mondale to Jackson as Nominee," *New York Times,* 10 July 1984, 1ff.

40. Incidentally, the pattern is almost reversed for vice-presidential candidates. During

the same period, the Democrats chose four southerners (Barkley, Sparkman, Kefauver, and Johnson) and three Catholics (Muskie, Shriver, and Ferraro); only Barkley and Johnson were on winning tickets. By contrast, both northern Protestants nominated by the Democrats (Humphrey and Mondale) were elected, even though Mondale was defeated in 1980.

41. Terry Eastland and William J. Bennett, *Counting by Race: Equality from the Founding Fathers to Bakke and Weber* (New York: Basic Books, 1979).

42. It surfaced first in 1972, because of McGovern's support for "free choice," and it became inescapable given the Supreme Court's decision in 1973 that abortion during the first trimester of pregnancy involves private rights protected by the Constitution (*Roe v. Wade*, 410 U.S. 113, 1973).

43. The Protestant right grumbles, from time to time, but for the moment it is content with a kind of ecumenism that concentrates fire on the main "secular humanist" enemy. Ribuffo, *The Old Christian Right*, 267-68.

44. For example, see the long debate on the "End of Catholicism," centering on Thomas Sheehan's critique of the "liberal consensus" in Catholic theology. *Commonweal* 111 (21 September 1984): 490-502.

45. Only 8 percent of Catholics cited abortion as a reason for their vote in 1984. *New York Times*, 25 November 1984, E2.

46. Ferraro helped make it clear that opposition to busing *need* not involve racism (although obviously it often does), since she strongly supports the integration of neighborhoods.

47. Leonard Silk, "The Bishops' Letter and U.S. Goals," *New York Times*, 14 November 1984, D2.

48. Paul Steidl-Meier, "A Reformist Document," *Commonweal* 111 (30 November 1984): 650.

49. J. Brian Benestad, *The Pursuit of a Just Social Order* (Washington, D.C.: Ethics and Public Policy Center, 1982).

50. Theodore White, "New Powers, New Politics," *New York Times Magazine*, 5 February 1984), 32, 34; Michael Novak, *The Rise of the Unmeltable Ethnics* (New York: Macmillan, 1971).

51. That Hispanics, a group defined by language, are at least a partial exception to the rule almost certainly underlines the distinction between favored and disfavored groups.

52. William V. Shannon, "Liberalism, Old and New," *New York Times*, 2 October 1976, 25.

53. According to Curtis Gans of the Committee for the Study of the American Electorate, the Republicans "are going to be a competitive party in the South, and maybe the dominant party in the next six years." *New York Times*, 11 November 1984, 53. For the long-term trend in this direction, see Bruce Campbell, "Patterns of Change in the Partisan Loyalties of Native Southerners, 1955-72," *Journal of Politics* 39 (1977): 730-61.

54. In choosing Ferraro as a running mate, of course, Mondale passed over the available southern candidates, and his choice of a woman was not well received in southern circles.

55. Benton Johnson, "Ascetic Protestantism and Political Preference," *Public Opinion Quarterly* 26 (1962): 35-46.

56. As Leo Ribuffo observes, however, Carter "barely qualified as an evangelical." *The Old Christian Right*, 262-63.

57. "Mr. Reagan's Civil Religion," 484; William G. McLoughlin, "Faith," *American Quarterly* 35 (1983): 101-15.

58. Adam Clymer, "Contradictory Lessons of the 1982 Election," *New York Times*, 4 November 1982, 1, 24.

59. *New York Times*, 11 November 1984, 30.

60. David Carlin, "The Abortion Debate: Rules for Liberals," *Commonweal* 111 (21 September 1984): 486-87.

61. Daniel Bell, *The Cultural Contradictions of Capitalism* (New York: Basic Books, 1976).

62. Sonia Orwell and Ian Angus, eds., *The Collected Essays, Journalism, and Letters of George Orwell* (New York: Harcourt Brace, 1968), 2: 15.

63. Bernice Buresh, "Students, Conservative, Fearful," *New York Times*, 4 November 1984, E25.

64. Serrin, "White Men Discover It's a Shrinking Market."

65. *Firefighters* v. *Stotts*, 103 S.Ct. 2451 (1983).

66. *New York Times*, 25 November 1984, E2.

67. White, "New Powers, New Politics," 34.

68. Kuttner is quoted from James Cook, "Ends and Means," *Forbes* 134 (17 December 1984): 140; see Kuttner's own *The Economic Illusion* (Boston: Houghton Mifflin, 1984).

69. For example, see Harry C. Boyte, *The Backyard Revolution: Understanding the New Citizen Movement* (Philadelphia: Temple University Press, 1980), on the neighborhoods movement.

70. Daniel Yankelovich, *New Rules: Searching for Fulfillment in a World Turned Upside Down* (New York: Random House, 1981), 251; the exact figure is 47 percent, up from 32 percent in 1973.

71. Sidney Verba and Norman Nie, *Participation in America* (New York: Harper & Row, 1972), 49.

Second Inaugural Address

RONALD W. REAGAN

Senator Mathias, Chief Justice Burger, Vice-President Bush, Speaker O'Neill, Senator Dole, Reverend Clergy, and members of my family and friends, and my fellow citizens:

This day has been made brighter with the presence here of one who for a time has been absent. Senator John Stennis, God bless you and welcome back.

There is, however, one who is not with us today. Representative Gillis Long of Louisiana left us last night. And I wonder if we could all join in a moment of silent prayer.

Amen.

There are no words to — adequate to — express my thanks for the great honor that you've bestowed on me. I will do my utmost to be deserving of your trust.

This is, as Senator Mathias told us, the 50th time that we, the people, have celebrated this historic occasion. When the first President, George Washington, placed his hand upon the Bible, he stood less than a single day's journey by horseback from raw, untamed wilderness. There were four million Americans in a Union of 13 states.

Today we are 60 times as many in a Union of 50 states. We've lighted the world with our inventions, gone to the aid of mankind wherever in the world there was a cry for help, journeyed to the moon and safely returned.

So much has changed. And yet we stand together as we did two centuries ago.

When I took this oath four years ago, I did so in a time of economic stress. Voices were raised saying that we had to look to our past for the greatness and glory. But we, the present-day Americans are not given to looking backward. In this blessed land, there is always a better tomorrow.

Four years ago I spoke to you of a new beginning, and we have accomplished that. But in another sense, our new beginning is a continuation of that beginning created two centuries ago when, for the first time in history, government, the people said, was not our master. It is our servant; its only power that which we, the people, allow it to have.

That system has never failed us. But for a time we failed the system. We asked things of government that government was not equipped to give. We yielded authority to the national government that properly belonged to states or to local governments or to the people themselves. We allowed taxes and inflation to rob us of our earnings and savings and watched the great industrial machine that had made us the most productive people on earth slow down and the number of unemployed increase.

By 1980 we knew it was time to renew our faith, to strive with all our strength toward the ultimate in individual freedom consistent with an orderly society.

We believed then and now [that] there are no limits to growth and human progress when men and women are free to follow their dreams. And we were right. And we were right to believe that. Tax rates have been reduced, inflation cut dramatically, and more people are employed than ever before in our history.

We are creating a nation once again vibrant, robust, and alive. But there are many mountains yet to climb. We will not rest until every American enjoys the fullness of freedom, dignity, and opportunity as our birthright. It is our birthright as citizens of this great republic.

And if we meet this challenge, these will be years when Americans have restored their confidence and tradition of progress; when our values of faith, family, work, and neighborhood were restated for a modern age; when our economy was finally freed from government's grip; when we made sincere efforts at meaningful arms reductions by rebuilding our defenses, our economy, and [by] developing new technologies helped preserve peace in a troubled world; when America courageously supported the struggle for individual liberty, self-government, and free enterprise throughout the world and turned the tide of history away from totalitarian darkness and into the warm sunlight of human freedom.

My fellow citizens, our nation is poised for greatness. We must do what we know is right and do it with all our might. Let history say of us, these were golden years—when the American Revolution was reborn, when freedom gained new life, and America reached for her best.

Our two-party system has solved us—served us, I should say—well over the years, but never better than in those times of great challenge, when we came together not as Democrats or Republicans but as Americans united in the common cause.

Two of our Founding Fathers, a Boston lawyer named Adams and a Virginia planter named Jefferson, members of that remarkable group who met in Independence Hall and dared to think they could start the world over again, left us an important lesson. They had become, in the years spent in government, bitter political rivals in the presidential election of 1800. Then years later, when both were retired and age had softened their anger, they began to speak to each other again through letters.

A bond was reestablished between those two who had helped create this government of ours.

In 1826, the 50th anniversary of the Declaration of Independence, they both died. They died on the same day, within a few hours of each other. And that day was the Fourth of July.

In one of those letters exchanged in the sunset of their lives, Jefferson wrote, "It carries me back to the times when, beset with difficulties and dangers, we were fellow laborers in the same cause, struggling for what is most valuable to man, his right of self-government. Laboring always at the same oar, with some wave ever ahead threatening to overwhelm us, and yet passing harmless we rode through the storm with heart and hand."

Well, with heart and hand, let us stand as one today: one people under God determined that our future shall be worthy of our past. As we do, we must not repeat the well-intentioned errors of our past. We must never again abuse the trust of working men and women by sending their earnings on a futile chase after the spiraling demands of a bloated federal establishment. You elected us in 1980 to end this prescription for disaster. And I don't believe you reelected us in 1984 to reverse course.

The heart of our efforts is one idea vindicated by 25 straight months of economic growth: freedom and incentives unleash the drive and entrepreneurial genius that are the core of human progress. We have begun to increase the rewards for work, savings, and investment; reduce the increase in the cost and size of government and its interference in people's lives.

We must simplify our tax system, make it more fair and bring the rates down for all who work and earn. We must think anew and move with a new boldness so every American who seeks work can find work; so the least among us shall have an equal chance to achieve the greatest things—to be heroes who heal our sick, feed the hungry, protect peace among nations, and leave this world a better place.

The time has come for a new American Emancipation, a great national drive to tear down economic barriers and liberate the spirit of enterprise in the most distressed areas of our country. My friends, together we can do this, and do it we must, so help me God.

From new freedom will spring new opportunities for growth, a more productive, fulfilled, and united people, and a stronger America, an America that
will lead the technological revolution and also open its mind and heart and
soul to the treasures of literature, music, and poetry, and the values of faith,
courage, and love.

A dynamic economy, with more citizens working and paying taxes, will
be our strongest tool to bring down budget deficits. But an almost unbroken
50 years of deficit spending has finally brought us to a time of reckoning.

We've come to a turning point, a moment for hard decisions. I have asked
the Cabinet and my staff a question and now I put the same question to all
of you. If not us, who? And if not now, when? It must be done by all of us
going forward with a program aimed at reaching a balanced budget. We can
then begin reducing the national debt.

I will shortly submit a budget to the Congress aimed at freezing government program spending for the next year. Beyond this, we must take further
steps to permanently control government's power to tax and spend.

We must act now to protect future generations from government's desire
to spend its citizens' money and tax them into servitude when the bills come
due. Let us make it unconstitutional for the federal government to spend more
than the federal government takes in.

We have already started returning to the people and to state and local governments responsibilities better handled by them. Now, there is a place for the
federal government in matters of social compassion. But our fundamental goals
must be to reduce dependency and upgrade the dignity of those who are infirm
or disadvantaged. And here a growing economy and support from family and
community offer our best chance for a society where compassion is a way of
life, where the old and infirm are cared for, the young and, yes, the unborn,
protected, and the unfortunate looked after and made self-sufficient.

Now there is another area where the federal government can play a part.
As an older American, I remember a time when people of different race, creed,
or ethnic origin in our land found hatred and prejudice installed in social custom and, yes, in law. There's no story more heartening in our history than the
progress that we've made toward the brotherhood of man that God intended
for us. Let us resolve: There will be no turning back or hesitation on the road
to an America rich in dignity and abundant with opportunity for all our citizens.

Let us resolve that we the people will build an American opportunity society
in which all of us—white and black, rich and poor, young and old—will go
forward together, arm in arm. Again, let us remember that, though our heritage is one of blood lines from every corner of the earth, we are all Americans
pledged to carry on this last best hope of man on earth.

And I have spoken of our domestic goals, and the limitations we should put on our national government. Now let me turn to a task that is the primary responsibility of national government—the safety and security of our people.

Today we utter no prayer more fervently than the ancient prayer for peace on earth. Yet history has shown that peace does not come, nor will our freedom be preserved, by good will alone. There are those in the world who scorn our vision of human dignity and freedom. One nation, the Soviet Union, has conducted the greatest military buildup in the history of man, building arsenals of awesome offensive weapons.

We've made progress in restoring our defense capability. But much remains to be done. There must be no wavering by us, nor any doubts by others, that America will meet her responsibilities to remain free, secure, and at peace.

There is only one way safely and legitimately to reduce the cost of national security, and that is to reduce the need for it. And this we're trying to do in negotiations with the Soviet Union. We're not just discussing limits on a further increase of nuclear weapons. We seek, instead, to reduce their number. We seek the total elimination, one day, of nuclear weapons from the face of the earth.

Now for decades we and the Soviets have lived under the threat of mutual assured destruction; if either resorted to the use of nuclear weapons, the other could retaliate and destroy the one who had started it. Is there either logic or morality in believing that if one side threatens to kill tens of millions of our people, our only recourse is to threaten killing tens of millions of theirs?

I have approved a research program to find, if we can, a security shield that will destroy nuclear missiles before they reach their target. It wouldn't kill people, it would destroy weapons. It wouldn't militarize space, it would help demilitarize the arsenals of earth. It would render nuclear weapons obsolete. We will meet with the Soviets hoping that we can agree on a way to rid the world of the threat of nuclear destruction.

We strive for peace and security, heartened by the changes all around us. Since the turn of the century, the number of democracies in the world has grown fourfold. Human freedom is on the march, and nowhere more so than in our own hemisphere. Freedom is one of the deepest and noblest aspirations of the human spirit. People worldwide hunger for the right of self-determination, for those inalienable rights that make for human dignity and progress.

America must remain freedom's staunchest friend, for freedom is our best ally, and it is the world's only hope to conquer poverty and preserve peace. Every blow we inflict against poverty will be a blow against its dark allies of oppression and war. Every victory for human freedom will be a victory for world peace.

So we go forward today a nation still mighty in its youth and powerful in its purpose. With our alliances strengthened, with our economy leading the world to a new age of economic expansion, we look to a future rich in possibilities. And all of this is because we worked and acted together, not as members of political parties, but as Americans.

My friends, we live in a world that's lit by lightning. So much is changing and will change, but so much endures and transcends time.

History is a ribbon, always unfurling; history is a journey. And as we continue on our journey we think of those who traveled before us. We stand again at the steps of this symbol of our democracy—or we would've been standing at the steps if it hadn't gotten so cold. Now, we're standing inside this symbol of our democracy, and we see and hear again the echoes of our past.

A general falls to his knees in the hard snow of Valley Forge; a lonely President paces the darkened halls and ponders his struggle to preserve the Union; the men of the Alamo call out encouragement to each other; a settler pushes west and sings a song, and the song echoes out forever and fills the unknowing air.

It is the American sound: It is hopeful, big-hearted, idealistic—daring, decent, and fair. That's our heritage, that's our song. We sing it still. For all our problems, our differences, we are together as of old. We raise our voices to the God who is the author of this most tender music. And may He continue to hold us close as we fill the world with our sound—in unity, affection, and love. One people under God, dedicated to the dream of freedom that He has placed in the human heart, called upon now to pass that dream on to a waiting and a hopeful world.

God bless you and may God bless America.

Index

The text of this book was set in Sabon. The first four chapters were transmitted via modem by the senior author from his IBM Personal Computer. The remaining chapters were set by the Chatham Composer. All material was processed by the Compugraphic Modular Component System. The graphic illustrations were prepared by Robert Sabol.

For indexing, the last three chapters were transmitted to the indexers via modem from the Chatham Composer to an IBM AT. All of the chapters were processed through MicroPro's StarIndex program and returned to the Chatham Composer for composition.